THE MAKING OF
QUADROPHENIA

SIMON WELLS

OMNIBUS PRESS

London / New York / Paris / Sydney / Copenhagen / Berlin / Madrid / Tokyo

THIS BOOK IS DEDICATED TO THE MEMORY OF
MARK COWAN 1965-2019

CONTENTS

FRANC RODDAM

QI was 18 in 1964, the same age as the lead character in Quadrophenia. It's astonishing to me that generation after generation of young people continue to have such a strong response to this film. Its impact is a testament to the brilliance of the original concept by Pete Townsend and The Who, the faultless acting of Phil Daniels and the massive contribution from the rest of the cast and crew, including my co-scriptwriters, Martin Stellman and Dave Humphries.

Quadrophenia is about teenage angst; it's a celebration of energy, and acknowledges every teenage generation's love of sex, drugs and rock and roll. It's also about friendship, love and family; it's about the struggle to discover who you are and where you fit in. It's a portrait of a young man who follows the mob and pays the price. He thinks he's found his place, only to see it all slip away and only then does he know who he really is. *Quadrophenia* really is a way of life – teenage life.

Franc Roddam
Director, *Quadrophenia*

LEFT: Franc Roddam in *Quadrophenia*'s editing suite, Lee International Studios, Shepperton, 1978

BILL CURBISHLEY

September 7th, 1978, was a very portentous day in many ways. I was on my way back from Polydor Records, quite elated, having finally signed the contract after many months of negotiation with the record company and their film division to finance two films for me to produce - *Quadrophenia* and *McVicar*. On arriving at my office, I was given the stunning news that Keith Moon was dead.

I didn't realise fully at that time that in a strange way part of *Quadrophenia* had died as well. There are quite a few facets of the lead character Jimmy that are attributable to or mirrored by the life and antics of Keith Moon. I've often wondered over the following years how Keith would have reacted to the movie that we completed.

At the very beginning of trying to get *Quadrophenia* up and running, I had decided along with my co-producer Roy Baird, that we should in the main use unknown actors and actresses, as for us the real star was *Quadrophenia*. The Who had released the album a number of years prior, and had toured extensively playing songs from the album, and for me there was no doubt that the work was firmly embedded in The Who fans' psyche and had been embraced globally by them in many ways.

With all this in mind we set about finding the director, and Roy asked me to look at a TV film called *Dummy*, starring Geraldine James, which had then been directed by a young director from the North East of England - Franc Roddam. Being a little bit sceptical of the arty-farty 'C' in his Christian name as opposed to a London 'K', I watched the TV drama. I at once felt that he was a very talented director and without any hesitation Roy and I approached his agent. Franc's fingerprints are all over the movie, through the development and casting, through post-production and editing. This is and was *his* film.

We settled on the cast of talented youngsters, and through the run up to the shooting stage there were lots of laughs to be had watching them become expert scooter riders, and developing the full Mod persona of some 15 years previous. At that time apart from Michael Elphick, nobody really knew the rest of the cast. Sting was a little known singer/songwriter, Toyah Willcox, Leslie Ash, Phil Daniels, Ray Winstone, Philip Davis... all young actors with dreams of stardom.

I remember we set off to film in Brighton at the end of September and we had to simulate summer. There's a beachside scene of summer tranquillity and heat where in fact it was a freezing cold day. Our stunt man, Peter Brayham, covered in grease and oil in an attempt to keep warm, begged for double money for the suffering that was being incurred swimming in the cold sea. We readily agreed and in fact paid him more than that.

Quadrophenia for me was a vastly different experience to the movie *Tommy*. I felt so much more at home with the cast and the working class backdrop that was created for the nucleus of the film. It was where I came from, where I spent my teenage years as a Mod, and I'd always felt that much of what occurred with Jimmy had been a part of my young life as well. Mods were industrious, never out of work, pre-occupied and obsessed with buying the right clothes, and walking the walk and talking the talk at weekends.

As a young Mod I had made many trips to Brighton with our little gang of teenagers, Chris Stamp and Mike Shaw amongst them, being two of my oldest friends going back to schooldays. Chris was the original manager of The Who along with Kit Lambert, and Mike Shaw was their lieutenant at Track Records. I really started handling things as early as 1972, when much in The Who camp had gone off the rails.

It was many years later that Chris told me that *Quadrophenia* was every bit the film he would like to have made, and he thought it was great that it was me in fact that had made it. Being an ex-manager he said jokingly that he 'knew talent when he saw it'.

Going back to the movie, I always felt that it might be a difficult transition for American audiences over and above other countries. In many countries we would subtitle, which was standard. But in the USA I was faced with a dilemma. We couldn't allow them to overdub with American voices, that would be sacrilege. And again to subtitle it would be to label it as a foreign movie which it most definitely was not. So I stuck to my guns and we kept the film in the form that it was in. I felt I had a master plan for launching it. I lined up a Who live tour to coincide with the release of the film, and instead of a support act at the beginning of each concert I ran a fifteen minute trailer of the movie. The plan was to open within 48 hours in cinemas in each city while everything was still fresh in the minds of 15 -20,000 fans who had attended The Who concert. The distributor World Northall did not obtain the cinemas in the way that we had asked, and the result was that the film had a staggered release across the country. However what did happen,

was that over a long period, it consistently did very well, played to good audiences, and became a landmark classic film.

Of course the film differs from Pete's original album which was condensed into 3 traumatic days in the life of a Mod. What we were able to do with the film was to come out from Jimmy's mind and build the large canvas of his environment and his social predicaments, and the struggle to come to terms with his family life, girls, the gang mentality, and the misguided credo 'all for one and one for all' that so devastatingly changes for him.

Looking back there's not much that I would change in the film. We got lucky in many ways. Finding such a great actor as Phil Daniels who became Jimmy and the terrific supporting cast is something that a producer hopes for but can never guarantee.

You could call the film a 'coming of age journey', 'a rites of passage' or any of the other clichés, but for me it was achieving a partial dream and releasing a cathartic explosion that I had held inside me since my own teenager years.

Bill Curbishley

ABOVE: Sting, *Quadrophenia*'s producer Bill Curbishley and director Franc Roddam outside Brighton's Grand Hotel, September 1978.

"QUADROPHENIA" 375

PROD.

DIRECTOR FRANC RODDAM | CAMERAMAN BRIAN TUFANO

SLATE 4-12 | TAKE 1

DATE Buney 1978 NIGHT INT

278 N

INTRODUCTION

'LOOK, I DON'T WANNA BE THE SAME AS EVERYBODY ELSE. THAT'S WHY I'M A MOD, SEE? I MEAN, YOU GOTTA BE SOMEBODY, AIN'T YA, OR YOU MIGHT AS WELL JUMP IN THE SEA AND DROWN.'
—PHIL DANIELS AS JIMMY IN *QUADROPHENIA*

One of *Quadrophenia*'s promotional taglines accompanying its cinema release in 1979 was the legend 'A Way of Life' – a lofty aspiration for the uninitiated maybe, but for its devotees, an absolute reality. While it's nearly four decades since *Quadrophenia* the film first saw the light of day, it's evident that it still occupies a warm place in the hearts and minds of those who've shared Jimmy the Mod's passionate search for identity.

Above all the other celebrated British youth films of the last fifty years, *Quadrophenia* still has the power to enchant and captivate audiences. But to the casual observer it presents a conundrum: why should a film over forty years old, set over a decade earlier, still continue to grab headlines and garner new audiences? Surely time would have taken its toll and consigned it to history? Films come and go, but *Quadrophenia* is still with us, alive and well in the twenty-first century. At the time of writing, the film is set to celebrate its fortieth anniversary, with a documentary, public events and a plethora of spin-offs all on the horizon. As many of the cast and crew have told me in recent months, the film has never been so popular.

To sum up *Quadrophenia*'s appeal in one cute soundbite is a nigh impossible task. While for the casual viewer it's just a film about Mods, for some it's a story based on The Who's concept album of 1973, and for others it's a film about the sixties. However, for those who associate closely with the picture the reality is far more involved. Given that it's a film set in the sixties, made in the late seventies, staffed by punks playing Mods with a contemporary rock band soundtrack from six years before, decoding the extraordinary appeal of *Quadrophenia* requires a diligent approach.

I've kept a keen eye on *Quadrophenia*'s journey over the years, and I'm still intrigued by the fervour and passion it generates among its followers (and, dare I say, its critics). Despite all the words expounded over the film since its release, the sharp reality is that *Quadrophenia* is not just a film about Mods – indeed, it could be argued that Mod is nothing more than an ambient backdrop to deeper, far more identifiable and perennial issues, spanning identity, love, alienation, mental health, adolescence and kinship. *Quadrophenia*'s themes are eternal, seemingly identifiable by generations both past and present, and well into the future.

To me, it's those qualities – plus its ferocious, exhilarating pace – that maintain *Quadrophenia*'s appeal, that defy time and the transitory nature of fickle fads. While *Quadrophenia* exists within a set

OPPOSITE: Dave Worrell's candid snap from Alfredo's Café, November 30th, 1978.

time period, this does little to obscure the film's broader themes. If indeed *Quadrophenia* had been a strictly historical document from the sixties, time would surely have consigned the picture to history, leaving it a quaint curio rather than the powerful social document we all know and love.

A few years ago I decided to take a serious look inside the making of the film and the multitude of tangents that have spun off it over the years. With this opportunity to try to decode Mod's greatest enigma, I immersed myself in the period that the film was set and made numerous trips to Brighton and London to follow in the footsteps of the cast and crew in 1978.

For most students of the film, *Quadrophenia* started out as a 1973 concept album by The Who, one of the most idiosyncratic bands of that era and the loudest exponents of the Modernist movement during the sixties. While retrospective in its approach, *Quadrophenia*'s echoes were not just from the spring of 1964, but came from other

eras and more existential sensibilities. Already I was spooked by the multitude of themes and dimensions that went into this piece of work. The film, its release coming two years after the punk onslaught of 1977, only added to the sense of disorientation.

The making of *Quadrophenia* occurred during late 1978, and it dovetailed with the tail end of the punk explosion and a rebirth of Modernism. British youth culture was in a spin, seemingly every movement was up for re-evaluation, and yet Mod with its forthright branding and direct manifesto won out. In hindsight, the speed at which *Quadrophenia* was committed to celluloid served to crystallise the energy of the moment. And in its swift transference, the filmmakers truly caught lightning in a bottle. While the semantics and emotional epithets may well have been drawn from the era in which it was set, there was no doubting that the anger and fury expressed on screen were more redolent of the atmosphere of 1978.

OPPOSITE: Jimmy on Sting's Vespa, September 1978.

ABOVE: Sting and followers alongside Brighton's Madeira Drive.

Quadrophenia's release in August 1979 was the crowning of the Mod summer. The film debuted amidst a blizzard of publicity and the film's target audience was already in place. Coinciding with the Mod revival's zenith that summer, *Quadrophenia* nationalised the neo-Mod movement more than any other element present at that time. Either too young or alienated by the high-brow intellectualising that surrounded the punk movement, many were swift to board the *Quadrophenia* express. Within weeks, what had been an anachronistic pursuit shared among a few diehards was now a modern-day phenomenon, with scooters, parkas, suits and ties an everyday sight across the UK.

The country was enduring an almost interminable 'Winter of Discontent', and *Quadrophenia* offered a brighter manifesto than any political party could muster. Given its arguably parochial themes and solid British heartbeat, *Quadrophenia* would also do remarkably well in overseas territories.

With cinema being the only way to view the film in 1979, once its route around the Odeons and Gaumonts of the UK had been exhausted, *Quadrophenia* endured in the minds and imagination of those who saw it rush past on screen. It would take several years for the first domestic video release to be issued, allowing many to see *Quadrophenia* from their living rooms. While the film had armed the neo-Mod scene with a blueprint for a lifestyle, the movement's diminishing status did little to neuter *Quadrophenia*'s cult status. Although the late eighties and nineties generation revelled in far more lurid colours and sounds, the film was still bedrock for many.

The rave culture slowly petered out in the early nineties, and Britpop would fully canonise *Quadrophenia*'s extraordinary influence – contemporising its appeal within a new generation hungry for anything sixties. The move from video to DVD brought a new legion of admirers, and with many following the fortunes and direction of bands such as Blur and Oasis, *Quadrophenia* became required watching.

With *Quadrophenia* available on a variety of digital platforms, beyond the viewing experience, a more tangible magic exists in the locations that once hosted its transference to film. Naturally, Brighton remains *Quadrophenia*'s emotional centre, and to this day the city plays host to hoards of devotees – many of them eager to retrace the footsteps Jimmy and his band of merry Mods made over forty years ago. Of little surprise, *Quadrophenia*'s famous alley has become the most identifiable signpost to the film's presence in Brighton, and is evidenced by the raft of foreign graffiti that covers the brickwork. *Quadrophenia* has become a global property.

Mod remains eternally cool and *Quadrophenia* retains its classic cult status – an association that looks set to endure throughout the twenty-first century. Having attended a sell-out night at London's Hammersmith Apollo in 2016, where 3,500 attendees shelled out upwards of £75 to attend a screening and Q&A, the enduring affection for the film is clearly undaunted by time.

For cast and crew, *Quadrophenia* remains a defining moment in their careers. A rite of passage for the film's young frontline actors, *Quadrophenia*'s main players are still in demand to recount their glory days on set. Given that the majority of the leading cast are now in their late fifties and sixties, it's fair to say that the film was, and remains, a signature moment for many of them.

With the aid of cast, crew and fans, I've been able to piece together the story of Britain's finest youth film and the effect it's had on everyone's lives, participants and viewers alike. While the history of other cult films is often littered with the weary and predictable torment, hurt and upset involved in bringing a story to the screen, *Quadrophenia* proved a joyous experience from beginning to end, and it's that joy that I wish to celebrate here.

Simon Wells
Forest Row, Sussex
November 2018

TOP OF THE

IT PARADE!

on your new

Lambretta 150
SPECIAL 'PACEMAKER'

You're certainly 'IT'—you're the star of a streamlined, dream-lined hit—when you ride the new LAMBRETTA 'PACEMAKER'. Hop on the top of the scooter pops—pull out the stops and W-H-O-O-M! You're really swingin'—on a *real* scooter with real performance.

For you—the light-hearted, easy-to-handle 'PACEMAKER' with thrilling extra power—right on the beat, right up your street—right on any road to anywhere. Yet the tax and insurance are exactly the same as for an ordinary 150cc. machine. Gear but NOT dear—it's HERE! . . . the NEW 150 'PACEMAKER'—go see it at your dealers now!

THE WORLD'S FINEST SCOOTER

CHAPTER ONE

'*QUADROPHENIA*'S LIKE OPENING A BOTTLE OF VINTAGE WINE. BEEN MANY YEARS SINCE I'VE WATCHED THIS MASTERPIECE AND IT'S MATURED BEYOND BELIEF. THE MARRIAGE OF WEST LONDON MOD CULTURE AND TOWNSHEND'S WRITING IS PURE GENIUS. I UNASHAMEDLY WEPT DURING THE FINAL MOMENTS.'
—COMMENT BY 'AHPOLLYOLLY' ON YOUTUBE WEBSITE, NOVEMBER 2011

While not represented in any conventional dictionary, the word 'Quadrophenia' has become the most popular byword for Modernism, a lifestyle forged in the early sixties and maintained throughout numerous revivals to the present day. Putting arguments from purists momentarily to one side, *Quadrophenia*, in all its dramatic mediums, remains a major reference point for a movement that shows no sign of flagging. For proof of this, a cursory search on Google informs one that there are over two million sites that reference the word 'Quadrophenia', while deeper in cyberspace there are numerous examples of how Pete Townshend's epic has been warmly adopted by its devotees. With multiple Facebook pages, chat rooms, YouTube reviews and location and trivia sites, the film has long outstripped its initial aims.

The tangible effect that *Quadrophenia* has had on its audience bolsters a belief that Mod is undoubtedly Britain's most enduring youth cult, above and beyond the other movements and their flaky manifestos over the decades. For many, even those now in their fifties and sixties, Modernism's template is enticing, fresh and perpetually attractive. While other youth cults have faded into obscurity and comic derision the Modernist ideology, in all its manifestations, still manages to attract new followers around the globe and is strongly (and vociferously) adhered to by those falling under its spell. The package of sharp looking and equally clear thinking hugely attractive, Mod proudly displays its bright colours – rarely slipping into sleazy or tacky diversions. In short, Mod's credo is about being cool, clean and hard; compromise is rarely, if ever, entertained.

For anyone not in step with the timeline, between the album and film of *Quadrophenia* there's a good six-year gap. Nonetheless, as befits the suspended timescale that hovers over the story, the genesis of *Quadrophenia* arose from the embers of the original Modernist movement, the radical philosophical experimentalism which occurred nearly half a century before The Who's somewhat hectic display on an Olympic running track in 2012.

While this book concerns itself with the film, it would be remiss to ignore its lengthy gestation period before filming began in 1978. Furthermore, it could be argued that the film of *Quadrophenia* was merely a stopping point in what was a work

in progress for Pete Townshend. As evidenced in the lavish packaging of the deluxe *Quadrophenia* album box set in 2011, the concept is evidently still active – its journey traversing above and beyond the vinyl, video and multitude of DVD formats that currently exist. With a tour, stage play, possible remake and sequel taking place, *Quadrophenia* is a living project, one whose future is destined to outlive its creators.

The stories of The Who and *Quadrophenia* are inextricably entwined, arguably more so than in terms of the band's other acclaimed rock opus, *Tommy*. The double album of *Quadrophenia*, released in 1973, was the band's sixth studio offering. With a back catalogue of numerous hit singles and albums, the release was hugely anticipated. The group's previous conceptual offering, *Tommy*, had elevated their status as a world-class act and yet it masked the long battle they had endured to secure that position (fiscal and otherwise). Overnight successes The Who were not, and with years of schlepping around the UK and other remote territories for very

ABOVE: Original Mods converge on Margate, May 1964.

little return, their rewards were hard won.

As has been long enshrined in legend, The Who first found a receptive audience in the burgeoning early sixties Mod scene. While never instinctive Mods like bands such as the Small Faces or The Action, The Who nonetheless adopted Modernism and the association attracted an instant audience, most of them cut from the same cloth as their West London fan base.

Like many musicians of the period, The Who's formative steps were fairly typical of the early sixties beat boom, an explosion that propelled many teenagers to pick up a guitar and wander onto a stage. Founder members Pete Townshend and John Entwistle were two such youngsters. Absorbed by the skiffle/trad craze of the late fifties, the pair performed with a Dixieland outfit called The Confederates, Townshend assuming banjo-playing duties and Entwistle employing the horn-playing skills he'd honed at school. While aware of the guitar-dominated scene led by the clinical moves of The Shadows, Townshend's tastes were already far broader and he was discovering the likes of Muddy Waters, John Lee Hooker and Bo Diddley – the earthy blues of the Mississippi Delta resonating strongly with teenagers such as Townshend.

Entwistle would later transfer his interest to bass, and during one sojourn around his home turf of Shepherd's Bush, West London, he came across singer Roger Daltrey, a guitarist who'd yet to explore his enormous vocal range. Instinctive and gruff, Daltrey was the protagonist of a band called The Detours. They were eager to seal a record contract and climb aboard the British beat boom, and they happened to be in need of a bassist at the time. Entwistle was in. In time, he would suggest that former Confederates colleague Pete Townshend would be suitable for rhythm guitar duties.

After a few personnel changes, The Detours chanced upon drummer extraordinaire and wild man Keith Moon in early 1964. Impressed by Moon's explosive and destructive drumming style, The Detours pulled him in and underwent a further transformation – becoming 'The Who'. (The name change was due to another band of the same name doing the rounds.) Name changed and drummer in situ, the combination of Townshend, Daltrey, Moon and Entwistle was forged.

And then the group came to the attention of one Peter Meaden, an unashamed Modernist who was in touch with this visceral movement exploding across London. Tuning in to the abrasive sound of these four teenagers, Meaden sensed an opportunity to secure Mod's first musical ambassadors.

Not that the media knew it, but for the best part of two years, Modernism had gained a large contingency of adherents, many of them basking quietly under the radar in their chosen lifestyle. Meaden was one of the primary 'faces' around town and his intelligence detected that the scene could travel much further than London's club land.

Mod was initially spawned in and around Soho – a melting pot of exotic influences that informed West London's most vibrant mile. The protagonists of the fledgling Modernist movement were largely drawn from the late fifties coffee bar culture – a scene that was populated largely by beatniks, students and dissenters revelling in a form of post-war Bohemia – and they shared a common bond: a healthy disdain of the skiffle/trad jazz scene, the latter, a crude movement whose main components were a fondness for baggy jumpers, pipe smoking and ruddy pursuits.

With more refined sounds emanating from London-based musicians such as Tubby Hayes and Ronnie Scott, an elevated clique, light years ahead of its peers, was being formulated. Intellectually, their tastes were rarefied (existentialist literature, jazz and European film); outwardly, they conveyed these interests in their sharply-styled fashion, an expression not witnessed by British youth since the tail end of the previous century (and then only to a select few).

THE STORIES OF THE WHO AND *QUADROPHENIA* ARE INEXTRICABLY ENTWINED, ARGUABLY MORE SO THAN IN TERMS OF THE BAND'S OTHER ACCLAIMED ROCK OPUS, *TOMMY*

From its inception, Mod fashion would assume a uniformity that was well outside dour British convention, drawing on the styles worn proudly by our European cousins. In reaction to the extravagant Edwardian-inspired styles draped over working-class English shoulders, the formative movers of the Modernist scene proudly showed off their unique identity, assuming an almost feminine approach to fashion sense that enchanted, as well as enraged, many.

Paul Anderson, author of *Mods: The New Religion*, describes the scene: 'The beatniks wanted to save the world, went on marches to ban the bomb, read poetry and preached from Ginsberg and Kerouac novels. The Modernist wanted that smart mohair number from Ben Harris the tailor,

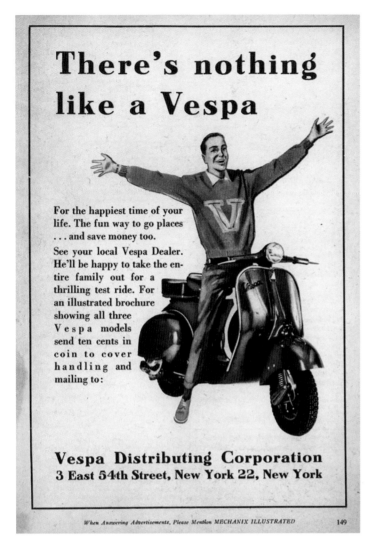

There's nothing like a Vespa

For the happiest time of your life. The fun way to go places ... and save money too.

See your local Vespa Dealer. He'll be happy to take the entire family out for a thrilling test ride. For an illustrated brochure showing all three Vespa models send ten cents in coin to cover handling and mailing to:

Vespa Distributing Corporation
3 East 54th Street, New York 22, New York

When Answering Advertisements, Please Mention MECHANIX ILLUSTRATED 149

ABOVE: Vespa mania hits New York.

those whip-cord slacks from Vince Man's Shop in Newburgh Street and a copy of Cannonball Adderley's *Somethin' Else* album.'

George Melly noted in his classic paean to youth culture, *Revolt into Style*, that Mod would 'accommodate a rapidly changing situation. Initially for instance "Mod" meant a very small group of young working-class boys who, at the height of the Trad boom, formed a small totally committed little mutual admiration society devoted to clothes.' And music journalist Paolo Hewitt, a noted authority on the scene, says of the primary moves of Modernism: 'It was a very sophisticated youth cult. I think in some terms it might have been a reaction to the Teddy Boys because Teddy Boys made themselves known with their quiff and their uniform. It was a

very outlandish uniform with the bootlace ties and the brogues – you spotted them straight away. With Mod, it was more about blending into society. You created a world within a world – no one knew about this world – it was completely secret.'

Music, too, would similarly evolve in line with the demands of its new audience. While modern jazz held its own in the basement bars of Soho, the Mod scene would soon sharpen its approach, introducing rawer sounds from R&B, blue beat and ska; the resultant sound becoming more raw and one that chimed with the frustrations of working-class culture. It was inevitable that many would attempt to emulate these sounds – to add a unique frisson of their own – and soon, home-grown personalities such as Georgie Fame and Zoot Money would put their own spin on things. Venues larger than coffee bars were soon required to cope with the acts and the frantic dancing that accompanied them.

Adding greatly to its appeal, the scene was discriminatory of neither race nor class, making it the most accessible youth movement to emerge in Britain – and a sharp affront to the, at times, racist Teddy Boy culture of the period. With full employment being enjoyed, many had access to disposable cash, and the recent introduction of hire purchase meant that many items previously inaccessible to the young working class were now within reach.

To sustain energy during all-night affairs, amphetamine pills would become an almost de rigueur accoutrement. Still legal and available via prescription (a hangover from the wartime years when they were used to dispel fatigue), these drugs would help to reduce weariness during the all-important weekend hours. Personal transport, a rare commodity in post-war Britain, would pull further on Italian influences. While the Rocker culture had claimed Norton and Triumph bikes as unwieldy chariots, understated Lambretta and Vespa scooters would become the preferred mode of transport for the Modernist movement.

Obviously, it was never decided as such, but these elements began to gel together into a lifestyle, with everyone involved feeling that they were part of something unique. Only later, when the tabloids began to expose the cruder elements of Mod's ascendancy, would the movement assume some sort of cult status. Peter Barnsley's feature in *Town Magazine* in October 1962 would, historically, be the first major article on the movement. Entitled 'Faces Without Shadows' (and subtitled 'Young men who live for clothes and pleasure'), with pictures from legendary snapper Don McCullin, the article would focus on three Stoke Newington Mods, one of whom was a pouting 15-year-old Marc Bolan. Nonetheless, despite the rich detail and scope of the feature, the journal's high-brow readership failed to be moved by the content and it sank without too much fuss. Nonetheless, the dye had been cast, forging the way from Modernist to Mod.

Unwittingly, it would be a television programme, Rediffusion's *Ready Steady Go!*, that would come to nationalise the movement from the dance floor of the audience-centric show based in London. First shown on August 9th, 1963, two key components of the show were fashion and dance, and many of the audience members were drawn from London's Mod club community. Predictably, these characters often stole the limelight from the bands on stage, their dress and dance sensibility sending frenzied signals to the nation's youth via cathode rays. These scenes painted vivid pictures for a generation of teenagers, and by late 1963 the Mod movement was set to poke its head above ground. Among many others watching these images were members of The Who and their then-manager Pete Meaden, a personality whose style and worldview rarely deviated from the Mod ethos.

Struck by Meaden's fanaticism, The Who changed their name to The High Numbers, the name leaving no illusions as to where they were coming from. In the ensuing metamorphosis, Meaden created the first overtly Mod band, and

as a result, a loyal following was instantly formed. Many of the kids who witnessed the band in the early days recognised that they were cut from the same cloth as their musical counterparts; they were instinctively and totally in tune with the ambitions of the group.

Townshend in particular was in awe of Meaden's attitude and lifestyle, and he revelled in the internal politics of the movement, well aware that its understated association with art and street-level semantics could furnish the band, and equally his songwriting, with innumerable possibilities.

'He grabbed at Mod straight away,' recalls Richard Barnes, Townshend's friend from art school days. 'It kind of almost answered all of his prayers. When Mod came along, I was quite surprised at how much he just went for it. It had the rules, it had the clothing – it was an unbelievably cool thing. And he was just so happy to discover it. I think it kind of fulfilled some need in him.'

Townshend and Meaden would feed each other with their shared interests: Townshend passing on his encyclopaedic knowledge of blues and soul, Meaden, his passion for the finery of Mod deportment and its sensibilities. 'I was always close to the greatest face of them all, Peter Meaden,' recalled Townshend later. 'If The Who hadn't got in the way I would have embraced the Mod movement far more deeply... I wanted to feel a part of something. I always have. The Mods allowed me that.'

Meaden's devotion to the movement and his belief in The High Numbers would extend to penning both sides of the group's first single, 'I'm The Face'/'Zoot Suit', a hymn of sorts to the lingo of the time and dripping in Mod epithets. While it was released a decade before the album *Quadrophenia* saw light, the single was a virtual manifesto of the landscape Townshend was later to reassess.

The excitement created by the single's release earned The High Numbers a couple of high-profile appearances (one with The Beatles) and yet, ultimately, the band were unable to escape their cult status. With Pete Meaden's stewardship drawing to a natural close, the ambitious Chris Stamp and artistic Kit Lambert took over responsibilities for the band in the summer of 1964. Although totally inexperienced in management, the pair retained most of Meaden's original premise for the group but pushed in a new direction to achieve wider recognition. The band name reverted to The Who. The music world was abuzz with the rewards to be made out of homespun compositions, and Townshend began constructing idiosyncratic songs inspired by the landscape and characters he'd come across during the group's evolution.

THIS NEW BREED OF PRETENDERS WAS FAR MORE INSTINCTIVE THAN THEIR PREDECESSORS. THE SHARP SUITS AND TAILORED GARMENTS THAT WERE ONCE DE RIGUEUR FOR THE EARLY MODERNISTS HAD BROADENED IN STYLE

Rebranded, the group began to crystallise their sound and, with Townshend's fertile mind articulating youthful confusion, their appeal grew, lifting them from the clubs, pubs and ballrooms of their locale to venues and far greater acclaim further afield. Like The Rolling Stones, The Kinks and The Pretty Things, The Who's uncompromising stance was seen as an affront to the Brian Epstein School of Show Business Deportment – not that it bothered any of these groups. While The Beatles found an eager audience for their clean-cut presentation and jaunty tunes, they had simultaneously alienated large swathes of the British youth, many of them suspicious of the Fab Four's saccharine exterior. Many reviewers of the time missed the inner semantics of songs such as 'I Can't Explain' or 'Anyway, Anyhow, Anywhere', but others lapped up the frustration pouring out of The Who. With

National Service, rationing and other wartime austerities finally consigned to the dustbin, the British youth were exercising new freedoms, with little respect being shown to protocol or convention. The self-destructive display and sound of The Who reflected the dissent that was being experienced around the nation. With politicians remote and seemingly unassailable, role models had fallen to the larger-than-life characters leaping off television, screen and vinyl.

Well before The Who's noisy emergence, seeds of the Modernist movement were already starting to germinate within an army of neophytes, many of them attracted to the bright livery and attitude of the movement. Others were excited by the cruder elements of the culture and were fired up at the chance to cut loose. Soon the media was picking up on the buzz and reporting, in sensationalist style, the extremities of tabloid Mod – the violence and the use of drugs.

Many who took to Mod via the tabloids' perception of the scene had little of the finesse that their predecessors had demanded and, despite adopting the Modernist uniform, they shared little of the original protagonists' view of Mod as an elevated lifestyle. These youngsters were still carrying a burning dissatisfaction brought on by years of austerity, and they leapt on the bandwagon in search of thrills and chaos. As a result of this growing nationwide hysteria, many original purists were sent scurrying back underground.

This new breed of pretenders was far more instinctive than their predecessors. The sharp suits and tailored garments that were once de rigueur for the early Modernists had broadened in style. As a result, desert boots, pullovers and polo tops came to supersede more rarefied tailored threads. Nonetheless, the scooter would still be maintained as the leading symbol of the movement.

While pop history would record a world smitten with the Mop Tops, their cheesy smiles and thumbs up, the reality was that many British youngsters found themselves alienated by something they felt

OPPOSITE AND NEXT SPREAD: The British media in a feeding frenzy over Mod seaside clashes, May 1964.

Daily Mirror

Scooter gangs 'beat up' Clacton

3d.   Monday, March 30, 1964   No. 18,746

'WILD ONES' INVADE SEASIDE—97 ARRESTS

By PAUL HUGHES

THE Wild Ones invaded a seaside town yesterday—1,000 fighting, drinking, roaring, rampaging teenagers on scooters and motor-cycles. By last night, after a day of riots and battles with police, ninety-seven of them had been arrested.

A desperate S O S went out from police at Clacton, Essex, as leather-jacketed youths and girls attacked people in the streets, turned over parked cars, broke into beach huts, smashed windows, and fought with rival gangs.

Police reinforcements from other Essex towns raced to the shattered resort, where fearful residents had locked themselves indoors.

By this time the centre of Clacton was jammed with screaming teenagers. Traffic was at a standstill.

Fought

The crowd was broken up by police and police dogs. Several policemen were injured as the teenagers fought them.

A number of arrests had already been made. Addresses had been taken, and messages sent to parents.

And worried mothers and fathers were beginning to arrive from the London area to bail out their sons and daughters.

The harassed police were glad to see them go. For the cells at Clacton police station were crammed with youngsters under arrest.

By last night the score of arrests and charges — still incomplete — included:

Thirty for assault on police and civilians; thirty for creating disturbances and fighting; ten for theft; and at least twenty for other offences, including drunk and disorderly, malicious damage and using obscene language.

Rough

Police said the court hearings would begin on April 27.

The Wild Ones—this was the title of a Marlon Brando film in which teenaged motor-cyclists terrorised a town—have caused trouble in Clacton before. But not on this scale.

They began arriving on Friday and Saturday and many slept rough on the beach, under the pier, in promenade shelters, and in beach huts they broke open.

Others spent the night roaring round the town on their scooters and motor-cycles.

Among incidents reported to the police were:

THE CLUB HOUSE of the local bowling club was broken into and wrecked and liquor and cigarettes stolen.

PENNY-IN-THE-SLOT weighing machines and 3d.-a-time telescopes on the promenade were thrown into the sea.

PARKED cars had panels kicked in and windows smashed.

A CHISEL was thrown through a police car window at a patrol driver.

WINDOWS of a new conference hall on the sea-front, due to be opened soon, were smashed.

A MAN who tried to stop

Youths in leather jackets help a police officer making inquiries last night into the rampage by gangs of teenagers at the seaside resort of Clacton. A police dog stands by.

Continued on Back Page

The Easter miracle of Alaska

'FEWER THAN 100' DIE

From BARRIE HARDING, New York, Sunday

THE earthquake which savaged Alaska is being described tonight as "The Easter Miracle."

For although the earthquake was one of the mightiest ever recorded, the death roll throughout Alaska is an amazingly light forty, with ninety-three injured.

Rescuers expect to find more bodies under the rubble of wrecked towns.

But they estimate that the final death roll will be fewer than 100.

Waves

Earlier reports put the number of dead in the hundreds or even thousands.

Today Hugh Wade, Alaska's Secretary of State, said: "Casualties are less than we ever dreamed they could be."

After the earthquake, which struck on Friday, giant waves travelling at a fantastic rate sped death and destruction as far as Crescent City, California, 2,000 miles away.

There ten people died and fifteen are missing. The tidal waves killed another six in Californian coastal towns and injured seventy more.

From the stricken Alaskan town of Anchorage (Pop. 48,000) a Mirror Correspondent cabled last night:—

A procession of US Air Force planes arrived today with aid for Alaska's five earthquake-shattered towns of Anchorage, Valdez, Seward, Whittier, and Kodiak.

They brought emergency Red Cross supplies, doctors, nurses and even a mobile hospital.

Meanwhile rescue workers were crawling through the buckled and bent buildings of Anchorage looking for dead and injured.

A huge hole has been clawed out of the main street, Fourth avenue. And one side of the street has sunk 30ft., taking with it stores, a cinema, a restaurant and small hotels.

Damage

Most of the fog-shrouded town is without heat, power, water or sewage facilities. Total damage is estimated at £71,000,000 and the townspeople are being warned to get typhoid injections.

But tonight there were fears for the safety of eighteen small Eskimo villages along the Alaskan coast. Officials said they were not sure whether the villages still existed.

PICTURES—PAGES FOUR AND FIVE

SUNDAY JOINT SAVED BY WIVES

THERE were no power cuts during the peak "Sunday lunch" period yesterday.

Yet a Central Electricity Board spokesman said on Saturday that cuts during much of the country were "almost inevitable" because of the power men's work-to-rule and overtime ban.

Why was the calculation wrong? A Board official said it was due to the housewives' "magnificent response" to an appeal to use electrical appliances as little as possible.

A nation-wide three per cent. voltage reduction helped.

Yesterday the Board also appealed to owners of outdoor illuminations—apart from street lighting—to switch them off.

A spokesman said: "Every kilowatt saved will conserve coal and help the Generating Board to meet the usual working-day demand on Tuesday."

Demands are pouring in from the men to union leaders urging them to carry on the ban.

He added that "power workers throughout the country" resent the Government setting up a court of inquiry to probe the dispute.

This was looked on, he said, as an attempt to delay settlement of the problem.

Last night a spokesman for the Power Workers' Editorial Committee — made up of shop stewards from all over Britain — said: Demands are pouring in from the men to union leaders urging them to carry on the ban.

Leaders of the five unions involved in the dispute—over a pay and hours' claim—meet tomorrow to decide whether to end the work-to-rule and overtime ban.

DAILY MIRROR, Monday, May 18, 1964 PAGE 13

Sticks, broken deckchairs, bottles . . Mirror Men see the savage battle on the sands

CHARGE OF THE MODS AT MARGATE

Charge! Armed with sticks, broken deckchairs and bottles, hundreds of T-shirted Mods race across the Margate beach

Wild Ones rampage in the High-street

REPORT by EDWARD VALE
PICTURES by Mirror Cameramen
BOB HOPE and ERIC PIPER

ALL through the night, the shouts and scuffles and smashing of glass had warned the people of Margate that their town had been picked on by the Mods and the Rockers for a Whitsun beat-up.

By 7 a.m., ordinary holidaymakers in sea-front boarding-houses were watching the rival thug gangs warming up with small-scale skirmishes.

And at 10.30 a.m., as the sun blazed on the white Margate sands, I saw the real battle blow up.

I was strolling along the promenade with Mirror photographer Eric Piper. Below the sea wall peaceful holiday-makers dozed or read their Sunday papers, or helped the kids with the sandcastles.

But 100 yards away down at the water's edge a mob of teenagers was ...

Stamping

There were about 500 of them. At first, they were just amusing themselves—kicking sand at each other, shouting, stamping and chanting like wild tribesmen.

Then the Mods spotted the Rockers ... about 100 of them, gathering on the sands near the promenade.

The Mods stopped their ... For a second, they did nothing. Then they charged up the beach.

Cameraman Piper and I moved in for a closer look. We found ourselves in a ... of flying bottles, deckchairs and lumps of wood.

Now the police moved in. There were six of them to part the 600 warring teenagers.

The gangs joined forces—and set about the police.

Truncheons flailed. Youths dropped on the beach.

In a few minutes, the 600 thugs had dwindled to about 400.

Then the Mods broke off the fight. They charged up from the beach and along the promenade ...

They swarmed into Margate's "Dreamland" amusement centre ... shouting and banging, as they ran out into the car park beyond.

Three hundred Mods went out through the car park exit before a police inspector and two guards got the gates shut. But 100 Mods were still shut in.

Hurled

Those on the outside hurled dustbin lids and milk bottles. Then they stood back and started chanting a count.

On "Three" the 100 charged the gates. The gates crashed open. The other 100 Mods flooded out of the car park ...

... owner and two girl assistants were getting ready for the Whitsun rush.

Five youths burst in, swept dozens of cakes and packets of biscuits off the counter, grabbed a red leather chair ... and stormed off to the neighbouring hardware shop.

The stolen cafe chair was thrust through the hardware shop window.

Next, one of the youths hurled the chair at the window of a council flat, where Alfred Tye, a 39-year-old clerk, was having breakfast with his 85-year-old father.

Mr. Tye threw his father to one side and leaped to the window.

Another youth saw him, went up to another window in the flat—kicked it in and ran away.

By now, extra police had reached Margate from neighbouring Ramsgate. Van loads of police went hunting the gang. At the top of High-street, they found their quarry.

The gang saw the vans. They ran away.

For two hours, all was quiet in Margate. But police reinforcements still poured in.

Dashing

By the afternoon there were around 100 police on duty in Margate.

At one stage, 100 teenagers marched to the town's railway station. A train was coming in.

Police turned the mob away.

But it looked as if Margate's troubles were not over yet.

Police were kept busy dashing around the town breaking up small fights.

Estimate

Then came word that more Rockers were heading for the town. By tea-time it was estimated that more than 1,000 teenaged thugs were in Margate.

A police spokesman announced: "The whole of the Margate force is tied down by this trouble, and we have reinforcements from fifty miles away."

What The Mirror Says—See Page 2.

Wild Ones fight on the white sands of Margate. One youth is caught. Another goes to help a friend pinned by a policeman.

Daily Mirror

3d. Monday, August 3, 1964 No. 18,854

Battle of Hastings—18 arrested

RIOT POLICE FLY TO SEASIDE

Torpedo boats attack a U.S. warship

THREE torpedo boats attacked an American destroyer 30 miles off the coast of Communist North Vietnam, in South-East Asia, yesterday.

They fired three torpedoes, and also attacked the destroyer with gunfire.

The destroyer, Maddox, fired back—and minutes later four jet fighters from the American aircraft carrier Ticonderoga ...

"Riot squad" police file quietly into the transport plane at Northolt. A few minutes later they were in the air on their way to the trouble town.

was close to a deception, and the popular Mod scene soon embraced those who resented the dominating influence of the Mersey Sound.

Groups of Mods were now collecting around the seaside towns of Great Britain, especially during Bank Holiday weekends. These gatherings were coordinated by word of mouth; news would spread like wildfire across the inner cities that something was about to happen. For those hemmed in by the city, any opportunity to flex their collective muscles by the seaside was too good to miss.

Also making their way to these locations were the Rockers, their unwieldy culture a throwback to the Teddy Boy scene that had consumed much of the fifties demob generation. Bagging the seaside landscape as their own, the Rockers viewed Mod as an antithesis, a photo negative of everything they stood for. Both tribes had already clashed at certain points in the inner-city arena, and it was only a matter of time before they would play out their differences on a larger stage.

These two warring factions would meet each other on the beaches, piers and promenades of places such as Brighton, Clacton, Hastings and Margate – normally the cosy domain of the British working-class family unit. In between beach towels, blankets and windbreakers, pitched battles erupted. These invasions caught the authorities on the hop, necessitating the emergency services to break up the violence and plan their operations like military exercises.

In the eyes of the media, this was the perfect filler for the vacuum of the 'Silly Season' – the period where hard news traditionally takes a summer breather. With impulsive youth seemingly on the rampage, Britain's freshly demobbed establishment was propelled into action; police, magistrates and the judiciary were primed to dish out exemplary sentences.

While not personally disposed to any of the violence that was breaking out in Britain, The Who were nonetheless present at many of the locations that hosted these clashes, Brighton being one of

them. For the sensitive and intuitive Townshend, images of the characters who were involved in these clashes would lodge in his subconscious for years, although with the unrelenting wave of experiences coming his way, he'd find little time to process these emotions until much later.

In a little over two years, The Who were indistinguishable from their early selves. 'My Generation', Townshend's classic homage to the frustrations of youth, saw the band leap to the top of the pop charts. With Daltrey's stuttering

phraseology resonating with amphetamine burnout, the song acted as a coda to the first instalment of the Mod movement. Folk, psychedelia and gentler sounds were starting to creep into the charts – Mod had become passé. Drugs such as marijuana and LSD were replacing amphetamines, and everything was changing, leaving Mod's monochrome palette behind.

As the turbulent decade of the sixties sped past, Modernism, as defined in the popular tabloid press, would start to dip at the tail end of 1965. In tandem, Townshend's writing was seeking broader pastures than the perimeters of Mod could offer. By the beginning of 1966, the band had largely abandoned their R&B sound and were exploring the possibilities generated by their own compositions.

By 1967, The Who had immersed themselves fully in psychedelia and were concentrating their activities way beyond the limitations of the UK. Following an explosive performance at the Monterey Pop Festival in June 1967, the group embarked on a more progressive route, one that was consuming all the major players of the time. *Tommy*, the group's seminal rock opera of 1969, would stand as one of the great collective anthems of the decade; its amorphous concept found huge favour with a generation revelling in ambiguity and metaphor. Coupled with the band's explosive stage presence, *Tommy* was purpose-built for the new genre of stadium rock. The Who's flirtation with the whimsy of psychedelia had left the band in danger of being stuck in limbo, but the group's dynamic appearance at the 1969 Woodstock Festival propelled them to the forefront of the decade's live performers. Given that The Beatles had long abandoned touring and the Stones were still attempting to recover their equilibrium after the Altamont tragedy, The Who became the world's premier touring outfit.

However, *Tommy*'s success threw up several dilemmas, not least a growing perception that they were now solely an album act. With their singles languishing in the lower reaches of the charts, there was a sense that *Tommy*'s success had defined The

Who as a concept act, with all the restrictions and expectations that the tag embodied. Concerned that *Tommy* could easily prove to be an albatross around their necks, Townshend decreed that a turnaround in style was required to dig them out of their funk.

In an era when experimentalism was to the fore, Townshend conceived *Lifehouse*, a futuristic fantasy set in a time way beyond contemporary music and envisaged as a 'celestial cacophony'. Ultimately, the complexity of the concepts overwhelmed Townshend and alienated those close to him. Despite *Lifehouse*'s ambitions being light years ahead of any other musical project of the period, it floundered.

Nonetheless, rising from the ashes of the project was the album *Who's Next*. Belying its simple presentation, the album was embraced warmly by the public and critics alike, the majority unaware of the album's tricky labour and delivery through the *Lifehouse* debacle.

Despite *Lifehouse*'s collapse, Townshend decided to mine rock operatics further, although in a new direction way beyond *Tommy*'s nebulous whimsy. Continually assessing his and the band's history, Townshend's brief was to look back, somewhat cathartically, at the legend of The Who – a project he provisionally entitled *Long Live Rock: Rock Is Dead*. This reflective approach was a re-evaluation that several bands of the period were undertaking, many of them tiring of and querying the cosy niche success had afforded them. Whereas The Beatles had turned full circle for their *Let It Be* sessions, the Stones were constantly striving to reassume their primary sound (their forays into contemporary rock having been mostly disastrous). Similarly terrified to be typecast by success, Townshend was eager to revisit the enthusiasm of the band's early days.

The concept of *Long Live Rock: Rock Is Dead* was based on the reflections of a fan of the band named Jimmy. Like *Lifehouse* before it, it would never get beyond the conceptual stage and many of the

OPPOSITE: Talking about their generation – The Who.

Who's next

ABOVE: Light relief
– the iconic cover
of *Who's Next*.

tracks were shelved before release. But a couple of the song's earmarked for the concept – 'Love, Reign O'er Me' and 'Is It In My Head?' – would survive for later release.

In between formulating plans for The Who's next stab at recording, Townshend was involved in rehearsals for a comeback show for an ailing Eric Clapton. Britain's finest virtuoso guitarist had just emerged from a disabling heroin addiction and, with Townshend's generous support, a group of close friends and associates had gathered together to help pull Clapton through his dilemma. During rehearsals for the show in Cleeve, Oxfordshire, Townshend had succumbed to a liking for the drug amyl nitrite – a chemical substance that produces a brief euphoric high. The flipside to the drug's ecstatic properties is a comedown similar to amphetamine withdrawal. During a low point after an amyl nitrite session, Townshend had an epiphany that took him back to a summer's night in August 1965 in Brighton – specifically the moments following a Who show at the Florida Rooms, a venue adjacent to Brighton's Aquarium. A stone's throw from the beach and

pier, the ballroom had become a popular spot on the South East's musical itinerary. With The Who appearing there, a large contingent of Mods had made the trip down to the coast to catch the vibe.

Townshend would elucidate this pivotal moment for the BBC in 2012: 'I had a flashback to when I was 19 years old. The Who had just played this amazing gig at the Aquarium Ballroom in Brighton and I was with my art school friend, Des Reed. After the gig we missed the train home, so we hung out and went down under the pier and there were all these boys in parkas with the fucking tide coming up around their feet; they didn't seem to understand they were going to drown. Under the pier, I was coming down from taking purple hearts – the fashionable uppers of the period. Sitting there at Cleeve that day, nine years later, the same feeling came flooding back; of feeling depressed, lost and hopeless, and I grabbed a notebook and quickly, while I was in this sad and lonely mood, I scribbled out the story… This was the story of a Mod called Jimmy. Jimmy was a normal boy with normal needs, passing through the normal things of childhood. But what made everything so much more complicated for him was that he had a bipolar problem: he was schizophrenic.'

Whether Townshend was actually aware of it or not, he'd tapped into a perennial reservoir of angst that every generation could identify with. While authors such as J.D. Salinger had crystallised teenage confusion in *The Catcher in the Rye*, Townshend charted the debilitating effects of mental illness through the medium of rock music – a revolutionary approach that, with the rare exception of some of Ray Davies's work, was unique at the time.

Townshend's decision to backdrop Jimmy's struggle with the British phenomenon of Mod was an audacious (if potentially ill-judged) move. The lifestyle having passed on nearly a decade before, there was the potential that it could serve to alienate the band, especially from the enormous American market that had adopted the band's progressive sound. And events in Britain had moved on considerably since the early sixties.

'The Mod movement of the sixties was almost forgotten at the time of the recording,' recalled Townshend, years later. 'Skinhead culture was springing up and was much more politically driven, albeit right-wing. The Mods I had known were all more gentle souls, effete in some ways, certainly intelligent and creative. What had happened to Jimmy? Where was he? What had he been through? Did he find what he was looking for?'

With his first-hand experience and observations of the Mod lifestyle, coupled with a gallery of characters he had encountered over the years, Townshend's project possessed enormous authority. The Who were the most idiosyncratic band to survive the sixties, and *Quadrophenia* would fulfil a multitude of aspirations, not least an assessment of Modernism, a cult that had engaged many but had yet to be contextualised.

Townshend built on the *Rock Is Dead: Long Live Rock* premise – to reflect the four personalities of The Who – and delved into the band's psyche. He aligned them with a quartet of themes for Jimmy and explained to Melvyn Bragg in 1974 how 'Jimmy's made up of four archetypal extreme personality types. One is a reflection of Roger's personality, which is tough and assertive. The other is Keith Moon's personality type, which is devil-may-care – 'I'll take anything, I'll eat anything, I'll jump off Tower Bridge – who cares?' The other is John Entwistle's aspect... a great secret romantic... The other side was [mine]... the mystical, frustrated seeker.'

With four musical overtures composed for each personality, the concept found immediate favour with the other band members.

Roger Daltrey: 'We got the essence of it, that this guy's got the personalities of every member of the band and it's just [based] on this one guy. And that was enough for me to say, "Great idea, let's go for it."'

While Townshend and Daltrey were publicly eager to promote the band's personalisation of *Quadrophenia*'s lead, there were other, more intimate, reflections pertinent to the concept.

'Jimmy's character was based on Pete Townshend,' recalled producer and Who manager Bill Curbishley to author John Hellier. 'It was based on me, it was based on Chris Stamp, it was based on [Pete] Meaden, it was based on a guy called Mike Shaw and many others from that time… We were all little streams that fed into a river! We all did the same things, we were all copying each other. "Jimmy" was a composite of all the different people that Townshend knew back in 1964.'

'WE GOT THE ESSENCE OF IT, THAT THIS GUY'S GOT THE PERSONALITIES OF EVERY MEMBER OF THE BAND AND IT'S JUST [BASED] ON THIS ONE GUY.'
ROGER DALTREY

With the band fully behind the project, Townshend's original blueprint began to blossom into a full visualised life of Jimmy. Jimmy was a deeply troubled soul whose only constant was the Modernist lifestyle he desperately hoped would reward him with the stability he craved. Through sixteen tracks and a library of prescient sound effects, Jimmy's odyssey takes him through a gamut of situations and emotions: from home life to workplace; from street to club; through drug highs and mental lows, love, rejection and betrayal before he finds himself under the big skies on a beach where a destiny of sorts presents itself. Whereas *Tommy* had relied solely on the songs to tell the story, *Quadrophenia*'s library of sounds demanded a greater connection with the themes of the narrative.

Recording for the album took place, in fairly arduous conditions, over a fifteen-month period before its eventual release in October 1973. With new and refined sonics continually evolving, the era of quadraphonic sound was set to hit home stereo systems. This heavily publicised separation of elements would dovetail neatly with Townshend's thematic presentation, although ultimately the quadraphonic sound approach would falter.

Nonetheless, if *Quadrophenia*'s intention was to display all facets of The Who, it succeeded in every sense. While the semantics of the piece correlated with the angst documented earlier in such compositions as 'I Can't Explain' and 'Anyway, Anyhow, Anywhere', the music itself bordered, at times, on anthemic. For Mods' rigid tastes, while the landscape was familiar, the music was sailing close to contemporary rock.

> **'WHEN I BOUGHT THE ALBUM, IT WAS LIKE A GUIDE TO LIFE: HOW TO DRESS, WHERE TO GO, IT WAS AS IMPORTANT AS THE MUSIC.'**
> **BRETT 'BUDDY' ASCOTT**

With American sensibilities an important consideration, Townshend was savvy enough to realise that a multi-media exposition would be required to underpin the more parochial details of the concept. A short essay, serving as the nuts and bolts of the story, was written by Townshend and included on the inside jacket of the sleeve. Written in a frenetic first-person narrative, the tale charted Jimmy's battle for survival.

To avoid overseas fans feeling excluded by the Britishness of the themes, Townshend commissioned photographer of the moment Ethan Russell to take a series of photographs for a lavish booklet to wrap around the two discs. With a cast of unknowns taking to the streets of South London to pose for Russell's lens, Jimmy's struggle for identity was processed into a monochrome reality. Despite having no captions, *Quadrophenia*'s visual representation served to furnish the curious and the neophyte with a virtual Haynes manual of the Mod lifestyle – and would become iconic.

OPPOSITE:
Quadrophenia's creator Pete Townshend takes the air at Brighton, September 1978.

Brett 'Buddy' Ascott, later drummer with Mod revivalists The Chords, recalls the effect the visuals had on him as a youngster growing up in the seventies: 'Quadrophenia is for me the epitome of the album packaging matching the music. When I bought the album, it was like a guide to life: how to dress, where to go, it was as important as the music... The booklet has two important points: it has the essay at the beginning which sets out the story – if you can't follow it from the music alone. And it's got the photographs, and the photographs are very important because they show a London and Brighton as [they were] in the sixties.'

The messages embedded in Quadrophenia's booklet made their way out to the four corners of the world, awakening many to the Mod ethos and confirming the validity of the movement to those who'd experienced the phenomenon first time around. Reviews were mixed, though, and while the album was hugely popular in the UK, commentators abroad were less convinced. This review from Lenny Kaye of Rolling Stone exemplifies this feeling:

'Quadrophenia is The Who at their most symmetrical, their most cinematic, ultimately their most maddening. Captained by Pete Townshend, they have put together a beautifully performed and magnificently recorded essay of a British youth mentality in which they played no little part, lushly endowed with black and white visuals and a heavy sensibility of the wet-suffused air of 1965... Nonetheless, the album fails to generate a total impact because of its own internal paradox:

OPPOSITE:
Quadrophenia UK album release 1973.

Instead of the four-sided interaction implicit in the title and overriding concept, Quadrophenia is itself the product of a singular (albeit brilliant) consciousness. The result is a static quality which the work never succeeds in fully overcoming. Townshend has taken great pains with the record, has carried it within him for over a year, has laboriously fitted each piece of its grand scale in place. Yet in winning the battle, he's lost the war and more's the pity... Quadrophenia falls short of the mark. Jimmy Livingston Seagull [sic], adrift on a stormless sea, with only his shattered wings and shared memories to keep him company – so close, and yet so far.'

Minor brickbats aside, Quadrophenia would hover over the top spot in both the UK and American charts for months, eventually going gold on both sides of the Atlantic. With Quadrophenia's songs filling a large part of the band's setlist, their 1973 US tour would preview the new material to sell-out crowds. Once the tour had drawn to a close, The Who would move on to other projects. It would take another four years for Quadrophenia to enchant a more receptive audience – ironically the generation that had missed it first time around.

If Quadrophenia the album succeeded in feeding its listeners with a multitude of imagery, like its predecessor Tommy it screamed for visual representation. Strangely, despite all their achievements in numerous disciplines, The Who were yet to exploit cinema. In just a few short years, all that would change. ●

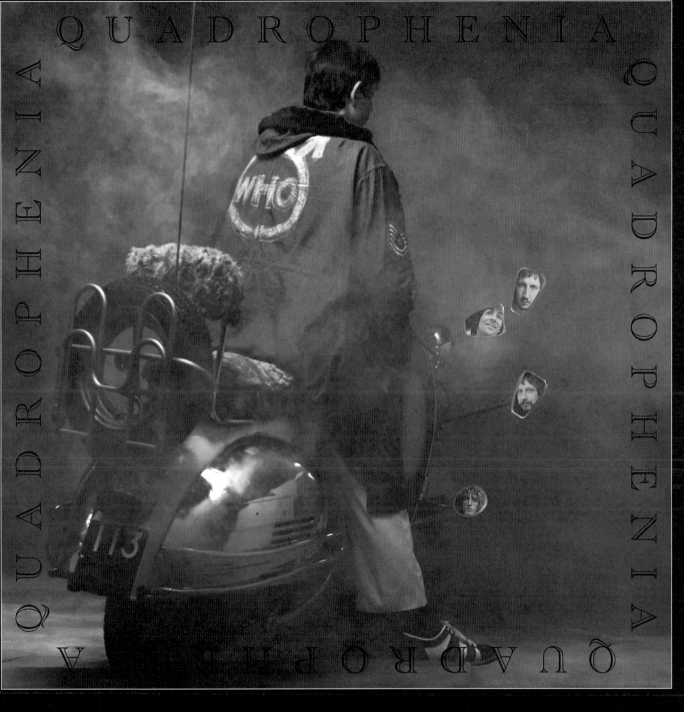

CHAPTER TWO

'I THINK SOME PEOPLE THOUGHT WE WERE GOING TO MAKE A DICK LESTER PICTURE, Y'KNOW, LIKE THE BEATLES. THEY GOT A BIT OF A SURPRISE.'

—ROY BAIRD, *QUADROPHENIA* FILM PRODUCER, 2005

QT he conclusion of the *Quadrophenia* tour in early 1974 brought the project to a momentary halt. Despite its vivid imagery and themes, the album did not kick-start a full-blown Modernist revival in Britain or abroad. Aside from a few diehards venturing to seaside locations on Bank Holidays to relive past glories, a major rekindling of the scene was not forthcoming. It was probably not that surprising. In a landscape dominated by glitter, permed hair, outlandish heels and flared satin trousers, a return towards a more conservative appearance was an unlikely proposition.

Nonetheless, it was somewhat predictable that the rich textures within *Quadrophenia* would inspire someone to animate them into a greater reality. Late in 1973, intrepid amateur filmmaker Dave Worrell did just that. Having been intrigued by the narrative of The Who's album, he wrote a screenplay around what he'd gleaned from the booklet and the sonics contained within.

'I was impressed by the music and the various sound effects which linked the tracks into a storyline,' reported Worrell to *Movie Maker* magazine in 1980. 'I had decided from the start to stick as closely as possible to the original storyline, but I had to cut the clashes between Mods and Rockers as these would have been far too more

expensive for me to recreate.'

Having collected a cast and crew, Worrell began the most ambitious task of creating a film that would join the dots together from *Quadrophenia*'s fragmented imagery – a project he'd entitle *For A Moment*. The necessary interiors collected from around his Birmingham locale, Worrell's team followed Jimmy's *Quadrophenia* trail, picking up locations in London, Brighton and further afield. With kind assistance from the guardians of Brighton's pier and the equally iconic Grand Hotel, Worrell created the first cinematic reflection of *Quadrophenia*.

Aware that the film would need an accompanying soundtrack, Worrell wrote to The Who's office, and following a labyrinth of referrals, would elicit a blessing from none other than Pete Townshend.

Despite its limitations in technical quality and budget, *For A Moment* spookily mirrors what would ultimately be realised some 4 years later in The Who's official film. Indeed, so startlingly similar would be some of the sequences captured by Worrell and Co., it would appear bizarre that no one in The Who's organisation had seen the film – but this is the case.

Just A Moment entered into a national amateur film competition during 1975, it received a three-star award. In 1977, just as *Quadrophenia* the movie

OPPOSITE AND NEXT SPREAD: Production shots from Dave Worrell's *Quadrophenia* themed film *For A Moment.*

was starting to be looked at seriously. Worrell's movie would receive a first prize in the BBC's Action 77 filmmakers competition, one of the judges being Monty Python star Terry Jones. While Worrell's film remains largely unseen for over 40 years, the filmmaker is now a successful author of movie-related books and also co-publisher of *Cinema Retro* magazine.

With no new group material scheduled for the immediate future, The Who found themselves in an unsettling state of flux – one not experienced since before their rise to fame. John Entwistle shuffled through the accumulation of discarded Who material to compile *Odds And Sods*. In between a few *Lifehouse* outtakes and other rarities, Pete Meaden's 'I'm The Face' received its largest audience to date, and elsewhere, Pete Townshend, Roger Daltrey and Keith Moon were actively pursuing a chance to expand beyond their Who personas; all three of them concentrating on solo projects. The announcement that *Tommy*, the band's most globally identifiable piece of work, was heading towards a cinematic interpretation ignited interest in the media and among fans. Expectations were high.

Remarkably, given their imaginative bent, film was a medium The Who hadn't previously contemplated, and many of their peers also failed to grasp the opportunities it presented. While The Beatles had redrawn the medium of the pop musical in the sixties, the Mop Tops singularly failed to advance beyond the cheeky adventures of *A Hard Day's Night* (1964) and *Help!* (1965). Inspired by the Fab Four's lead, a handful of other musicians had made perfunctory forays into cinema in search of creative and financial glory, but, with a few notable exceptions – The Dave Clark Five's *Catch Us If You Can* (1965), The Monkees' *Head* (1968) and Mick Jagger in *Performance* (1970) – most were met with derision and viewed as little more than cheap exploitative fodder designed to prolong ailing musical careers. While The Who had appeared in the documentary works of auteurs such as D.A.

ABOVE: *Tommy*
on its journey to
enchant the world's
cinemas.

Pennebaker (*Monterey Pop*, 1968) and Michael Wadleigh (*Woodstock*, 1970), their potential on film was uncharted territory.

Discussions about committing *Tommy* to the big screen had been active since the late sixties. Open to suggestions about just where an adaptation might go, Townshend had already had a series of conversations with director Ken Russell – a larger-than-life personality who'd loudly welcomed rock music's explosive manifesto and viewed the genre as a natural extension to musical innovation of the past. Russell's controversial direction of productions such as *Women in Love* (1969) and, notably, *The Devils* (1971), eclipsed much of his earlier work for television, a medium that had allowed the director space to commit the life stories of a host of composers to screen. With The Who arguably the first band of rock musicians to seriously mine the landscape of contemporary operatics, a collaboration with an auteur such as Russell was seen as dangerously exciting.

Predictably, a buzz developed; the word in the industry suggested that the film of *Tommy* would be far greater than a simple exposition of the 1969 album. Daltrey bagged the lead role, and rumours were rife that a galaxy of stars from the worlds of music and film were to be part of Russell's interpretation. Adding considerable gravitas to the project, Townshend agreed to coordinate and reinterpret the original album. Taking a large part of 1974 to arrange and score, and consumed by the complexities of soundtrack arrangements, Townshend cut back The Who's touring and recording schedule to an absolute minimum.

Over a hectic twelve weeks, and with a budget exceeded by twice its original forecast, *Tommy* was completed by the summer of 1974. Backed by a publicity campaign of over $100,000, *Tommy*'s transference to the screen proved to be an unusually exciting experience for many. Despite some critics passing over the film, audiences and fans of the group heaped praise on *Tommy*'s inventive presentation. Internationally, it lit up numerous territories, its vibrant imagery transcending any parochial restrictions. Townshend's experience of working with Ken Russell proved salutatory, however – it was one, he declared, that he didn't wish to repeat.

Regardless of the mixed critical reception, returns from *Tommy*, especially from America, were enormous; the film grossed over $2 million in just one month and went on to make $16 million in 1975 alone. The Who's reputation was given a further boost by the film's global distribution and soundtrack release, and their subsequent touring programme saw the group playing larger arenas with box office records broken everywhere.

Of all the band members, it was Daltrey who appeared most energised by the filming process.

Immediately after completing work on *Tommy*, he reconnected with Ken Russell to film the life of Franz Liszt, *Lisztomania*. Daltrey, under Russell's wayward direction, would competently weave his way through a series of vignettes from the German composer's life.

Meanwhile, The Who's recording oeuvre appeared to have fallen into a rut. The patchy *Who By Numbers* collection of 1975 hinted at unsettling energies, and the group decided to scale down their activities after a decade of non-stop touring and recording. With film work and solo offerings from all four members reducing their live appearances, some critics were suggesting that they were lacking the direction that drove their previous work. Adding to the malaise, Townshend and Daltrey were trading differences in the media and Keith Moon's behaviour was hitting new heights of excess. The immediate future of The Who appeared to be in doubt.

The group began to look seriously at their business interests. Bill Curbishley assumed a greater presence in The Who's managerial future. He had previously worked alongside Chris Stamp on The Who's label, Track Records, in the early seventies – organising tours for the band and other artists on the label's roster. An unashamed first generation Mod, during the sixties Curbishley had travelled frequently from his native East End to Brighton and other points on the Mod dial. A friend and former business associate of Pete Meaden, Curbishley was intimately aware of the territory that Townshend spoke of in *Quadrophenia* and was hugely instrumental in realising its potential.

Securing management duties for The Who in 1974, Curbishley and his wife Jackie formed Trinifold Ltd, a music publishing group with a particular interest in The Who's output. The success of *Tommy* was opening up new possibilities, and expanding the group's catalogue in a variety of cinematic directions became a priority. Thus, The Who Films Ltd, a division dedicated to exploiting any potential cinema projects, was formed; it was a wise move

that would wrestle production control away from corporate organisations. To house and develop these new interests, the group acquired property within the Shepperton Studios film complex.

Curbishley persuaded Polydor to take a serious look at the potential of Who film-related projects. With Townshend's music and Daltrey's acting prowess, it appeared to be an obvious and marketable rite of passage. Curbishley had an influential advocate who shared a similar vision for The Who's transference to screen, in old friend and then-managing director of the record label Polydor, Fred Haayen. A fan of The Who, Haayen had been instrumental in signing them to Polydor and immediately green-lighted *Quadrophenia*'s pre-production as well as giving the go-ahead for *McVicar*, a powerful screen adaptation of the life and times of former gangster and 'public enemy number one', John McVicar.

Another project that was due for exploitation was a retrospective anthology of the group to date, to be brought to the screen. On the face of it, the project appeared to be a fairly simple task. To chart the group's history, American director Jeff Stein had located a huge arsenal of archive footage. Stein was a personality who'd been known to the group for some years, and he'd impressed them with a brief show-reel of clips he'd compiled in advance of the project. Unfortunately, the film's ascendancy was stalled by the red tape required to license the clips, but, with a soundtrack album to be released in tandem, the omens were good for the film's

LEFT:
Quadrophenia's future director Franc Roddam.

THE WHO

The Kids Are Alright

You've heard the sounds. Now live the life. Because only seeing is believing!

MUSIC FROM THE SOUNDTRACK AVAILABLE ON Polydor RECORDS AND TAPES

ROCK FILMS LIMITED PRESENTS A JEFF STEIN FILM starring **THE WHO/ROGER DALTREY/PETE TOWNSHEND/JOHN ENTWISTLE/KEITH MOON** in **THE KIDS ARE ALRIGHT** AA/Edited by Ed Rothkowitz/Producers: Tony Klinger/Bill Curbishley/Executive Producer Sydney Rose/Conceived and Directed by Jeff Stein
RELEASED BY BRENT WALKER FILM DISTRIBUTORS LTD.

ABOVE: *The Kids Are Alright*, The Who's 1979 visual retrospective – compiled as *Quadrophenia* went into active production.

financial success. Provisionally entitled *The Kids Are Alright*, this was a chance to reassess The Who's history, visually, musically and thematically, and in an era where home video was an expensive luxury, the reality for fans was that the only chance of witnessing The Who's extraordinary presence was going to a concert.

Alongside work on *The Kids Are Alright*, *Quadrophenia* was now in the first stages of pre-production. *Tommy* was still rewarding The Who with enormous returns, and a chance to build on that film's success appeared to be a formality. In preparation, former manager and associate Chris Stamp completed a treatment of *Quadrophenia*. However, despite his connections with the film industry, it was considered nothing more than a template. It appears that Townshend had a hand in contributing ideas to Stamp's treatment,

although much of what was written harked back to the concepts of the original album. Reportedly mixed into this early draft was a hefty dose of existentialism, an interest that was ever present for both Stamp and Townshend at the time.

Discussing the original draft with *NME* in 1979, Townshend emphasised that 'there was no riot scene at all, not at all. For me, *Quadrophenia* was all about what was going on in the kid's head. The threat: "I'll do anything, I'll go anywhere", and what you are dealing with is a little wimp. Who's fucking useless. Who couldn't fight anybody… It was a study in spiritual desperation.'

With the project stumbling towards fruition, several issues started to become apparent. Whereas *Tommy* was still being eulogised by remnants of the Love generation, *Quadrophenia*'s fusion of psychosis and rock operatics, underpinned by a distinctly British theme, was going to be a much harder sell, especially to the fickle minds of young America – a territory pivotal to the financial success of the film.

Britain's teenage landscape had been scarcely reflected in cinema during the first half of the seventies. The industry was struggling to assume any sense of integrity, and those filmmakers who hadn't escaped abroad appeared content to churn out an endless and unpalatable diet of end-of-the-pier sitcom adaptations, soft-porn romps and trash horror adaptations. British musically-themed films of the seventies were largely of a similar standard and aimed to have a cheap commercial appeal, for example, Cliff Richard in *Take Me High* (1973), Marc Bolan's *Born to Boogie* (1973) and the Gary Glitter documentary, *Remember Me This Way* (1974). Slade's *Flame* (1975), a fictionalised account of the sixties pop landscape, was a rare imaginative beacon and won a small but vocal army of admirers. Less convincing but eminently watchable was David Essex's *That'll Be The Day* (1973). Despite featuring Keith Moon in a hysterical cameo, a new Townshend composition ('Long Live Rock') and several atmospheric hints at alienation à la *Quadrophenia*, the film's plot was stodgily linear. The sequel, *Stardust* (1974), offered little more, other than to prove that nostalgia had a market. With seemingly only a few prepared to take a serious stab at capturing rock culture onscreen, the canvas (in Britain at least) was still largely blank.

Despite the youth market being largely shunned by the film industry, a few exceptional films did surface. *Kes* (1970), directed by Ken Loach, was perhaps the finest and most intelligent example of what could be achieved. Moving, visceral and authentic, Kes succeeded in portraying the hopelessness and brutality of early seventies life, although its focus was not on the rocky landscape of gang mentality and its attendant clothes and affiliations. *Melody* (1971) was an unashamedly romantic and charming look at pre-teen life in working-class London. Warm and affectionate,

the film succeeded in capturing the twilight world of puberty, but its brief was never to challenge its audience.

A closer inspection of youthful highs and lows was captured in Barney Platts-Mills' extraordinary debut, *Bronco Bullfrog*, released in 1969. Made on a ridiculously low budget of just £18,000, the film was shot, guerrilla-style, in just six weeks. Staffed entirely with non-professional actors and hopefuls from local acting schools, *Bronco Bullfrog* was a series of imaginative monochrome snaps of London's East End that captured the sharp reality of existence.

Bronco Bullfrog inadvertently allowed the uniform of the time to drip onto the celluloid. Capturing the cusp of the skinhead movement as it morphed into the broader seudehead culture, the main characters' dress sense bore echoes of sixties Modernism. In many ways, both cinematically and

ABOVE: *Bronco Bullfrog*, made in 1969 and often cited as a thematic predecessor to *Quadrophenia*.

thematically, *Bronco Bullfrog* acted as a powerful blueprint for *Quadrophenia's* screen realisation, although it would take several decades before the film was seriously evaluated.

The moribund landscape of the early seventies was an unforgiving environment. Culture and fashion had become complacent and laissez-faire, and with only the occasional example of daring displayed by footballers and the occasional actor, rock music and its associated cultures had lost its collective mojo. Those in the higher tiers of rock music were wallowing in drugs, esoteric philosophies and flaky self-indulgence, and there was little for the average kid on the street to identify with.

At actual street level, things weren't much better. While only scant traces of Mod existed at the beginning of the decade, the skinhead cult of the early seventies had also swiftly run out of steam. Glam rock and glitter dominated, and unease was haunting Britain's streets. By 1976, the stockpile of resentment, anxiety and anger exploded in a way that hadn't been experienced since the early sixties.

The punk explosion of 1976 having ripped up everything that had gone before, concept albums and rock operatics were viewed with derision. Like many who'd come through the original Mod scene, Pete Townshend viewed punk as a brilliant piece of revolutionary synchronicity and a close reflection of the movement that had transformed Britain's dismal landscape during the sixties. Intrigued by punk's gobbing army of dissenters, Townshend became fascinated with the burgeoning scene exploding across London.

At the pinnacle of the movement stood The Sex Pistols, led and largely articulated by that most intelligent and sharp-tongued dissident John Lydon, aka Johnny Rotten. Punk revelled in its ability to provoke every tier of the establishment, and while the most obvious targets in its sight were the ruling class and pillars of authority, pompous rock stars, especially those who'd revelled in affluent complacency, were also up for summary execution.

Although they would have viewed any association with the past as anachronistic, the Pistols shared much of the angst, frustration and revolutionary qualities of The Who in their earliest phase. But punk's protagonists were publicly deriding anything that reeked of stadium-driven rock, and The Who could well have been lumped in with the other dinosaurs. Nonetheless, with the immediate destiny of The Who unclear, Townshend viewed the movement with great excitement; its confrontational and stark manifestos forced him to rethink his own status and that of the band.

'Punk freed me,' he recalled in 1987. 'It allowed me to be myself. It dignified me, in a way, to be cast to one side. I felt very uneasy with the way that The Who were inevitably on the road to mega-stardom. I believed that the punk movement would free me from that. It did. It freed me from it, that it was all crap and that the bottom line was that it was all crap.'

Fuelled by memories of their formative days, Townshend and Moon started to visit the clubs. Claustrophobic, reeking of filth and fury and fuelled by amphetamines, it was a virtual throwback to the early Mod club scene. Bolstering the belief that the punks were the bastard sons of the original Mods, the Pistols included a few Who, Creation and Small Faces hits in their setlist. Well over a decade since these clubs had hosted the original Mod scene, here it was again, rebooted and rebranded for the seventies. While many of the new punk bands had leapt onto the bandwagon with scant interest in music or culture, others had passed through the ranks of pub rock before morphing into the scene. Many of those acts owed a huge debt to their contemporaries of the sixties, The Who included. While trashing the past was a fashionable pursuit for those riding punk's new wave, the reality was that the scene was not dissimilar to that of its Mod predecessors.

The Jam were one band who proudly wore their influences to The Who and Modernism unashamedly on their sleeves. Strictly on the fringes of punk's battleground, Paul Weller, an 18-year-old from suburban Surrey, had spent years regretting not having been part of the original Modernist movement. With punk slowly yielding

to the more creative new wave scene, Weller and his compatriots arrived – nattily dressed in suits and ties. The influence of The Jam on *Quadrophenia*'s later success cannot be overstated, and while Weller and Co. duly doffed their collective hats to the punk ethos, their smart and uncluttered presence was already igniting a Mod revival around the country.

Despite several attempts to meet with Weller, it wasn't until late 1980 that Townshend held an audience with his young pretender. Townshend had already collided with many luminaries from the punk movement, the Pistols included. Johnny Rotten, then the nation's chief bogeyman, maintained an omnipresence across Britain during 1977. Famed for his untamed and dynamic performances, Rotten's persona belied a sharp and sensitive intelligence. While few would dare to suggest that his charisma would ever be brilliantly conveyed on screen, others – Pete Townshend included – were already sizing up his spindly frame and unique facial expressions for more imaginative use later on.

⊙ 'PUNK FREED ME. IT ALLOWED ME TO BE MYSELF. IT DIGNIFIED ME, IN A WAY, TO BE CAST TO ONE SIDE.'
PETE TOWNSHEND

With this major outpouring of anger coming to a head across the nation, there was a strong probability that Britain's youth would chime with a film version of *Quadrophenia*. Despite the project's association with sixties Modernism, the themes of angst and frustration were no different to what was being experienced then in seventies Britain – and *Quadrophenia* had a transatlantic bedfellow shadowing the film's pre-production.

Yes, *Saturday Night Fever* was dripping in flares, big blow-dried hair and disco (and not least its atmospheric New York location), but the film had its roots in the landscape that *Quadrophenia* drew from. Journalist Nik Cohn's original story – a

DUMMY
PRIX ITALIA 1979

Q 'I PUT A PS ON THE LETTER SAYING I COULD WRITE THEM A SCRIPT FOR *QUADROPHENIA* IF THEY WERE INTERESTED AND THAT'S WHERE IT ALL STARTED.'

ALAN FLETCHER

commissioned feature in *The New York Times* – was, in essence, a work of fiction, but the protagonist was created from a sixties Mod Cohn had known in The Who's old stomping ground of Shepherd's Bush – a character he described as a 'one-time king' of London's Goldhawk Road. The project was firmly in The Who's slipstream, and the sheer potential of the story saw it being snapped up by film producer and Bee Gees manager Robert Stigwood, who had also produced *Tommy*.

Back in England, and with events moving furiously at street level, *Quadrophenia*'s early pre-production was running quietly in tandem with the Mod resurgence that was now gathering momentum. Many who had felt alienated by the punk explosion were looking backwards for smarter

inspiration. *Quadrophenia* the film was little more than a potential film in 1977, its collision with the imminent Mod revival, pure synchronicity.

Despite talk of *Quadrophenia*'s transference to screen over the years, and with treatments from both Townshend and Chris Stamp to hand, ultimately the spark to the project being considered in earnest came from a simple fan letter to Pete Townshend.

Alan Fletcher was a first generation Mod who'd grown through the ranks of the fifties beatnik scene. A native of Stockton-on-Tees in the North of England, he had witnessed first-hand Mod's enlivening of working-class Britain and he was keen to chronicle his experience through literature and the medium of film. When The Who publicly announced their intention to explore cinematic possibilities beyond *Tommy*, he sent Townshend a script, entitled *Two Stroke Sonata*.

'Well, it all started with a film script I'd written in the mid-seventies,' reflected Fletcher to the Sohostrut website in 2011. 'I had tried to get it produced on TV, with some encouraging "reviews" but with no offer of production. I saw Townshend on television one night and he was saying they were getting into films so I sent the script to him asking him if they were able to produce it. I put a PS on the letter saying I could write them a script for *Quadrophenia* if they were interested and that's where it all started.'

Duly inspired by the possibilities, Fletcher began writing *Quadrophenia*'s first draft. His script was warmly received by Townshend and Bill Curbishley (who would later produce *Quadrophenia*). The practicalities of transferring Fletcher's concept to the screen proved to be insurmountable, but his blueprint was enough for The Who's management to start thinking seriously about employing professional scriptwriters.

Several of Fletcher's vignettes survived for the finished product, though: the character of Steph, while not defined in name as such, was his creation; as was a humorous moment when two of Jimmy's crowd find themselves sharing a Brighton beach hut with some sleeping Rockers – a scenario drawn from a real incident that occurred in Yarmouth during the sixties; and Jimmy's old school friend turned Rocker getting beaten up by Mods was also Fletcher's idea.

Given his encyclopaedic knowledge of Mod culture, Alan Fletcher was retained as a consultant for the entirety of the project and, with the possibility of a *Quadrophenia* novelisation, commissioned to dramatise the finished script into book form once the film was released.

There had been other approaches that were later claimed as possible influences on *Quadrophenia*'s future appearance on film. One was a storyline by original Mod and early Who fan 'Irish' Jack Lyons. He had been one of their most ardent fans in an era when the line between artists and admirers was thin.

During the band's formative days back in Shepherd's Bush, Lyons and Townshend kept up an enthusiastic line of communication concerning the rich palette of emotions that Mods were experiencing. Lyons' association with The Who would endure over the years and, when the *Quadrophenia* album appeared, he was inspired to write his own response to what he'd heard and seen

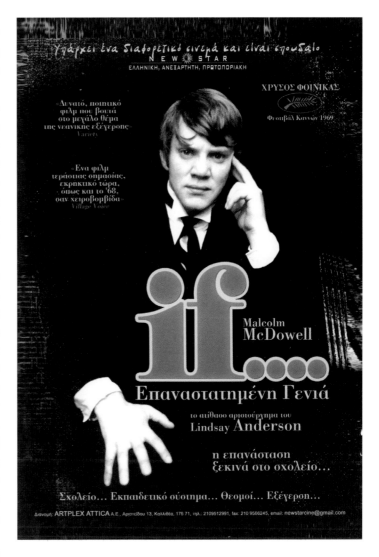

in the album's booklet. Claiming that *Quadrophenia* was akin to 'an apple tree planted in my head', Lyons produced five copies of his take on Jimmy's life: one for himself and the rest for each member of The Who. While Lyons' observations were never considered a basis for a screenplay, elements of what he was writing about were deemed worthy of preserving, and a copy was filed away for use later on. Once pre-production began, Lyons' association with The Who's early days bore fruit – he was duly courted for consultancy duties.

Enter producer Roy Baird, a character who carried a wealth of film experience from his earliest days at Elstree Studios. Having endured the trials

ABOVE: A bona fide classic, Lindsay Anderson's *If...* (1968) boasted future *Quadrophenia* producer Roy Baird on its credits.

and tribulations of post-war British cinema, by the early seventies he was considered the finest first assistant director in the industry. He then moved into producing.

Baird had strong links with some of the most challenging British films, not least with Lindsay Anderson's revolutionary schoolboy satire *If...*, which he worked on in 1968. Some six years before, he'd acted as a first assistant director on the cult classic *The Leather Boys* – arguably the first film to seriously assess early sixties British gang culture. An assistant producer on the James Bond spoof *Casino Royale* (1967), Baird had also been an executive producer on the rock-centric drama *That'll Be The Day* (1973). He had come to The Who's attention during *Tommy* and then *Lisztomania*, and subsequently forged a management partnership with The Who's manager Bill Curbishley, a relationship that would form the bedrock of the band's film wing.

The Who Films Ltd would assume hands-on production duties for both *Quadrophenia* and *The Kids Are Alright*. The latter production requiring only a small portion of contemporary material; more creative concerns were being invested in *Quadrophenia*. Anticipating a huge amount of by-product from the associated soundtracks, Polytel (the German company that oversaw the group's record label Polydor) pumped $2 million into *Quadrophenia*. With the promise of distribution from the (then) influential Brent Walker organisation, the all-important finance was now in place. All that was needed was a finished script and a director.

Both Roy Baird and Bill Curbishley were actively talking up *Quadrophenia*, and the script was entering yet another round of revisions. Whereas Townshend's original concept employed a nebulous,

thematic approach, *Quadrophenia* would call for a much more tangible exposition of the protagonist's environs and, equally, an exploration of the angst that underpinned his every move.

With The Who's music serving as the aural landscape, *Quadrophenia* the film was conceived to process the story into a tangible reality. Given that an intrinsic part of the movement was based on attention to detail, there was a risk that every frame of the completed film would be examined with a fastidious eye. In 1978 Mod was still relatively fresh in people's memories, and as a result, an enormous amount of effort went into ensuring the detail of the picture would be as authentic as the movement that spawned it.

TIME WAS NOW OF THE ESSENCE. YET NO SCRIPT HAD BEEN COMPLETED, AND THERE WAS ALSO THE PRESSING ISSUE OF FINDING A DIRECTOR WHO COULD MANAGE THE PICTURE'S DEMANDS

Time was now of the essence. Yet no script had been completed, and there was also the pressing issue of finding a director who could manage the picture's demands. Nic Roeg (of *Performance* and *Walkabout* fame) and Alan Parker were early candidates, but, for reasons unknown, they were unable to commit. On November 9th, 1977, an explosive television drama entitled *Dummy* handed *Quadrophenia* its director. At *Dummy*'s helm was 31-year-old Franc Roddam and it was his energetic presence that would ultimately transform *Quadrophenia*'s beginnings into a reality. ●

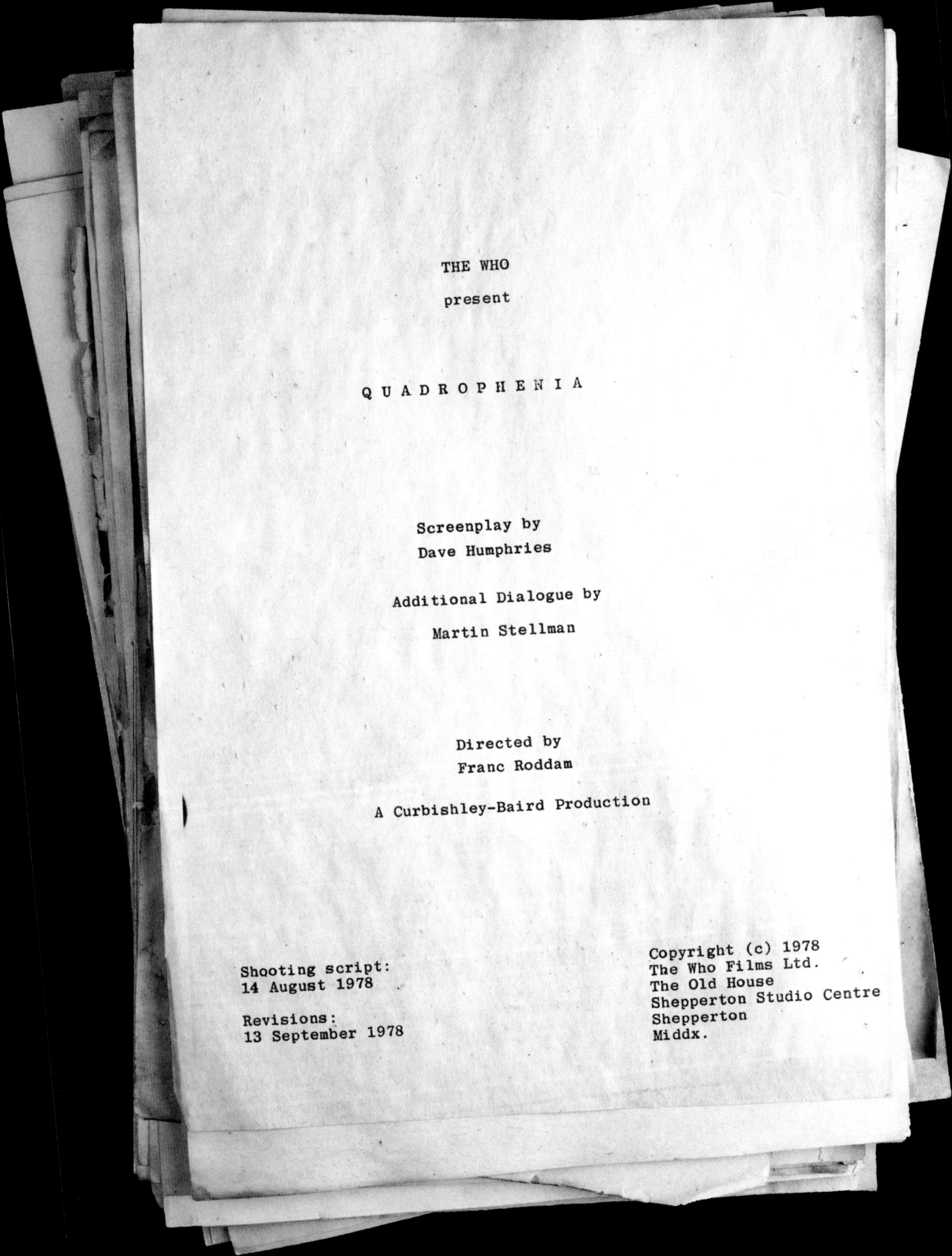

THE WHO

present

Q U A D R O P H E N I A

Screenplay by

Dave Humphries

Additional Dialogue by

Martin Stellman

Directed by

Franc Roddam

A Curbishley-Baird Production

Shooting script:
14 August 1978

Revisions:
13 September 1978

Copyright (c) 1978
The Who Films Ltd.
The Old House
Shepperton Studio Centre
Shepperton
Middx.

CHAPTER THREE

'JIMMY, A YOUNG MOD IN HIS LATE TEENS, RIDES THROUGH THE NIGHT STREETS OF THE SHEPHERD'S BUSH AREA ON HIS SCOOTER, COMPLETE WITH WING MIRRORS, PENNANTS AND MOD REGALIA. JIMMY IS SERENE, WEAVING AND CRUISING ALONG THE ROAD; UNTIL, ONE BY ONE, THE REAR VIEW MIRRORS BLAZE WITH HEADLIGHTS... BRIEFLY JIMMY IS TRAILED, SURROUNDED AND BUZZED BY A PACK OF HALF-A-DOZEN ROCKERS IN THEIR HELMETS AND LEATHERS, RIDING TRIUMPHS, NORTONS AND ROADROCKETS. AFTER SOME TAUNTS AND JEERS, UNINTELLIGIBLE AMID THE NOISE OF THEIR BIKES, THEY SURGE AWAY FROM HIM...'

—THE OPENING SCENE FROM *QUADROPHENIA*'S SCRIPT

By 1978 Franc Roddam was being referred to as one of the most exciting filmmakers of his generation. Born in Norton, Durham, England on April 29th, 1946, Roddam's early years were backdropped by the magic of film. With two cinemas at the end of his street, the youngster became smitten by the infinite possibilities of the medium.

Roddam lived in the North of England during his teens and then, eschewing the expected route of working in the local shipyard, became something of a beatnik and followed the hippie trail around India, Egypt, Libya and Turkey.

Back on home turf, Roddam began to process his dreams of working in the cinema. He gravitated to the London Film School in central London in the late sixties. Based in Shelton Street, Covent Garden, coincidentally the college was situated close to where *Quadrophenia* would begin its celluloid ride.

Once he had graduated, Roddam cut his directorial teeth on a host of commercials before moving into television. He first came to national prominence courtesy of some incisive documentary work for the BBC – then at its creative peak in the sixties and early seventies. His first documentary was *The Fight*, a revealing look at the preparations for a heavyweight boxing bout between Joe Bugner and Joe Frazier in London in 1973. The following year, Roddam was at the helm of a 12-part documentary series entitled *The Family*. With enormous viewing

OPPOSITE: *Quadrophenia*'s shooting script revised just days before shooting was due to commence.

figures and predictable interest from the tabloids, the real-life dramas of the Watkins family made for groundbreaking television, fly-on-the-wall productions still being in their infancy in the seventies.

Roddam's promise confirmed by *The Family*'s daring approach, he moved on to other similarly challenging pieces of work. In 1975, he directed a remarkable documentary for the BBC's *Inside Story* series – *Mini*. This 45-minute feature focused on a troubled child arsonist beset with numerous issues. No one knew it at the time, but *Mini* was to strike an oblique reference to *Quadrophenia* later on. Roddam was then commissioned by actor Dustin Hoffman to make a short film about his ballerina wife Anne, entitled *Dancer*. In 1977 Roddam would direct one of the most controversial dramas in television history, ATV's *Dummy*. The BBC had a reputation for producing most of the pioneering TV dramas of the sixties and seventies, but independent television occasionally rose to the occasion, *Dummy* being one of the finest examples.

Based on a true story, *Dummy* charted the dismal fortunes of a deaf-mute girl named only as Sandra X (played by Geraldine James). The film follows Sandra's poverty-stricken life, from her manipulation and degradation to eventual prostitution on the streets of Bradford, North Yorkshire, before her deeply disturbing fate. Utilising stark realism, any lines between fiction and reality were disturbingly blurred.

With *Dummy*'s pre-publicity quoting Roddam as saying that he wanted to 'expand the margins of your tolerance', on the night of November 9th, 1977, over fourteen million people tuned in. Ninety minutes later, and with questions already being tabled in Parliament, the nation leant back and took a deep breath. *Dummy* went on to be a landmark in British television drama, winning a coveted Prix Italia Drama Prize among other accolades.

Quadrophenia's co-producer Roy Baird was one of the fourteen million who'd watched *Dummy* that November evening. Roddam's name kept coming up in conversation during the months that followed, and coincidentally, two luminaries of British film direction, Alan Parker and David Puttnam, also championed Roddam's suitability for *Quadrophenia*. Baird secured a copy of *Dummy*, and a screening was held in The Who's production office during the spring of 1978.

'Roy Baird came to me and suggested we watched *Dummy*,' reported Bill Curbishley to the author in 2012. 'We thought Franc had done a great job, we called him down to London, met him and immediately thought he was right.'

The early part of 1978 was consumed with the usual rubber-stamping of financing for the picture. By the beginning of June, the green light was on for active pre-production to begin.

'I got contracted on 13th June, 1978,' recalled Roddam later, 'and we were filming on 26th September.' His task at the helm of the production was immense: he had just over three months to complete a script, cast the film, gather a crew and secure locations. If that wasn't a hectic enough schedule, there were plenty of landmines to negotiate before the camera started rolling.

As well as being keen to work on his first full-length feature film, Roddam had another good reason to associate himself with the project. Following one of his jaunts abroad as a teenager, he'd returned to England in the mid-sixties to find that his home turf had undergone something of a Mod conversion. 'I had come back from travelling in Istanbul at the end of one summer,' he told the author in 1999. 'Suddenly everyone was a Mod. There were Mod weddings, Mod parties. With a lot of the scenes, I borrowed events that happened to me and my friends and also little things, like putting the Durex on the fingers, were all incidents from the lives of people I knew.'

Equally, the street violence he'd witnessed as a youngster growing up in the North would serve to imbue *Quadrophenia* with a gritty authenticity. 'I come from a violent town,' he said to *NME* in

1979. 'So I did get involved in a lot of street fights. I also think I know the ambitions of that group of people. I know the economic problems. So I didn't have to do much research except to remind myself, to make sure my memory wasn't being distorted by affection or disaffection.'

Some fourteen years later and armed with his personal experience of the original Mod landscape, Roddam duly devoted the next three months of his life to bringing *Quadrophenia* to life. Contractually on board and with the film's pre-production advancing at a furious pace, there was no looking back.

'The whole thing was a rollercoaster,' he told the BBC in 2004. 'We rushed through this. Roy [Baird] was very cool and he said to me, "More or less, I trust you. Do what you want in terms of the story." Pete Townshend also gave me the same sort of freedom.'

Townshend and Roddam forged an excellent rapport on their first meeting – sharing many opinions on British society and how punk had revolutionised the nation's youth – but, despite the conviviality, it's evident that Townshend had his own firm ideas for the film's screen adaptation, which were at odds with Roddam's vision. Keen to energise the storyline with the early fury of The Who, Roddam wasn't convinced that an operatic treatment (*Tommy*-style) would best serve the reality of the piece. 'I didn't want to make a rock opera for several reasons,' he admitted to *NME* in 1979. 'I didn't think the subject was a rock-opera type and I'm not that kind of director anyway. I've been brought up in the school of realism, so therefore I couldn't be a Ken Russell.'

'When I met Pete,' he recalled in 2004, 'he wanted to do it like *Tommy*. He brought me some orchestration tapes with strings and violins. I said, "No, that is *Tommy* – this is *Quadrophenia*. This is about street kids, this is going to be about rock and roll; this is going to be very raw and that suits my style as a filmmaker." And he immediately kind of folded in the nicest possible way and said:

"Make the film you want to make, I'm with you." And I felt that was an incredible freedom to be given to me.'

In addition to his encounters with Townshend, Roddam found himself clashing with the other members of The Who in the run-up to filming. Mid-1978 found the group in a good space. With film projects *Quadrophenia*, *The Kids Are Alright*, and Daltrey's solo vehicles, *McVicar* and *The Legacy*, in production, as well as sessions for their album *Who Are You* taking place, the group were enjoying a busy renewal of activity.

Roddam has since recalled that Entwistle was generally happy with the supposed direction of

⦿ 'I DIDN'T WANT TO MAKE A ROCK OPERA FOR SEVERAL REASONS. I DIDN'T THINK THE SUBJECT WAS A ROCK-OPERA TYPE AND I'M NOT THAT KIND OF DIRECTOR ANYWAY.'
FRANC RODDAM

the picture and was looking forward to reworking the music for the film. Daltrey, the most film-conscious of the group, was concerned that the fashions of the time be properly attended to and made numerous suggestions as to its stylistic direction. This would extend to ensuring that the young band earmarked for the film were as authentic as possible.

Of little surprise, Roddam's meeting with Keith Moon was extraordinary in every sense of the word. By the beginning of 1978, although Moon's mental health and weight were spiralling out of control, he was on a high following his cameo in Mae West's final film, *Sextette*. Roddam's discussions with the other members of The Who had been positive and constructive: a meeting with 'Moon the Loon' was a far more challenging prospect.

Their meeting occurred during the race to

ABOVE: Keith Moon from his album *Two Sides Of The Moon*.

finalise the film's pre-production. Arriving in a vintage Rolls-Royce, Moon was dressed in jodhpurs, wearing a monocle, and accompanied by a minder (a character famed, allegedly, for having once thrown someone down an elevator shaft). The odds were stacked against Roddam.

'Moonie was the last to come,' he recalled for the BBC. 'He arrived in a big old Rolls-Royce with an eight-foot bodyguard who insisted on sitting in on the meeting. Every time I spoke the bodyguard laughed at me… [Moon] liked to talk like Long John Silver in *Treasure Island*, and he said to me, "I've got a great idea. Why don't we direct the film together?" and I said, "Yeah, okay, as long as I can drum on the next Who album."'

Roddam's succinct reply would serve to neuter any further demands from Moon and the drummer would have no further input to *Quadrophenia*'s development. While his health had been a cause for concern for several years, no one had any inkling as to where events would take him in the next few months.

As the creator of *Quadrophenia*, Townshend was acutely aware of how important the authenticity of the picture had to be, especially bearing in mind its financial limitations. 'The biggest danger is that it could come out looking like *That'll Be The Day* or *Stardust*,' Townshend commented prior to filming, 'because low-production British pictures have that look about them. I suppose I'm banking on the fact that Franc Roddam is, I think, the only British TV director who's going to make that transition to film. If he does pull it off, I don't think there's going to be any stopping him.'

With Roddam's direction confirmed by all four members of the band, he could now turn to the job in earnest. However, before any active pre-production could take place, he had to look seriously at the script. With only the fragmentary segments and insights from Pete Townshend, Chris Stamp and 'Irish' Jack Lyons, the need for a tangible and credible document was paramount to satisfy the financiers that a script was ready. Alan Fletcher's draft had found some favour with Townshend and Curbishley, but producer Roy Baird wasn't too enamoured with it. Baird told Roddam that he had three weeks to have a script prepared for filming. The director's workload was mounting. He began scouting around for the right individual, someone who could write a script quickly, and with conviction.

Barrie Keeffe, later to achieve considerable acclaim for writing *The Long Good Friday* (1980), was a popular choice of the production team, but he was busy with a play at the National Theatre and had to pass. At the suggestion of Roddam, Dave Humphries, a writer with a lengthy television CV, was brought in. In addition to his work on *The Professionals* and other popular crime shows of the period, Humphries had already demonstrated his understanding of rock culture through his contribution to Slade's *Flame*, a project that had gleaned enormous (if not financial) interest. Less impressive was his script for the Joan Collins romp, *The Stud*, filmed prior to his *Quadrophenia* duties...

Finally in possession of all the written fragments that had been stockpiled over the years for *Quadrophenia*, Humphries set about attempting to stitch a script together.

To ensure the script's authenticity, 'Irish' Jack Lyons was flown from Ireland to London and then interviewed by Humphries and others involved in the film's production about his early days on the Shepherd's Bush Mod scene. An interesting vignette of those hectic pre-production days was drawn from Lyons' later reflections for the website, thewho.net.

'Irish' Jack Lyons: 'They interviewed me a million times and I was placed in a claustrophobic 10x8 basement cell, deep in the bowels of Essex

Music on Poland Street, without any windows or air ducts. It was in that stifling environment that I spent my days typing up reams and reams of typical Mod situations and scenarios as I remembered them. This entire inspired product was finding its way over to David Humphries, who was operating at the Trinifold office, in a room much better furnished and roomier than the holding cell where I had been incarcerated. So one day I thought to myself, "I'll take a wander over there to the office and see how *Quadrophenia* is coming along." I arrived and popped my head around the door to say hello to Mike Shaw [*Quadrophenia*'s musical director]. He shared a bit of small talk before adding that I should go and have a chat with Dave Humphries in the next room. So I said, "I will." I tapped on the door, heard the word, "Come!" and pushed open the door. I was immediately surrounded by a much larger executive room than my own, where I found dear old David Humphries typing feverishly with one hand and using the index finger of the other to guide him through each line of an earlier *Quadrophenia* story I myself had written! I thought, "Hey, this is bloody great! You know, he's actually dictating from my own *Quadrophenia* storyline."'

Also popping into The Who's production offices around this time was Pete Meaden. Still allied, in a mainly social context, to the group, he'd been monitoring the journey of Jimmy's psychosis being processed for the screen. Reports have suggested that Meaden had read a treatment and thought that the character of Jimmy was based solely on him, but both Townshend and Curbishley confirm that the protagonist was based on the mixture of characters who informed the original album concept.

Humphries had busily worked in Alan Fletcher's original script with Townshend, Chris Stamp and Lyons' treatments, but the results reportedly lacked a gritty reality that would appeal to audiences. With less than two months until filming was scheduled to begin, Roddam decided to comprehensively rewrite the script, an incredible act of faith that could easily have pushed the shooting schedule further back.

Humphries' script ran to 220 pages (somewhere in the region of three hours' screen time), but *Quadrophenia* was not expected to run longer than 120 minutes. A lot of heavy revision was required to bring it in under time. To assist with the mammoth task of rewriting the script as well as the other demands of pre-production, Roddam called upon an associate of his, Martin Stellman, to assist with the extensive rewrites.

A freelance journalist, musician and playwright, Stellman had recently graduated from the National Film and Television School after studying at Bristol University. In 1978 he was dividing his time between writing and establishing drama workshops in impoverished areas of London. One of the film projects he was developing was entitled *Babylon*, a candid and vivid exposition of black youth culture in mid-seventies South London. With the project being mooted for a prime slot in the BBC's respected *Play for Today* drama season, Roddam's name was mooted as a potential director. When Roddam met with Stellman to discuss *Babylon*'s screen future, the pair formed an instant connection. With *Babylon* yet to go into production, Roddam brought in Stellman to help rework the *Quadrophenia* script.

Martin Stellman: 'Franc rung me up and said, "I've got a script by this guy Dave Humphries and I think you could do a really good job on it. Can you have a look?" Of course, I was extremely excited by the prospect of working with The Who. I read the script and it was pretty skeletal. Franc said: "I'm really quite worried about this as I've got a very short amount of preparation time and it really needs work." I could really see that it was kind of sketchy and perfunctory in many ways. There was very little character development, which was one of the areas which most worried me. Equally, there was very little of the sense of the period.'

Stellman began to draw from his own recollections of the sixties and the energy generated by the Mod movement, sensing that behind the obvious signs of rebellion lay a rejection of post-war austerity. 'I wasn't a scooter-riding Mod,' he recalls, 'but I had been on the inside fringes of the movement; certainly with the clothes and the music. The explosion of the mid-sixties was just extraordinary; it was a kind of vibe that I could understand. It was this thing about adolescent rebellion and it was the fact that you could not only rebel, but there was a whole culture that you could belong to, which was one of the very first times that working-class youth could speak out. Previously, it had been the family, the church or the Empire. With Mod, you put on these clothes, dressed in these nice suits, took these drugs and you'd listen to this music. It was a religion.'

To embed the screenplay in fact, Stellman utilised his journalistic contacts to visit archives and newspaper libraries where he scoured reams of cuttings, archive photos and original documents from the era. Adding considerable verisimilitude to the theme, some of the dialogue and vox pops captured from the time of the 1964 riots worked their way, verbatim, into the script.

Roddam, now consumed with all manner of pre-production duties, delegated a lot of the work to Stellman, the pair touching base periodically to assess their progress. Martin Stellman: 'We had an initial session where we talked a lot and that went on for a few days. I then went away for two or three weeks at a friend's place in Surrey to do the dialogue and major scenes. Then I came back and had another session with Franc and then went away to do more work on it.'

By August 18th, 1978, the Roddam/Stellman collaboration had thoroughly revised Dave Humphries' original script down to 119 pages, leaving a mere twenty per cent of the original document (although, presumably for contractual reasons, Humphries received a principal writing credit).

While respecting Pete Townshend's original concept for *Quadrophenia*, what Roddam and Stellman delivered was arguably the most vibrant and believable portrayal of British youth culture of the twentieth century. A visual as well as emotional tour de force, *Quadrophenia* was more than a straightforward exposition of sixties British Mod culture. Above and beyond the themes of teenage alienation, gang culture and identity, embedded in *Quadrophenia*'s landscape was a strong voice for the working class.

'We wanted to rewrite history in favour of the working class,' states Roddam. 'What we wanted to do was to say, "The emotions of the smaller people are as big and as important as the emotions of the dukes and kings." We were rooted in that. Certainly, when Martin and I worked on the script together – that was the brief.'

Furthermore, the writers wanted to document the austerity of post-war Britain, an angle that many filmmakers had spectacularly failed to assess previously. 'It was on the cusp of the old England,' recalls Martin Stellman. If you look at the film's subtext, there's lots of stuff which refers to the older Britain, echoes of the Empire. So there was this kind of sense where England didn't really know where it was going, but the Mods knew where they were going.'

While maintaining elements of Townshend's original theme, the script would prove far more coherent than the nebulous framework that held *Quadrophenia*'s album together. Nonetheless, there obviously had to be a continuum with the album and its music (especially when there was a new soundtrack album to promote). There were 'fixed' points where the music should come in, but it was left to the filmmakers to determine the appropriate moments to insert the musical interludes.

What was being constructed was an extra ordinary testament to youth, in all its grit, glamour and flaws. Whereas America had embraced the romance of gang culture in *West Side Story* and more recently the youthful energy and excitement of *Saturday Night Fever*, Britain would have its first believable youth film in *Quadrophenia*.

At its core, *Quadrophenia* centres on the life of Jimmy Cooper, a sixties teenager with a strong allegiance to the Mod scene. Despite the drudgery of his home life and lowly post-room job, time spent with fellow Mod travellers Dave, Chalky and Spider elevates his otherwise dreary and predictable life. Adding a constant sparkle to the gang's roistering around town is a heavy indulgence in drugs and (the hope of) sexual encounters.

> **'IF YOU LOOK AT THE FILM'S SUBTEXT, THERE'S LOTS OF STUFF WHICH REFERS TO THE OLDER BRITAIN, ECHOES OF THE EMPIRE.'**
> **MARTIN STELLMAN**

Struggling with mental health issues, Jimmy's fractured inner self starts to chip away at his equilibrium. Compounding this, his attraction to teenage femme fatale Steph presents a host of emotional landmines.

In between episodes of mad partying and drug-fuelled petty violence, an altercation with some bikers results in Jimmy's old friend (now a greaser), Kevin, being beaten to a pulp. Violence, a component of the Mods' landscape ultimately casts a shadow of doubt over Jimmy's allegiances.

A chance to escape London for the excitement of Brighton one Bank Holiday weekend gives Jimmy and his cohorts the opportunity to cut loose from their urban environment. Realising the Mod dream of unity, Jimmy and his pals engage in a seaside battle with their Rocker nemeses across Brighton's promenade, beach and backstreets. As the violence reaches fever pitch, Jimmy and Steph finally consummate their relationship in an alleyway.

ABOVE: Leslie Ash and Phil Daniels, the calm before the storm.

This joyous moment proves to be short-lived. Thanks to his Mod gear, and being in the wrong place at the wrong time, Jimmy is collared by the police and charged for his participation in the affray. Later, he finds himself in the dock with Ace Face, the ultra-Mod's self-assured presence going some way to ease the pain of Jimmy's fine.

Having returned home, Jimmy's mood plummets. Confronted by his irate mother, the revelation of his nefarious behaviour finds him exiled from the family home. In a vortex of rejection, he quits his job, only then to find out that Steph has paired off with his best mate Dave. Following a violent confrontation with Dave and a brutal brush-off from Steph, his scooter is written off in a road accident.

Every atom of his being in distress, Jimmy returns to Brighton in a desperate attempt to recapture some of the magic he experienced during the Bank Holiday. Despite the physical landscape being the same, the ecstasy and unity that accompanied his previous visit fail to materialise. The sight of Ace Face's scooter outside a Brighton hotel revives him momentarily. However, his fantasy soon dissolves when he discovers that Ace Face is nothing more than a subservient bell boy employed at the hotel.

To represent his feeling of betrayal and rejection of his Mod dreams, Jimmy steals Ace Face's scooter and takes it to a nearby clifftop. An emotional drive along the cliff edge followed by a brief moment of reflection allows him a final attempt to assert his identity. Finding nothing to articulate his state of mind, he symbolically drives the scooter off the cliff. However, it is clear that Jimmy does not follow in the scooter's trajectory. *Roll credits…*

While a lot of the script was reworked as filming

progressed, there were a few key moments that did not, ultimately, make it into the final cut.

By far the biggest revelation in the original shooting script is that Jimmy's surname was Haines, not Cooper. Digging deep into the period around its creation, it could well be seen as a nod to one of the film's earliest champions, Polydor president Fred Haayen. For those who have charted the picture's history it is a surprising change to Cooper, and as is evident in the shooting script of September 1978, it was a last-minute alteration. However, on viewing Roddam's résumé, (as with many directors) it's evident that he liked to keep a form of continuity with his previous work. The surname of Haines was originated during Dave Humphries' tenure; Roddam replaced Jimmy's middle and surname with those of the little boy in his 1975 documentary, *Mini*.

Michael Cooper, a ferociously intelligent 11-year-old hailing from a tiny mining village in County Durham, held the dubious claim of being Britain's youngest arsonist. Failed by his family and then the care system, Michael's struggle had touched Roddam. Now recognising echoes of the vulnerability of Jimmy, he was eager to name-check him in *Quadrophenia*.

The script completed, it was duly formatted to meet the requirements of shooting. To give the document a greater resonance than just words, an outtake shot from the photo session of *Quadrophenia*'s 1973 album booklet was pasted on the front and back of the script.

Townshend had some initial reservations about the direction the script was now taking, but he conceded that the film required a harder, grittier exterior to carry the piece through.

'I didn't feel the script went deep enough into Jimmy's psychosis,' Townshend revealed in 2009. 'I was sad that it didn't precisely follow the song-cycle structure. However, I also knew that there was no story in place on the album, just a journey that was deliberately left vague and open so that people listening could get inside it. The film needed a story, and Franc and his writer came up with one.'

With Townshend's opinions taken into consideration and a working template of the script completed, Roddam now turned his attention to casting. He had to be quick. There were only a few weeks to go before shooting was due to start, and a cast of hundreds had to be found to bring Jimmy and his cohorts' story to life. ●

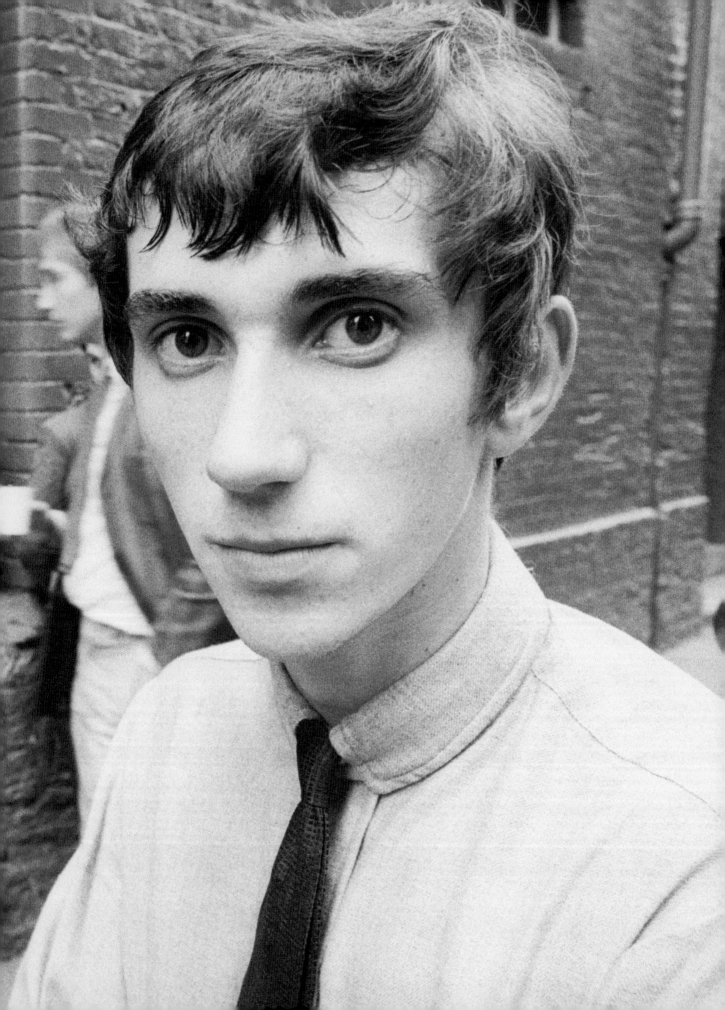

CHAPTER FOUR

'I SAW THOUSANDS OF PEOPLE. WE DID IMPROVISATIONS WITH EVERY ONE OF THEM; GOT THEM DOWN TO A HUNDRED, THEN WE GOT THEM DOWN TO FORTY, AND THEN WE GOT THEM DOWN TO TEN AND THE ONES WE DIDN'T USE IN THE FIRST TEN, WE USED IN THE SECOND FORTY AND THE ONES IN THE FIRST FORTY BECAME EXTRAS. EVERYBODY WE SAW WAS IN THE MOVIE.'

—FRANC RODDAM

'IT TRANSPIRED THAT I WAS GOING TO APPEAR IN A £2 MILLION MOVIE. AND I'D NEVER EVEN BEEN IN A SCHOOL PLAY.'

—GORDON SUMNER AKA STING

QCasting was now ready to begin in earnest. Who would play the role of Jimmy? Given that *Quadrophenia*'s protagonist would occupy virtually every scene, the decision was vital. With the modest budget precluding any high-profile 'stars', the production team's brief was to find young, instinctive actors with a believable, streetwise presence.

'We felt that the star here was *Quadrophenia*,' Bill Curbishley told the author in 2014. 'It was the brand that was the star, as were The Who. With that in mind, we cast it that way.'

Casting directors Patsy Pollock and Esta Charkham brought a wealth of experience, and to give the production some early publicity, Pete Townshend personally contacted *The Sun* newspaper in July 1978 to see if their enormous readership could help find the film's all-important central character. Elsewhere, agents were already getting wind of *Quadrophenia*'s imminent production and were bombarding the casting directors with photos and CVs. One such advance revealed a young actor by the name of Philip (Phil) William Daniels, aged 19 and brimming with talent and enthusiasm. It was later revealed that Daniels' mum had cut out *The Sun*'s advert and posted it to Africa, where her son was filming *Zulu Dawn*. However, Daniels' agent was one step ahead of his mum and had already put him up for the role.

Despite his tender years, Daniels had already built up a sizeable catalogue of film and TV work before *Quadrophenia* arrived. He had stumbled into acting quite by chance courtesy of Anna Scher, a character whose maverick presence in

OPPOSITE: Phil Daniels during filming in London, October 20th, 1978.

seventies North London changed many young lives. To arrest the boredom of long summer holidays, Scher had set up workshops in empty schools under the banner of 'Amateur Children's Theatre'. Engaging numerous latchkey children, Scher became an important figure for many seeking a happy distraction, Phil Daniels among them.

'I was 13,' recalled Daniels in 2012. 'Anna Scher came to my old primary school in King's Cross. A mate's sister went to one of her drama groups and we had to go and pick her up… We went there and there were all these lovely girls of our age. And it was amazing, because I went to an all-boys' school and it was all pretty suppressed and we were all lads together, and so it was quite eye-catching really. So we got dragged in to go and sit in the back of this drama group, watching people being trees and playing certain role games and got involved.'

Future actors such as Linda Robson, Pauline Quirke, John Blundell, Trevor Laird, Dexter Fletcher and Spandau Ballet stars Gary and Martin Kemp within his peer group, Daniels soon elevated himself from giggling at the back of a hall to taking an active part in proceedings. Stung by the acting bug, within a few short months Daniels found himself faced with a life-changing career move. Apart from his interest in drama, music ran a close second. Prior to the punk explosion of 1976, Daniels played guitar in Renoir – a band that included Daniels' close friend Trevor Laird and Gary Kemp.

His talent soon outstripped youth club and school productions, and he transferred to television. Like many of Scher's drama group, in 1975 Daniels took part in ITV's landmark youth programme, the improvisational comedy show *You Must Be Joking* – a virtual showcase for Scher's alumni. One memorable moment in the series saw Daniels and Gary Kemp duetting on a version of the band America's classic song 'Sandman'.

Further TV work followed: a bit part in a BBC

production of *Falstaff* and then more substantial roles in children's series such as *Four Idle Hands*, *The Flockton Flyer* and *The Molly Wopsies*. In 1975, as part of a BBC community drama initiative, Daniels was cast alongside a young actress named Toyah Wilcox in a production called *Glitter*, a surreal piece of television drama that expanded the talent of everyone involved in it. A small part in *The Naked Civil Servant*, a homage to the extraordinary actor and writer Quentin Crisp, pointed towards greater things.

In 1976 Daniels secured his first cinematic role in Alan Parker's adolescent romp *Bugsy Malone* – a production that employed many graduates from Scher's talent school. Following a small part in the Glenda Jackson-led *The Class of Miss MacMichael*, in 1977 Daniels received his most challenging role to date as Richards in Alan Clarke's brutal drama of seventies borstal life, *Scum*. Banned from a television screening at the behest of the BBC censor, Daniels – along with equally talented youngster Ray Winstone – would have to wait several years to reshoot the film for the cinema. Less substantial but with wide coverage, he featured in a popular TV commercial for Olympus cameras, comically mocking the popularity of one David Bailey.

In early 1978 Daniels received a choice part in *Zulu Dawn* and found himself on location in Africa alongside Peter O'Toole, Nigel Davenport, Burt Lancaster and Bob Hoskins.

Quadrophenia's casting desk now awash with hundreds of photographs and résumés, Phil Daniels' profile was evidently considered worthy of further investigation. He received a phone call from casting director Patsy Pollock while on location in Africa. After his filming on *Zulu Dawn* drew to a close, the actor returned to London to prepare for an audition for *Quadrophenia*. (The invite had not revealed which role he was up for.)

Daniels' return to the UK from Africa was not without incident. While filming there, Daniels, along with co-stars Denholm Elliott and Bob

ABOVE: Phil Davis flanked by Toyah Wilcox and Mark Wingett.

Hoskins, had caught a tropical virus after spending a few nights with his indigenous co-stars in a township – the idea had been to highlight the poor conditions the extras were enduring. While this act of solidarity may have highlighted the issue, it left Daniels with a serious infection. His tongue was split in half, and a yellow discharge in his mouth meant he was unable to eat, so by the time of his return to Britain, Daniels' weight had plummeted, leaving him drawn and emaciated.

Nonetheless, in true showbiz-trooper tradition, there was no way Daniels was going to miss this audition. Requiring some moral, as well as physical, support, Phil brought with him his friend and fellow Renoir bandmate, Trevor Laird – who would also join *Quadrophenia*'s main cast. On first sight, Daniels' physical state shocked Franc Roddam,

and although it suited the amphetamine-driven persona required for a bona fide Mod, Roddam was not initially convinced.

Actor Philip (Phil) Davis was also invited to attend preliminary auditions for the lead role. At 24, he was slightly older than the age the script called for, but his talent, mercurial looks and understanding of *Quadrophenia*'s landscape ensured he would be perfect for a part. His resemblance to a young Roger Daltrey may also have been a factor. Born in 1953, raised on a council estate in Grays, Essex, Davis harboured early aspirations to enter the dramatic profession and he learned early on how to deflect the jibes of his peer group (his thespian inclinations earned him the nickname 'Shakespeare').

'Everybody thought I was mad,' Davis recalled

to the *Guardian* in 2012. 'You wait for kids to grow out of it, they want to be captain of the England squad or go to the moon, and it felt like that. When I was a kid I felt like I was a nutcase, born in the wrong place at the wrong time.'

Davis persevered and soon gravitated to small theatrical parts and then to television. His first film role was in a musical adaptation of Charles Dickens' *The Old Curiosity Shop*, in 1975. Following a brief period of inactivity in 1976, he was offered a plum role in the theatrical version of Barrie Keeffe's extraordinary drama, *Gotcha*. The tale of a disaffected teenager who held two of his teachers hostage elevated Davis's profile enormously, as did its eventual transference to television. It was Keeffe, an early contender for *Quadrophenia* script duties, who informed Davis of the film's imminent production.

Daniels and Davis were required to attend a more formal screen test in the following weeks. This would take place at Wembley Studios, and such was the breakneck pace, auditions, improvisations and screen tests were running simultaneously.

Despite the competency of both Daniels and Davis's auditions, others with less theatrical provenance were considered for *Quadrophenia*'s lead. One, reportedly, was Jimmy Pursey, the self-appointed leader of disenfranchised youth who headed the chaotic Sham 69. Pursey's spirited performances endured the tail end of punk's first burst with considerable gusto. With several hits detailing the bleak landscape of English wastelands, Sham 69 attracted a sizeable following – many alienated personalities finding favour with Pursey and Co.'s desperate cries for acknowledgement. Pursey's audition was reportedly so emotionally challenging, the punk star was reduced to tears during an improvisation with Garry Cooper. Another name thrown into the melee for parts was Tony James, guitarist in the Billy Idol-led Generation X.

The production team's desire to link the Mod past with the punk present managed, briefly, to court interest from the highest level of the punk kingdom. John Lydon was, by the summer of 1978, on the cusp of a new direction, the Pistols having imploded in a blizzard of in-fighting and controversy. Lydon had dispensed with the Rotten tag and was looking to build his career with a new band, Public Image aka PiL (the Ltd was added later). The band hired studio space in Pete Townshend's Eel Pie Studios in Soho, and between Townshend and Lydon a friendship of sorts developed. One particular night, as *Quadrophenia*'s casting was in progress, Townshend, Lydon and Franc Roddam decided to hit the road for a night out in London. According to Roddam, the evening started early, as did the drinking.

'Johnny has an extraordinary capacity to drink lager,' recalled Roddam. 'He would get a can of lager, blow the dust off the top and down it in one hit. And he could drink about sixteen of them. Pete thought he would try and keep up with him, and he wasn't drinking at the time. He had a full bottle of vodka in his hand, and off we went into the night.'

Suitably refreshed, the trio piled into Townshend's car and drove off in the direction of the popular North London venue, the Music Machine (later known as the Camden Palace and then KOKO).

'Johnny Rotten liked to drink and so did I,' recalled Townshend later. 'We went out and got pissed and I drove my car the wrong way around a roundabout. We went to the Camden Palais together and I got stopped by the police and they hauled us out.'

Somehow managing to bypass any sustained police interest, Roddam, Townshend and Lydon made it to the Camden venue. Not surprisingly, Lydon was greeted as a visiting deity, and going some way to confirm this, he proceeded to cut off chunks of his hair and hand them around to his admirers. Bizarre antics aside, Lydon impressed

Roddam enough to have him seriously considered for the role of Jimmy. 'I was very tempted to use him,' said Roddam to the BBC in 2003. 'I thought, "Punk is very strong. He's the king of punk, he's the ambassador of punk and if we had him in the film we could link the past with the present."'

Lydon's global notoriety masked his relatively quiet upbringing in North London, a landscape he shared with Phil Daniels. A face on the streets of Islington during the early seventies, Lydon was known in the district for his outlandish behaviour and the eccentric band of characters he hung around with. Bearing witness to Lydon and his coterie was Phil Daniels. The latter's allegiance to Chelsea F.C. drew little respect from Lydon, an ardent Arsenal supporter. Their differences had resulted in many verbal spats across North London streets and terraces, and their paths now crossed again during screen tests for *Quadrophenia*.

'There's history there,' Trevor Laird told the author in 1999. 'We all grew up in the same manor. Lydon used to come in and say, "Oh, there's that wanker who can barely act and supports Chelsea." Daniels would say, "Oh, there's that wanker who can't sing at all and supports Arsenal."'

With *Quadrophenia*'s casting in full swing, Toyah Wilcox would now make herself known. On the first rungs of an acting career, Wilcox had had a life-changing experience courtesy of punk. Based in a South London squat at the time, she immersed herself in the new wave explosion occurring across the city. Her talents spanned many mediums; she'd taken to singing, had formed her own band, and acting was providing a living of sorts. She'd also received critical acclaim for her role in Derek Jarman's oblique homage to punk, the brilliantly splintered and eclectic *Jubilee* (1977). Word of *Quadrophenia*'s transference to film reached Wilcox, and she lobbied her agent to get her a part.

After having met Wilcox, Roddam was noncommittal about a role for her, but gauged that her unusual presence might best be suited to steering Lydon through the delicate manoeuvres required for a formal audition.

'Roddam asked if I would be prepared to give some acting tips to the possible lead to get him through the screen test,' Wilcox recalled later. 'It was Johnny Rotten. I thought, "This is going to be horrible – what can I do?" I idolised this man, yet was completely scared of meeting him. I didn't want to say no because I wanted to be in the film.'

'Johnny came to join us for a drink,' she recalled, 'and he was the sweetest, most politest gentleman and very shy. We shared a cab back and I talked to him about my little punk band and I felt such an idiot. I got him to drop me off in Sloane Square as I didn't want him to see my tatty squat in Battersea. The next day I arrived at his flat off the King's Road which, being very naïve, I expected to be very grand. It wasn't. It was just like my squat. I felt such a dork. We went to Shepperton and we did the screen test.'

Much to everyone's surprise, Lydon made several concessions to meet the demands of the screen test, to the extent of wearing a suit and having his hair conventionally styled.

'I thought Johnny Rotten was fucking brilliant,' confirms Toyah Wilcox. 'He was conscientious, he knew his lines and he was on the ball.'

According to Trevor Laird, who was present for other duties on *Quadrophenia*, one of Lydon's screen tests involved the recreation of a scene where he'd confront a Rocker. It had to be abandoned after Lydon smashed a wine bottle and held it to a terrified actor's throat. While Daniels and Davis made extraordinary moves in front of the camera, the raw brutality of Lydon's explosive audition impressed the casting team. The producers, too. With the so-called 'King of Punk' on board, the publicity was going to be plentiful.

The politics of filmmaking requiring concessions to satisfy insurers, once Lydon's involvement was being talked up, sensitive antennas began to quiver. With questions from financiers being raised as to whether Lydon would be able to commit to a three-month shoot with 14-hour days, some serious decisions needed to be made. Sadly for Lydon's prospective film career, *Quadrophenia* did not employ his talents.

Franc Roddam: 'They'd seen him [Lydon] spitting on photographs of the Queen, puking up and they said, "We can't rely on this guy to turn up sixty days in a row on a set." So they wouldn't let me use him.'

In later years, Lydon would characteristically brush aside the whole *Quadrophenia* experience, claiming he was never interested in the first place. This left Roddam to focus on the other characters who were in the pipeline for the role of Jimmy. Aware that Daniels' initial auditions had been marred by his poor health, Roddam invited the young actor back for a meeting – not for a further try-out on celluloid but a re-enactment of a scene from the recently completed script.

'I saw Phil this time and he looked better,' remembers Roddam. 'His tongue was clean [laughs] and he [was] well and healthy, and then he did this performance which was just fantastic,

and I knew I could really work with him and we were going to be great partners.'

Roddam's intuition was correct. Daniels' age, London street sensibility and presence combined perfectly. Furthermore, his aura was slightly out of kilter with the archetypal Mod look – a perverse quality which in itself would lend him a detachment that the role of Jimmy demanded. The shooting dates fast approaching, the relief was palpable; *Quadrophenia*'s lead had been secured.

However, there was still an associate cast to be determined. The script called for nine main protagonists, plus an associate ensemble that would (with extras) run into hundreds. A lot of work was needed to be done to bring everyone in on

> **◎ 'THEY'D SEEN HIM [LYDON] SPITTING ON PHOTOGRAPHS OF THE QUEEN, PUKING UP AND THEY SAID, "WE CAN'T RELY ON THIS GUY TO TURN UP SIXTY DAYS IN A ROW ON A SET."'**
>
> **FRANC RODDAM**

HOW TO BEGIN A GARDEN . . . Don't miss Saturday's Sun!

HE'S OUR WHO FILM STAR!

■ ONE of the stars of The Who's latest rock opera film, Quadrophenia, is a caretaker's son from London's King's Cross.

Phil Daniels, 19, was chosen by The Who's Pete Townshend from thousands of hopefuls who wrote in to The Sun in July.

We asked readers to help Townshend find Britain's answer to John Travolta for his follow-up film to Tommy.

Our offices were swamped by letters and

photographs. And Daniels's agent read our story and phoned Townshend.

Daniels says: " I was in Africa filming at the time.

" My mum saw the story and sent me a copy of The Sun, but by that time my agent had already put me up for it."

Quadrophenia tells the story of a young Mod in the early Sixties.

PHIL DANIELS
Big chance

time. While the casting directors were competent enough to secure most of the leads, others were on the lookout for suitable character actors.

Next to Jimmy, the role of Steph called for a hugely stylish individual. The love interest was originally created by Alan Fletcher in his early draft script; his initial description of her was as 'a cool Mod crop princess'. After some reworking by Roddam and Stellman, Steph's character was created, the name coming from a niece of the director.

The picture's leading lady required a character that was identifiable to anyone who'd been through the ups and downs of teenage romance. Furthermore, she'd have to engender an abrasive and brittle exterior, a quality that would underpin her visual beauty on screen.

Despite the high expectations the role of Steph demanded, native South Londoner Leslie Ash came through the audition process with honours. Just turned 18, the girl who arrived at the auditions was a supremely confident individual, whose promise had been noted from an early age. Appearing in a clutch of adverts aged just 4 years old, she'd earmarked her career in lights, although in which medium she wasn't entirely sure.

Enrolled at the renowned Italia Conti Academy in London, by the age of 14 Ash had already scored a few moments in children's media, the most sustained being a Children's Film Foundation production, *The Boy with Two Heads*. Later, she'd act while taking on modelling work, at one point being photographed by the doyen of British fashion photography, David Bailey. At the age of 16, she appeared on the covers of teen magazines such as *Jackie* and although her heart was set on a singing career, she maintained a fairly active presence in acting.

In 1978 a small role in the racy British film comedy *Rosie Dixon – Night Nurse* gave Ash her first moment in cinema. Her agent knew Franc Roddam socially, and so Ash duly attended auditions for *Quadrophenia*, impressing the director that she had the right qualities and provincial beauty for the film's leading lady.

'In the town I came from,' recalled Roddam in 1999, 'every now and then you'd get a very pretty little girl who everybody fancies. Leslie's like that and very South London. So even though she didn't have much experience as an actress she was the real McCoy. She'd left home at 15, got herself a flat, earned her own money; she was quite hard in some ways.'

Ash's precocious attitude was quickly revealed when she made it clear to the casting directors that she wouldn't consent to the crop haircut designated for the role. Ash would get her way and her barnet remained untouched, Ash going for what she called the 'Jane Asher look'.

The all-important roles of Steph and Jimmy secured, the associate cast could now be gathered. Everyone who'd made it to the audition

OPPOSITE: Leslie Ash in repose at Brighton, September 1978 and (above) a cover star for *Jackie* magazine..

stage was sensibly kept on the production books, allowing all the roles to be eventually filled within the associate cast.

'I had this wonderful group of people,' reflects Roddam. 'I had about forty to fifty people who were the core of my film. Some of them became the top six lead roles; some of them became the second lead characters; and some of them became special extras, but they were all together all of the time.'

Jimmy's best mate and fellow traveller on the Mod carousel would be known as Dave. More in keeping with Townshend's original working-class vision of Jimmy, Dave was cast as a dustman whose penchant for chaos and outrageousness frequently upstaged the film's lead.

One character up for the part was Mark Wingett; at 16, he was one of the youngest members of the prospective cast. Hailing from Melton Mowbray, Leicestershire, on moving down to the South Coast in his teens, he was eager to break into dramatic mediums. Acting would prove to be a necessary diversion for young Wingett; at that point he was earning 40p an hour on a petrol station forecourt. In pursuance of his dreams, Wingett had joined the National Youth Theatre and was using every opportunity to build on his future career.

Playing the lead in one of the National Youth Theatre's productions, Wingett's spiky presence was observed by *Quadrophenia*'s casting directors. 'I had a lead in one of the plays,' he remembered in 2011. 'Patsy Pollock and Esta Charkham came to see it. About twenty of us from the Youth Theatre came up to see Franc. We spent half a day doing different scenarios and acting different things. At the end of the first day, I remember Franc giving me this black-and-white album called *Quadrophenia*, with the photos in the middle of it. They were looking for this person called Dave. I went away and he called six of us back the next day, and he [Roddam] offered me the job on the spot – which is extraordinary.'

Like many of his vintage, Wingett was infused with the punk spirit that had enlivened every nook and cranny of teenage Britain. While his future screen role depicted a Mod to the core, off set Wingett looked every part the spirit of 1977, sporting tight trousers, dog collars and spiky hair. His persona reflected his energetic *Quadrophenia* alter ego. Reportedly a fan of Sid Vicious, his fascination with the doomed Sex Pistol would prove fortuitous for the production later on.

Despite not securing the lead role, Phil Davis's promise was never going to be passed over, and he was offered a key role, that of Chalky, one of Jimmy's chief partners in crime and a character destined to feature in many adventures. 'I was a little disappointed obviously,' recalled Davis to the author on not securing *Quadrophenia*'s prize role. 'But Chalky was a great part and I liked Phil Daniels. So we were off.'

Toyah Wilcox's determination to secure a role, too, had not gone unnoticed.

Having already shepherded John Lydon through his screen test, Wilcox was determined to make her own mark. Frequently turning up unannounced at the production offices in Wembley, she was convinced that her persistence would land her a role: 'I was so egotistical and arrogant at that age, very cocky. I asked Franc Roddam what part I'd got and he said I didn't have one.'

With rejection an anathema to her, she heard that the part of Monkey – an exuberant female Mod – was yet to be cast. With this knowledge to hand, she upped her offensive.

'I demanded the part,' she recalled years later. '[Roddam] called Phil Daniels into the room and said, "If you kiss him now, you can be Monkey." It was no problem whatsoever. I just grabbed him and snogged him and that secured the role.'

Though not initially part of the script, the part of Ferdy, a black drug-dealing Mod, proved to be pivotal and controversial. Phil Daniels' friend Trevor Laird, a 20-year-old from Islington, ultimately got

OPPOSITE: Cool, clean and hard. Mark Wingett relaxes in Brighton's Beach Café, September 1978.

the part, although how he came to the attention of the production crew was completely by chance.

Born in 1957, Laird, like Phil Daniels, hailed from North London. Another Scher alumnus, on leaving school he'd decided that a career in the arts was for him. Laird had gravitated towards acting, appearing in a couple of drama slots for the BBC. Shadowing Phil Daniels at one of his auditions, Pete Townshend happened to be present and wondered if Laird would be up for a part, remarking that the youngster reminded him of a drug-dealing character who had been on the fringes of The Who's early circle, a character named Winston. Duly inspired by Townshend's interest, Roddam cast Laird as Ferdy with Martin Stellman duly writing in the character's sequences in the script.

'I had slight problems with that role at first,' Laird commented to the author in 1999. 'I was a young kid, 20 years old, just beginning to tiptoe through the whole black identity thing. Stellman told me he'd really wanted to make my character Caribbean. In 1964 I probably would have had a West Indian accent, but at the time, being a Londoner, I wanted to be one of the lads.'

Gary Shail was another individual who appeared tailor-made for Quadrophenia's gritty landscape. Hailing from the South East of England, Shail had trained at the Arts Educational School and, like many, was absorbed in the punk lifestyle. Aged 18 when he arrived for Quadrophenia's auditions, despite his punkish exterior, his slender build initially turned off Roddam's interest. 'Franc didn't think I wasn't hard enough to be a Mod,' recalls Shail today. 'At that time I was doing serious martial arts.'

'Shail came into the room,' recalled Roddam in an interview in 1999. 'He was really coming full-on saying, "I want to be in your film." I said, "Look, you're great but I just don't think you've got the strength, you're a bit too young-looking." "Stand there! Stand there!" he howled. "Go on, attack me! Attack me! Kick me!" "For fuck's sake," I

muttered, and took a big fucking kick at him. He did a backward somersault and landed about ten feet away.'

Shail was duly handed the role of Finger, a key member of Quadrophenia's lead cast. However, Shail's alter ego received a name change to the slightly more palatable moniker of Spider. Names aside, his winning of the part impressed many, not least his mum.

'At that time I was a punk,' Shail related to author Jonny Bance in 2012. 'My mum was most impressed that instead of wearing all the leather trousers and having pink hair I had to go through a complete transformation! Smart suit and haircut to look like a cool, well-dressed Mod from the sixties.'

With the main ensemble decided, there were a few other personalities who played less visual supporting roles. Garry Cooper, originally earmarked for a more iconic role, was cast as Peter Fenton (Steph's part-time boyfriend). The actor had featured in several high-profile stage roles before landing a part in Quadrophenia.

From the start, it was clear that the most iconic cast member was going to be Ace Face, the uber-Mod who was head and shoulders above his peers in style, dress and dance steps. Harking back to Pete Townshend's album concept, the script brought Ace Face's huge reputation to life. The original script first introduced Ace Face on a Brighton dance floor and its directions were explicit in depicting his majestic presence.

OPPOSITE: 'Message in a Bottle'. Sting rehearsing between takes, September 1978.

> The main attraction for many
> of them is THE ACE, a handsome,
> impeccably-groomed MOD who is
> dominating the crowded dance
> floor with his grace and
> agility… dancing more or less
> by himself and to himself, he
> holds the crowd in thrall.

QUADROPHENIA
A WAY OF LIFE
UN FILM DE FRANC RODDAM

Garry Cooper was initially earmarked by Roddam for Ace Face and yet, despite his statuesque profile and imposing presence, the director sensed that the role called for someone with an altogether more otherworldly presence. For a while, actor John Altman was a contender, and it's rumoured that Adam Ant was also a possibility.

But it was one Gordon Matthew Thomas Sumner, a 27-year-old former teacher and musician with new wave band The Police, who was highlighted as a candidate. Dreams of stardom aside, Sumner – married and with a young child – had been working as a humble cleaner, as Franc Roddam confirmed to the BBC in 2005.

Franc Roddam: 'A woman who worked in the accounts department said, "You're looking for a super guy? There's a guy who cleans my house and he's an unemployed teacher who's wanting to be a rock musician." The casting director then brought him in.'

ABOVE: Garry Cooper with Leslie Ash.

A call duly went out, and Sumner, who preferred to call himself by his stage name Sting, conferred with his wife, actress Frances Tomelty. She encouraged him to audition for the part. (It later transpired that Tomelty was friends with casting director Esta Charkham.) Sumner raced over to *Quadrophenia*'s production offices in his work clothes, 'looking like a garage mechanic'. Despite his commanding stage presence, Sting had never acted in his life.

'I went down to the studio,' he recalled to *Melody Maker* in 1979. 'I met Franc Roddam and sat around discussing Hermann Hesse's *The Glass Bead Game*, I think. Suddenly, he said, "You're perfect. You look perfect." I got the job that day. It transpired during the conversation that followed that I was going to appear in a £2 million movie. And I'd never even been in a school play.'

Sting's blond shag and steely blue eyes were evidently perfect for Ace Face. Similarly, Roddam's vision of linking the Mod past with the punk/new wave present was embodied in Sting; his band The Police were about to explode. Privately, however, Sting wasn't entirely in step with the concept of youth movements.

'I am in my mid-twenties and I've never actually been part of a youth cult,' he admitted soon after filming *Quadrophenia*. 'If anything, I feel it is what's wrong with society that they feel they have to wear some sort of uniform to live fulfilled and happy lives. The opposite is true; get rid of the uniforms and you can be yourself.'

Nonetheless, as Ace Face, Sting would have to at least appear as though he identified with the Mod movement, and it was vital to test his physical mettle – if only to see if he could handle the extremities that would occur once filming started. During auditions, Roddam quietly conferred with two actors who had been selected for possible roles: John Blundell, later cast as the chief Rocker in the Brighton sequences, and Ray Burdis. Both had come off hugely combative roles in the BBC's version of *Scum* and had the appropriate presence to challenge any cocky pretender, regardless of how cool he appeared.

John Blundell: 'Franc sent a message saying, "Can you come down to Pinewood? I'm doing *Quadrophenia*; I want you to go through some improvisations with someone." Ray and I jumped on a train and went down there. When we arrived Franc said, "Now, I want you to have a look at this guy doing an improvisation. He's not really an actor, but let me know what you think." This guy came in, quite unusual-looking, with short spiky blond hair, and it was Sting.'

With a brief to intimidate the physically slight musician, they laid into Sting, drawing out the

necessary resistance during improvisations.

'We did... a couple of situations Franc had suggested,' recalls Blundell today. 'Franc sent this guy out. We sat down and Franc asked us what we thought of him. We said, "He's unusual, not much of an actor, but he's okay!"'

'He remained very, very cool and started intimidating them back,' recalled Roddam. 'I thought, "Great, now I've got my Ace Face." He was slightly older and he had that self-possession thing and it just worked. He also had a very different look and he stood out from everybody else.'

'Ace is very much part of my own character,' Sting recalled later. 'I have a very, very strong ego. Ace is very, very close to my personality when I'm onstage.'

The role of Ace Face finally secured, the finer points of pre-production could begin in earnest. The clock was ticking. ●

"QUADROPHENIA"

Domestic Version
Export Script

EASTMANCOLOUR   ASPECT RATIO 1.85
STANDARD PROJECTION at 24 FRAMES PER SECOND

PRODUCED BY: ROY BAIRD & BILL CURBISHLEY

DIRECTED BY: FRANC RODDAM

TOTAL NUMBER OF REELS: TWELVE.

EXHIBITION FOOTAGE: 10849 –
                       72 Allowance for 12ft.
                 ——— leaders on 'A' Reels
          10777 Feet.

          3284.830 Metres.

RUNNING TIME: 1 hour 59⅔ minutes

NOTE: FIRST ACTION FRAME on all 'A'
Reels is set at: 12'0 for
measurements and on 'B' Reels
at: 0'0

4th April 1979   Printed in England   P – H CINEGRAPHICS LTD.
                                             Pinewood Studios

CHAPTER FIVE

'WE WERE WALKING AROUND LONDON ACTING LIKE MODS AND MEETING MODS, WHILE EVERYONE WAS ACTING LIKE PUNK ROCKERS. WE WERE AHEAD OF OUR TIME AND BEHIND IT TOO.'

—PHIL DANIELS

Quadrophenia's frontline cast signed up, the casting process for the supporting roles now began. It was clear from the start that Jimmy's parents were crucial, having to remain detached and disapproving of the antics of their errant son.

The role of Jimmy's dad would be given to 31-year-old Michael Elphick. A presence in the theatre since the age of 15, Elphick displayed a maturity on screen well beyond his years. While he'd go on to find enormous success in both film and television, as Jimmy's long-suffering father he was handed numerous opportunities to stretch his creative limbs. The role called for numerous confrontations with his son, but also a level of empathy. Interestingly, one late-night ramble between father and son about the family history was partially drawn from director Roddam's own background.

'My Irish mother's uncles used to go to church on Sunday,' said Roddam in 2012. 'Afterwards they would have a good drink up, and one of them fell down a well in the garden and ended in a river about a mile away.'

The role of Jimmy's mother had been given to actress Amanda Barrie, an actress with a sizeable portfolio of work dating from the sixties that included playing alongside Patrick McGoohan in *Danger Man* and leading-lady status in *Carry On*

Cabby and *Carry On Cleopatra*. Unfortunately her *Quadrophenia* audition awkwardly coincided with a host of personal issues, and while she'd carry the audition, fortune would not reward Barrie in the ensuing weeks.

Some notable cameo roles included Hugh Lloyd as Jimmy's post-room manager, Mr Cale. A veteran of numerous comedy productions (not least as a foil to Tony Hancock) and now in the twilight of his career, Lloyd's presence resonated with a bygone era. The suave Benjamin Whitrow was supremely cast as Jimmy's boss, Mr Fulford, railing against Jimmy's free-range behaviour at work. Already a veteran of numerous stage and TV dramas, Whitrow's most popular moment was as Chief Superintendent Braithwaite in ITV's *The Sweeney*.

A quiet aristocratic presence was witnessed in Jeremy Child (actually Sir Coles John Jeremy Child, 3rd Baronet). Cast in a minor role as an advertising executive, Child added some upper-class gravitas to a scene in the agency's toilet. A veteran of numerous productions, Child had already made a memorable entrée to cult cinema in Peter Watkins' pop tragedy *Privilege* in 1967.

Jimmy's workplace also served to introduce one Timothy Spall: the 21-year-old cast as a hapless projectionist. Spall's acting career was in its formative stages, and *Quadrophenia* presented

OPPOSITE AND NEXT SPREADS: Production ephemera from *Quadrophenia*.

him with his first cinema role. Like many, he was propelled into frontline acting work courtesy of *Quadrophenia*.

Reading-born John Altman was another young actor whose potential appeared limitless. He'd been brought in to audition for the enigmatic part of Ace Face but found a place instead in the supporting cast as Mod Johnny Fagin. A proviso to Altman's casting was that he (and others) would have to be receptive to improvisations and rewrites as filming took place. He was a familiar presence throughout the film, featuring in both the Brighton and London sequences.

A scene devised by Alan Fletcher during the very first incarnation of *Quadrophenia*'s film script featured Jimmy's childhood friend, the ex-soldier turned leather-clad Rocker Kevin Herriot. His dismal roughing-up served to throw up an emotional dilemma for Jimmy and would prove pivotal in Jimmy's eventual rejection of the Mod philosophy. Auditions for someone who could handle this brief but key role brought 21-year-old Ray Winstone into the *Quadrophenia* fold.

Winstone had gone a long way to embellish his credentials as a teenage hard man as Carlin in Alan Clarke's startling portrayal of borstal life, the 1977 television drama *Scum*. Also starring Phil Daniels, *Scum* had been banned by the BBC, the Corporation doubtless fearful of a political backlash due to the picture's violent and challenging content. However, it was remade as a film a few years later and eventually shown on Channel 4. Winstone's gritty presence stole both productions.

Hailing from a tough East End background, Winstone excelled in amateur boxing, training at the legendary Repton Boxing Club from the age of 12. Such was his prowess in the ring, the youngster won numerous awards during his teenage years. In 1975 a change of focus led Ray to sign up at London's Corona Theatre School. This landed him a few television roles and resulting in his securing the lead in *Scum*. The film's controversial embargo meant that a disillusioned Ray was forced to seek work outside acting, and he took on anything from stallholder to sales rep. Ironically, it was talk of *Scum*'s cinema revival that reignited Winstone's acting career. With *Quadrophenia* offering him a chance to build on his already enormous potential, Winstone's cheerful and uncompromising presence proved perfect for the role of the doomed Rocker.

In the run-up to shooting, other actors such as Gary Holton, Daniel Peacock, Julian Firth and Perry Benson were also signed up to make brief appearances.

With the script calling for the main cast to be dependent on each other, Roddam set about creating a gang in preparation for what lay ahead. In touch with the chemistry that bonds young minds together, he was eager to gauge how the cast related to each other, both on and off set. In pursuance of this, Roddam was granted a month for preparation and team building, a commodity rarely afforded to a production with such a modest budget.

'The most useful thing was that we really got to know each other,' remembered Phil Davis to the author. 'The kind of gang theme of "who liked who" and "whose favourite with each other", we really got that going.'

'Because they weren't expensive actors,' explains Roddam, 'Roy Baird let me have them for a month before, which is very unusual. I had forty people for a month before we started shooting.'

For the punk kids of 1978, revisiting the Mod world of the sixties required special tutoring. Aware that looking at books and clippings wouldn't be sufficient for the task ahead, those linked with The Who's fan base called up some of the group's earliest Mod acolytes in West London to help with research. Fourteen years on, some of these characters were still actively maintaining the Mod ethos and were happy to school *Quadrophenia*'s cast in the finer points of deportment and etiquette. As well as being responsible for the bulk of the film's sound remixing, it was John Entwistle who was largely instrumental in forging a link between *Quadrophenia*'s cast and the original London Mods.

'We went to parties in their houses,' Toyah Wilcox recalled later. '[We] learned how to do the dances and learned about the drug cultures of the time. A lot of us were living quite wildly at the time, and we really got into it, burning the candle at both ends.'

'We were introduced to a couple of old Mods,' recalled Phil Davis to the author in 2012. 'One was a bloke called Tommy who lived in Fulham. He threw a party for us and they were playing all the old Mod tunes and they were telling us what was hip and what wasn't and showing us all the different dances. A big bag of blues [amphetamines] appeared and we all had a go. We were up all night, eyes out on stalks. To be clear, the producers were not encouraging us to take drugs, this was our own thing, but we wanted to throw ourselves at the Mod culture. And we did. We were young. We watched sixties movies. All manner of stuff went on.'

Toyah Wilcox: 'I can remember being driven on the back of a scooter around Peckham at about 90 mph at four in the morning by this old couple who were showing us the life.'

Trevor Laird also recalled Entwistle's role in this vital preparation, personally shepherding cast members to meet members of The Who's original fan base and view some of the key locations in their past.

While the mass of memories from this period could fill an entire book, most of the cast vividly recall one party with some of the original Mods. The action took place on all floors of the house, and Sting made a bizarre, wholly impromptu appearance.

'I'll never forget at one of these parties,' recalled Trevor Laird in 1999, 'in the house of an old Mod called Mickey, Sting suddenly appeared at the top of the stairs – swimming, murmuring, "I've got to get there, I've got to get there."'

'We met a load of geezers down in Shepherd's Bush,' said Gary Shail in 2011 of the partying cum

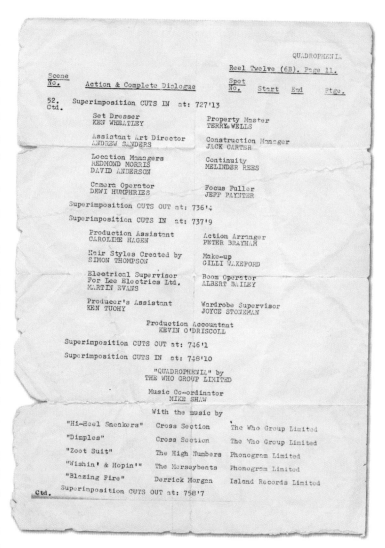

> ⊙ 'I CAN REMEMBER BEING DRIVEN ON THE BACK OF A SCOOTER AROUND PECKHAM AT ABOUT 90 MPH AT FOUR IN THE MORNING BY THIS OLD COUPLE WHO WERE SHOWING US THE LIFE.'
> **TOYAH WILCOX**

method research. 'They all had half-fingers that had been mashed up in the sixties wars with the Rockers. They were giving us pills and all that shit, and we all got mashed.'

Aside from the partying, Mark Wingett described the whirlwind of preparation that sixties.) The film's producers took the acquisition of clothes very seriously. One company approached to secure the necessary period pieces was Contemporary Wardrobes. More than just a clothes-hire operation, they'd earned a reputation for supplying genuine period-piece items for films and other productions. Despite their rather lofty title, most of their business was generated from a market stall in London's Portobello Road. Overseen by two former Mods, tailors Jack English and Roger Burton, they recalled their delight at being called in for fashion duties on the film for a Who fanzine in 1979.

'Getting the costumes together was pure joy because we were part of the Mod era and our hearts are still there,' reported Jack English. 'We were at the actual Brighton riot portrayed in the film. Those were the days when a guy spent an hour getting the knot in his tie just right, afraid to sit down on the bus in case his suit got creased. There were only about 300 guys in the whole of London who could then afford authentic Mod suits, and for the film we located a wonderful genuine silk John Michael exclusive... For *Quadrophenia*, we had to research the right shape.'

For Jimmy's all-important suit, Dave Wax Outfitters in Hammersmith were employed. Such was the importance placed on Jimmy's Brighton uniform, its tailor, Mitch Wax, took nearly ten days to perfect the garment. Such was the timeless appearance of the tailors' premises, they would be utilised for filming later on.

Dancing was as integral to the Mod lifestyle as clothes and drugs, and an authentic dancing style was essential. To facilitate this, Roddam called in Gillian (Gillie) Gregory, a choreographer who'd previously taught classical ballet and tap dancing, and whose résumé included tutelage on films such as *Tommy* and *Bugsy Malone*. Initial rehearsals took place at the London Dance Centre in Covent Garden.

Unfortunately, from all accounts, Gregory's choreography wasn't sufficient to mirror the

occurred prior to filming. 'We'd get picked up in a car and taken to the strip club in Soho... above it was a dance studio, and we were given dancing lessons for two weeks... Franc would say, "Right, tonight we're going off to the Nashville Rooms [a famous West London punk venue] to watch a band," and we'd all turn up there. Or we'd go to the Southgate Royalty [a North London dancehall] to see how we all interacted together.'

Vital to the Mod lifestyle were clothes and dance. (Toyah Wilcox, abandoning her overtly punk look for the role, remembers rummaging around in her mother's wardrobe for anything idiosyncratic moves of the Mod generation. It was felt that a club floor-level approach was required, and a fortuitous meeting with legendary club DJ and counterculture icon Jeff Dexter helped. A character who had been at the sharp end of many defining events during the sixties and seventies, Dexter first came to prominence for his legendary club nights around London's Mod compass: the Flamingo and Scene clubs in particular. Although he hadn't danced professionally since 1965, his experience of both style and the era was without question.

'It was kind of a strange thing to be requested to come and do all the dances I used to do all those years ago,' recalled Dexter to the BBC in 1978. 'I had to take on the team and start off by teaching them the Twist, the Pony, the Locomotion and all the real idiot dances of the time. I explained to them how stupid most of the dances were, how long they lasted and how dancing developed into individual styles.'

Such was his authority, Dexter was signed up to oversee an entire club sequence in which scores of extras had to strut their collective stuff. Sting's enigmatic Ace Face required some genre-defining footsteps, and Dexter spent a considerable time with the actor in an attempt to get everything right, first at a dance studio in London's Covent Garden and then later on set.

In the run-up to filming, Sting had been modest in revealing details of his other life in music to fellow cast members. This coyness prompted an amusing revelation which Gary Shail related to the author in 2014: 'We were rehearsing in this dance studio and Sting walked in wearing his classic green flight suit. On his lapel he had a little badge that just said "Police" and I said, "What's that?" and he said, "That's the name of my band," and I said, "What a fucking stupid name for a band!"'

Convincing dance steps aside, competent scooter riding was also essential for *Quadrophenia*'s Mod pretenders and so tutoring on how best to operate the tricky vehicles was obligatory. Knowing how important the confident

manoeuvring of scooters would be to the authenticity of the film, Roddam allocated a hefty chunk of the pre-production budget to acquire a large contingency of two-wheeled transport.

In preparation for scooter-riding duties, the main cast, including Leslie Ash and Toyah Wilcox, were shunted over to police training headquarters at Hendon, North London; the brief – to get them acquainted with conventional bikes before transferring them to the more Mod-friendly Lambrettas and Vespas.

Hendon had the benefit of a large driving circuit, a place where novice cadets could practise their skills on two wheels. For some of *Quadrophenia*'s cast, it was the first time they'd ventured out on two wheels, let alone dealt with the subtle quirks of a scooter. With just one week set aside to learn the ins and outs, this intensive period led to some amusing moments, especially concerning Leslie Ash, as Phil Daniels and Toyah Wilcox would later recall.

'We went to the Hendon police place,' recalled Phil Daniels in 2008, 'and got taught by some big fat copper about how to ride our bikes. He used to get Leslie Ash onto the back because he fancied her. I mean, when you are about 19, they're the

ABOVE: Sixties counter culture icon Jeff Dexter was brought in as a special advisor for *Quadrophenia*'s dance sequences.

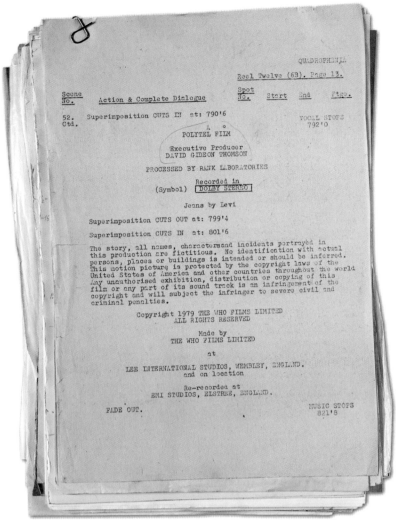

The story, all names, characters and incidents portrayed in this production are fictitious. No identification with actual persons, places or buildings is intended or should be inferred. This motion picture is protected by the copyright laws of the United States of America and other countries throughout the world. Any unauthorised exhibition, distribution or copying of this film or any part of its sound track is an infringement of the copyright and will subject the infringer to severe civil and criminal penalties.

riding sessions, the vehicles provided at Hendon were in fact conventional motorbikes with an engine capacity of 125cc. The more complex riding of scooters would come later on the open road. For Trevor Laird, who'd never ridden any sort of two-wheeled device, he was spared the embarrassment and was allowed to ride pillion for several moments.

In between numerous hiccups and adventures, a bond within the main players was growing. 'We all became very good buddies, very quickly,' reported Phil Daniels to the BBC in 2005. 'We all hung around together, Franc encouraged this. He encouraged the depraved sides of our nature. He was not one for tucking us into bed of a night-time.'

Indeed, Roddam's background did inspire the direction the film was going to take. 'When I made *Quadrophenia*,' he recalled later, 'I said, "I'm going to shoot it in the same way that I make a documentary. I'm going to let the actors have the space, they're going to decide the movement, I'm going to move like they move and the camera [will] move like they move."'

Given its frenetic schedule, *Quadrophenia* required a director of photography with enough agility and street-level empathy to successfully transfer the action onto celluloid with conviction. Enter Brian Tufano, then a 39-year-old veteran of the British film and television industry. Hailing from the same turf as The Who, Tufano had worked his way up from being a 16-year-old trainee projectionist at the BBC to production assistant. His evident talent saw him later transfer to the BBC's acclaimed documentary division, where he contributed to high-end productions such as *Panorama*, *Omnibus* and *Man Alive*, and a number of short dramas. *Quadrophenia* was his first foray into full-length films.

To keep a sense of order without compromising the necessarily violent scenes, stunt coordinator Peter Brayham was called in to manage the action. Violence and motorcycle stunts were key components of this hugely energetic film, and

best bits – y'know what I mean? Free bike rides and all that.'

'One of my first images is Leslie Ash going arse over tit falling off a scooter,' remembered Toyah Wilcox later. 'I think she used the brake as the accelerator and it kind of flipped her.'

Seemingly impeccable in most disciplines, it appears that Sting's bike riding was well below par for what was ultimately required. 'They wanted me to do a wheelie moving along,' recalled Sting to the *Daily Mirror* in 1979. 'By the time I'd smashed two scooters they decided not to use that shot in the film.'

Memories may well be a little faulty forty years on, as the reality was that for these initial 'scooter'-

OPPOSITE: Sting's Vespa being made ready for action.

only someone of his vast experience could be relied upon to ensure that all the physical action could be contained safely. An actor as well as a stunt coordinator, Brayham had featured in the James Bond epic *From Russia with Love* and *Lisztomania*, and appeared in the cult classic *The Prisoner* and Gerry Anderson drama *UFO*. Well schooled in marshalling challenging situations, there were times on *Quadrophenia* that tested even his extensive skills.

While Roddam had the freedom to hire scooters and motorbikes for pre-production, it was obvious that the detail of Jimmy and Ace Face's vehicles would come under immediate and close scrutiny once the film was shown in cinemas. Mods, renowned for their ultra-obsessive attention to detail, would quickly spot any slight chink in authenticity once blown up on the big screen.

With a brief to be faithful in every respect to the lead vehicles, the film producers approached Sterling Scooters, a small establishment based in West Drayton, Middlesex, to supply some of the all-important pieces of machinery. With Phil Daniels' vehicle occupying a large part of the screen time, it was decided that two identical scooters were required in case of any damage or incapacity once filming started.

However, the ultimate choice went against the grain of the theme. Jimmy's scooter was a 1967 Lambretta LI 150 model, series 3. Although the lyrics on the *Quadrophenia* album solely referenced a 'GS Scooter' on the track 'I've Had Enough', it was decided early on that Jimmy's vehicle had to be in line with those of his cohorts.

While evidently vintage, Jimmy's Lambretta hailed from the period 1967–8, a full three years beyond the film's timescale. As a result, the scooter's original number plate, an 'F' registration (dating from August 1967), had to be clipped to deflect any anorak complaints. The rest of the plate – KRU 251 – remained intact, indicating an unusual registration to those who monitored such things.

Much like the character who rode it, Ace Face's scooter had to upstage all the others. The machine was dressed in numerous mirrors and other livery befitting its celebrity. Given that it was due to meet an inglorious fate at the film's finale, five contemporary Rally GS vehicles were purchased from Sterling Scooters and re-dressed to assume the look of their sixties counterparts – the Vespa GS 160.

The rest of the cast needed suitably vintage transport, too. Original vehicles from the period proved hard to source, so a host of contemporary scooters was acquired and distressed to convey the period. One of the consultants employed to flush out any old parts from dealers across the country was William Woodhouse, a former aircraft engineer and a member of the Vespa Club of Great Britain. 'We had lots of trouble hunting around dealers finding the mirrors and lights,' he recalled in 2011. 'You had to find five sets that all looked the same.'

Nonetheless, Woodhouse succeeded. Overlooked in previous appreciations of the film, it was Woodhouse's idea to give Sting's vehicle its unique number plate – VCB 160 – a curious assignation and the subject of much debate among *Quadrophenia*'s aficionados. In 2009 Williams finally revealed the plate's somewhat unique derivation to reporter Jennifer Scott: 'I was in the Vespa Club of Britain. That's the reason I put its initials on there. I was just advertising the Vespa Club for free! The original bike they wanted was a Vespa 160, which is where the numbers came from. All the film's fans thought the numbers had a special meaning behind them.'

The Brighton shoot required other vehicles for the ancillary cast, so a call went out to members of the scooter fraternity throughout the UK club network – most notably, Bournemouth's Modrapheniacs. However, inviting hard-core scooter fanatics to get involved with the production raised several issues, not least a belief that the production crew were seemingly eager to compromise authenticity over style. Reportedly,

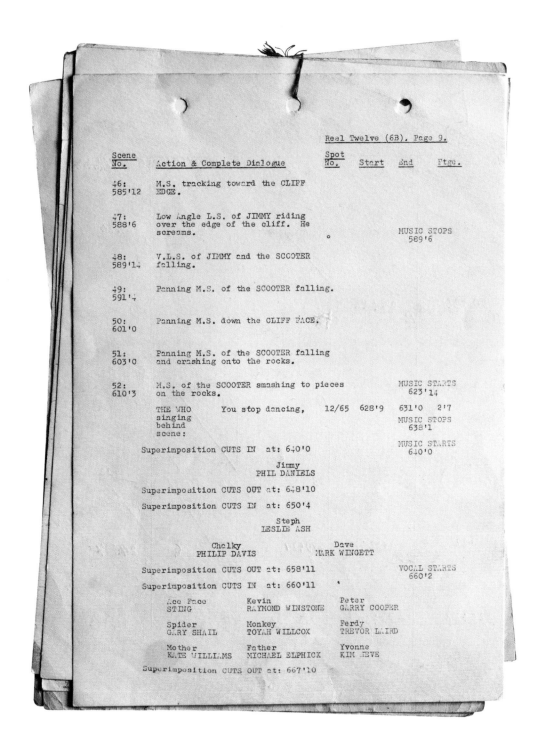

```
                                        Reel Twelve (6B). Page 9.

Scene                                   Spot
No.     Action & Complete Dialogue      No.    Start    End    Ftge.

46:     M.S. tracking toward the CLIFF
585'12  EDGE.

47:     Low Angle L.S. of JIMMY riding
588'6   over the edge of the cliff. He                        MUSIC STOPS
        screams.                          o                    589'6

48:     V.L.S. of JIMMY and the SCOOTER
589'14  falling.

49:     Panning M.S. of the SCOOTER falling.
591'4

50:     Panning M.S. down the CLIFF FACE.
601'0

51:     Panning M.S. of the SCOOTER falling
603'0   and crashing onto the rocks.

52:     M.S. of the SCOOTER smashing to pieces               MUSIC STARTS
610'3   on the rocks.                                          623'14

        THE WHO       You stop dancing,  12/65  628'9  631'0   2'7
        singing                                        MUSIC STOPS
        behind                                          638'1
        scene:
                                                       MUSIC STARTS
        Superimposition CUTS IN  at: 640'0              640'0

                              Jimmy
                           PHIL DANIELS

        Superimposition CUTS OUT at: 648'10

        Superimposition CUTS IN  at: 650'4

                               Steph
                            LESLIE ASH

                Chalky                  Dave
              PHILIP DAVIS            MARK WINGETT

        Superimposition CUTS OUT at: 658'11           VOCAL STARTS
                                                        660'2
        Superimposition CUTS IN  at: 660'11    '

          Ace Face        Kevin              Peter
           STING          RAYMOND WINSTONE   GARRY COOPER

           Spider         Monkey             Ferdy
          GARY SHAIL      TOYAH WILLCOX      TREVOR LAIRD

           Mother         Father             Yvonne
          KATE WILLIAMS   MICHAEL ELPHICK    KIM NEVE

        Superimposition CUTS OUT at: 667'10
```

this led to several scooter aficionados leaving the production early on. Nonetheless, others were excited about their vehicles featuring in the film and happily acquiesced.

In tandem with securing the period artefacts for the film, there was the considerable task of finding locations. For a production that was scheduled to be filmed in genuine settings, a huge amount of work had to be undertaken to secure believable exteriors and backdrops. Consumed with scriptwriting, casting and other issues, Franc Roddam delegated the nuts-and-bolts production workload and sent a team of professional location scouts to London and the South Coast to secure the best exteriors.

Brighton was central to the film's theme, of

ABOVE: Some examples of production notes from *Quadrophenia*.

course; frustratingly, early approaches to the town were met with a less than positive response from the stuffy local authorities. Mindful of the havoc that had occurred on their beaches just fourteen years ago, Brighton Council initially blocked the use of the town for filming, arguing that the beach-fight scenes could be enormously provocative and detrimental to the town's image. Genuine riots involving punks and Teddy Boys at seaside resorts the year before had revived banner headlines and delicate sensitivities. The thought of any rioting, however fictional, was a problem for Brighton's nervous guardians.

'Brighton Council would not give us permission to shoot here,' recalled Roddam in 2007, 'so we started looking around at Scarborough, Weston-super-Mare – all these other towns that had piers. But in the end I thought, "One: [Brighton] is the most beautiful-looking town," and "Two: we should be faithful to the album."' So I persisted and said to my producer Roy Baird, "Look, I want to do it here. You've got to make it happen."'

On Roddam's insistence, Quadrophenia's big guns travelled down to Brighton to ensure that the iconic South Coast location was cleared for filming use. 'We were very lucky,' Roy Baird reflected to the BBC in 2007. 'The completion guarantee for the film was put up by a gentleman called Jimmy Swan. Jimmy's friend was a chairman of Brighton and Hove Albion Football Club, whose friend was a [police] chief superintendent. So I go to Brighton, go to a little cocktail party and meet the Chief of Police, and he said, "They can't stop you, y'know? The council can't stop you shooting. I can stop you but they can't." So I said, "They said we can't go on the beach." And he said, "They can't stop you going on the beach." So I thought this was sounding really good. So he said, "You can carry on as long as you don't break the law."'

The Police Chief having tacitly green-lighted permission to use Brighton for filming, Roddam and his team drew up a comprehensive map to detail where all the action would take place. 'This

was a massive team effort,' recalled Roddam to the BBC in 2007. 'We had a lot of people who were very enthusiastic about making this film. We had a very fine art director called Simon Holland. I remember I said to him, "Can you get me big maps of the streets, big blueprints?" I remember myself and a lot of other people strategising the riot and working it out… It was just very efficient. It was my first film, my first feature, I wanted to succeed, I was fiercely determined.'

With no objections from the police, permission from Brighton's local authority was less equivocal. Filming on the streets and a section of the beach was deemed permissible, but there was one important caveat: namely, that no filming would be allowed on either the Palace Pier or the West Pier. Mindful that, in 1974, shooting for Ken Russell's Tommy had razed nearby Portsmouth's South Parade Pier, there were concerns that the electricity required for filming might have a similar effect on these two iconic landmarks of the Brighton landscape. This restriction caused a few headaches for the production team, especially as a key scene towards the end of the film called for an expressive use of a pier.

This quandary not immediately soluble, Roddam and his team had to look elsewhere. Portsmouth, still reeling from the Ken Russell incident, was obviously out of bounds, while other South Coast piers were not up for the task. One potential location was situated some 200 miles away at Weston-super-Mare. Roddam and his art department duly headed off to the West Country after a day of pre-production had been completed in London.

'I went to Weston-super-Mare,' Roddam told the author in 2012. 'We finished work on a Friday night, got this long train journey and arrived at 11.30 p.m. Everything's closed up and there's a guy waiting for us at the pier, a doorman, and he's telling us he'd written a book called Revolving Doors. Anyway, Weston-super-Mare was going to be very difficult to get the production down there. So I went back to Brighton and decided to look at the pier, rather than be on the pier. It did me a favour.'

While Roddam and his immediate production team were consumed with all manner of casting, scriptwriting and other duties, as well as doing everything they could to secure clearances and permissions, others in *Quadrophenia*'s crew were not sharing their imagination or stamina. With shooting dates imminent, it soon became apparent that the location scouts had made only a perfunctory effort at securing clearances. It was a tip-off from the film's art director, Simon Holland, that only a few of the locations for filming had been sourced – the worst omissions occurring at the key Brighton shoot – that revealed the lackadaisical approach.

'I remember my frustration with the guys I was working with,' recalled Roddam. 'They kept bringing me locations that were good for parking because the locations guy's first thought is, "Is it good for parking so [I] can get all the vehicles there?" And my first thought was, "Does it look good on screen?" This was my first feature and these were all seasoned guys I was working with, and they got a little bit lazy, and they kept showing me locations in Barnes. This guy lived in Barnes, which is a suburb of London, and I said, "Look, it's good for parking and it's good for Barnes, but it's no fucking good for me. So get it right!"'

Despite Roddam's protestations, the location scouts were unmoved by the demands of a first-time film director. The British film industry now well beyond its halcyon days of the sixties, some were still lamenting the lavish hospitality and complacent ambience of the glory days. With the clock ticking, it soon became apparent that only a few sites had been cleared for filming. In Brighton, where the most intense preparation was to take place, only two out of twenty-four locations had been secured. With the scouts ensconced in a hotel on the South Coast and reportedly dining at fancy restaurants in the district, an incensed Roddam got wind of their behaviour and shot down to their Brighton accommodation to find out what was going on.

'I burst into the room,' he recalled in 2008. '[I said] "Guys, I hear you haven't got the locations?" And they said, "Yeah well…" and I went ape-shit. I said, "I don't want you to breathe. I don't want you to eat. I don't want you to shit. You find all those fucking locations for me or I am going to come back here and you're all fucking fired, the whole lot of you. This picture's going down because you haven't got what I've asked of you. Your job is to get what I ask!" One guy jumped up and took off his jacket. I remember (and I must have been out of my mind) I picked up a wine bottle and I said, "Get the fucking locations!" Anyway, I went away and came back a few days later and they'd got nineteen of the twenty-two that were missing.'

Less problematic in terms of clearance was the setting for the film's finale. This took the production team to Beachy Head, just outside Eastbourne, East Sussex. For reasons best known to those who scheduled the timetable, they shot the final scenes of *Quadrophenia* first, bringing Phil Daniels to the location for three days of shooting. September 1978 saw the heaviest amount of pre-production for *Quadrophenia*, with filming due to start at the end of the month. However, no one was aware that tragic events in The Who's immediate circle were about to threaten the entire production ●

CHAPTER SIX

'SOMEONE SUGGESTED PUTTING "THIS FILM IS DEDICATED TO THE MEMORY OF KEITH MOON" ON *QUADROPHENIA* AND I SAID: "YOU DON'T NEED TO SAY IT; *QUADROPHENIA* IS KEITH MOON."'
—PETE TOWNSHEND

QPete Meaden's visionary outlook for Mod (and by extension *Quadrophenia*) had shadowed The Who's formative movements. Although he had maintained an interest in music and promotion, and possessed a CV that included working with the likes of The Rolling Stones, Captain Beefheart and Chuck Berry, work had petered out. The seventies were especially barren, and Meaden had suffered from depression. His mental illness compounded by drink and drug abuse, Meaden eventually died of a barbiturate overdose at his parents' home in Enfield, North London on July 29th, 1978, sadly just a few weeks before *Quadrophenia* started filming. Reportedly, he had been privy to the creation of the script, and although he was not formally consulted about the film's production, he had held on to the belief that the lead character was based on his glory days back in the sixties.

Although they paid for his funeral, members of The Who were unable to attend. Adding further irony, Pete Meaden was buried in Southgate Cemetery, a stone's throw away from one of *Quadrophenia*'s imminent locations, the Tower Ballroom, an environment he would have been more than at home with during his Mod heyday.

Despite the sadness of Meaden's passing, work on *Quadrophenia* had to continue. The film budget was relatively modest, and everyone was acutely aware of the strict conditions attached to bringing the picture in on time. Financed in part by The Who's record company, Polydor, the resulting fortunes of the film were largely dependent on the continuing activities of the band, not least the scheduling of two albums to tie in with *Quadrophenia*, namely the film's soundtrack and the group's anthology, *The Kids Are Alright*. With all four members of the group still in their mid-thirties, the band's immediate future was not considered in doubt. However, no one was prepared for what occurred in the first week of September 1978.

Keith Moon's perilous physical and mental health had given cause for serious concern over the

THIS IS one of the last pictures of Keith Moon, the wild man of rock.

The 31-year-old tearaway drummer of The Who pop group was at a party with his girl friend Annette Waller-Lax, which was thrown by Paul McCartney on Wednesday night.

It was Annette who found Moon dead of a suspected drug overdose early yesterday.

The party's over: Picture special, Pages 2 and 3

OPPOSITE: Phil Daniels ready and waiting, Beachy Head, September 26th, 1978.

LEFT: News breaks of Keith Moon's death, September 7th, 1978.

years, and during the mid-seventies his diminishing health had prompted a temporary respite from his heavy roistering. With only a few recording sessions and other film-related work for The Who, Moon had busied himself with other projects.

Outside work, Moon was enjoying a rare attempt at domesticity with his girlfriend, Swedish model Annette Walter-Lax. From the sanctuary of the couple's Mayfair flat at 9 Curzon Place, the pair occasionally ventured out to party. On September 6th, Keith and Annette attended a star-studded reception in honour of Buddy Holly, a gathering hosted by ex-Beatle Paul McCartney. Appearing convivial and relaxed, the pair enjoyed the party and then made their way home, where they stayed up for most of the night. Moon had recently sought medical advice regarding his alcoholism and had been prescribed medication to curb his addiction. In need of some stabilising influence, at some point Moon inadvertently took thirty-two tablets of Clomethiazole, a sedative aimed to combat the symptoms of alcohol withdrawal. A usual dose amounted to just one tablet, with a daily maximum of three. Moon's massive overdose cut him down. Despite input from the emergency services, Moon was pronounced dead the following afternoon.

News of his passing spread like wildfire throughout The Who's tight-knit circle. After the public announcement, the press devoted banner-page headlines to the drummer's short but hugely eventful life. Beyond the obvious sadness, the future of the group without Moon was clearly in question.

There was also the pressing issue of *Quadrophenia*. *The Kids Are Alright* required post-production work and *Quadrophenia* was on the cusp of shooting. At the time of Moon's death, co-producer Roy Baird was in Los Angeles to discuss the film's US release and distribution. In between meetings, he received an urgent call from the film's production offices that would call for prompt action.

Baird recalled for the BBC in 2007 how 'suddenly an operator came through and said, "Sorry, but we've got a very important call coming through

from London." It was Bill Curbishley, and he said, "I've got very bad news; Keith's dead." It was a huge shock. So I got on a plane and came back, and we thought that was the end of the film. As it was being financed by the record company, they probably thought, "No Keith Moon, no Who." So that was a big problem. It could have been the end of the film before it started.'

However, assurances came through from the group and their management that, despite Moon's enormous loss to both the group and their fans, The Who would continue. The statement reassured the record company and filming remained on target for the end of September 1978, but the shock of Moon's death hung like a pall over everything.

The cast was ready to travel to Brighton, but there were still hundreds of extras to be contracted for the many crowd scenes. While conventional extras agencies were tapped for most of the background personnel, others came via different routes. Some were drawn from scooter and biker fraternities across the country. Others with less specific roles came from Brighton's Job Centre. With the promise of £10 a day, there was the added bonus of an extra £5 if you brought along a scooter or motorbike. Predictably, Mods totally outnumbered their Rocker counterparts in the employment queue, leading the advert to be removed and a more selective recruitment having to take place.

Given that those masquerading as policemen would have more demanding roles, they were drawn from a specialist agency in London. Numbering around thirty, these fake policemen were hired on the basis that they would be required for two days' shooting. Briefed in advance that there would be some realistic scenes to contend with, stunt arrangers attempted to allay any worries that they'd have to suffer anything too rigorous. To further placate delicate dispositions, these extras were told in advance that the weaponry employed by rioting Mods and Rockers (deckchairs, sticks, stones and other beach paraphernalia) would be made out of balsa wood, and potatoes would be used

as stones. Unfortunately, these briefings served to relax the extras a little too much. This would lead to problems later, especially given that a distinctly violent reality was required during the riot scenes.

There was little respite for Franc Roddam during shooting. It was clear that there would be few of the trappings that normally accompanied a director on a major feature film. 'Roy [Baird] said to me, "You're not going to have a director's chair." I said, "I always wanted a director's chair," and he said to me, "You won't have time to sit down."'

Despite *Quadrophenia*'s troubled gestation, after three months of hectic preparation, filming started on schedule on Tuesday, September 26th, 1978, at Beachy Head, near Eastbourne. While it might seem illogical, the first shots to be captured were those for the riots and Jimmy's finale. Within film circles (particularly those on tight budgets), filming the most expensive scenes first made good sense, especially if the money ran out later. Equally,

with daylight at a premium in late September, for a film set in May it was vital to capture the exteriors before autumn and diminishing daylight took a greater hold.

The set-up for the Beachy Head shoot required a variety of props, stuntmen and other machinery, but much of the usual bulky hardware present on film sets was abandoned in favour of more organic equipment. Normally, moving shots, especially of vehicles, are captured on what is known as a 'dolly' – a device engineered to take the bumps out of uneven terrain. However, Roddam insisted that Jimmy's iconic ride along the cliffs was to be tracked from the rear of a converted Citroën 2CV, a temperamental French vehicle that was famous for its fuel economy and light weight. While not as smooth as the dolly device, it gave a greater sense of realism to the emotional ride along the cliff's edge.

Only Phil Daniels was required for filming these

ABOVE: Mod Mayhem! A recreation of an iconic moment on Marine Parade, September 1978.

sequences on Beachy Head, so the main cast gathered together back at the Brighton base. This, Daniels' first leading role, meant he would have to endure a virtual baptism of fire, slip immediately into Jimmy's frazzled state, so that he could taper his characterisation for the rest of the film.

Phil Daniels: 'I think for an actor there's a lot to be said for doing the end of a film first, because you know where you are going to go. I knew where I was going to end my part, so could build up to that.'

The dramatic coastline of Beachy Head had rarely been utilised in modern cinema, although the car in *Chitty Chitty Bang Bang* had sailed off the cliff in 1968. The nearby lighthouse had a modest televisual history, most notably in Patrick McGoohan's cult series, *The Prisoner* (1967). More discreetly, in 1986 the coastline featured in the equally cultish BBC television series *The Life and Loves of a She-Devil*, and the clifftop location would feature in the Bond film *The Living Daylights*, *Harry Potter: The Goblet of Fire* and *Pearl Harbor* in the future.

To establish a safe route along the cliff edge, a stuntman took a few test runs before Daniels mounted his vehicle. However, the scooter's tyre tracks dug hard into the early morning dew, scoring the grass. While they proved useful for Daniels to follow later on, these impressions – especially from above – inadvertently caused an indelible imprint on the cliff edge for the entirety of the Beachy Head shoot, something that cinematic technology (certainly by 1978 standards) proved impossible to erase. With no means to eradicate the tracks, the filmmakers had to grin and bear it.

In glorious weather, Daniels began his first few sorties, at several points getting dangerously close to the cliff edge. Its sheer drop over 540 feet at one point, he had to call on every atom of his scooter training back at Hendon, although there was nothing that could prepare him for Beachy Head's unpredictable terrain.

With just a few weeks of tuition, even for a competent scooter rider, riding the cliff edge at Beachy Head called for considerable expertise.

OPPOSITE: 'Here above sea and sand'. Phil Daniels alongside Beachy Head.

*Jimmy — Sc 170 —
Jacket open, Parka open
& Zipped about 6" from bottom*

*Jimmy — Sc 170 (for make up
Tie loose at collar.*

*Sc 170 Jimmy on stand in
Scooter.*

ABOVE: Production Polaroid's from Beachy Head.

While a stunt double undertook some of the more exacting moves, Daniels found himself traversing part of the journey.

Youthful bravado to the fore, at one point Daniels came off the scooter – thankfully away from the cliff edge – and required medical attention. This hiccup proving salutary, he received some timely advice from one of the production staff.

Phil Daniels: 'Ray Corbett, the first assistant director, a wise old owl who had been in the business for years, put me right. "Look, Phil, if you fell over the cliff, right, you'd be dead. They'd pay out straight away on the insurance and some other geezer would be playing your part tomorrow. So let me give you a few words of advice: take it easy. Let the stuntman do all that. You look after yourself."'

While these hiccups were occurring on solid ground, Roddam was otherwise occupied hovering over Beachy Head in a helicopter with a cameraman. 'I remember being in the helicopter and being terrified,' he recalled in 2008. '[The pilot] used to play games and he'd swoop off the edge. This guy was wild. He'd sit there smoking a pipe dressed in a navel raincoat with a huge moustache… His idea of seeing whether we were cool enough to fly with him was to put the helicopter down on the edge of the cliff, half hanging over, half on the cliff, and rock the helicopter back and forth to see if we were cool enough. He then let the helicopter fall off the cliff and started the engine about a third of the way down… It was quite a wild moment.'

Following the completion of all the shots along the cliff's edge, the iconic scene of the scooter going into mid-air was ready to be captured. This proved problematic in more ways than one, especially in terms of the safety of those attempting to film it. Well before shooting had started, Eastbourne's local authority had to be consulted about clearance for this controversial shot. The beach roped off by security, and with boats maintaining a watching eye, the council also insisted that any vehicle destined to be launched should be free of all fuels and lubricants. Furthermore, once filming had finished, the beach would have to be systematically swept for any residual parts that had come off the vehicles on impact.

While on dry land, Sting's scooter was as authentic as could be achieved; for its spectacular demise it had to be subtly different. With the likelihood of more than one take for the final sequence required, scooter engineer William Woodhouse had prepared a couple of Vespas for the sequence. In addition to getting the right weight balance for the

scooter's launch, there was another, more practical demand to be addressed.

'I had to make one bike without engines to go off the cliff,' explained recalled Woodhouse to the This Is Nottingham website in 2009.'The filmmakers didn't want the weight because they had to get the bike back. The council wouldn't allow them to leave the wreckage on the beach!'

The bike's exact trajectory was of particular concern, especially with a film crew at the base of the cliff and a helicopter and cameraman also attempting to track it from above. To ease the vehicle's passage, only the bare shell of the Vespa was used on its launch into the air. To facilitate its curving trajectory, a ramp was built close to the cliff edge. On cue, the scooter was propelled into the air via a winch tied to a Range Rover driving in the other direction.

Evidently, the ultimate direction of the flying scooter had been the source of much debate in *Quadrophenia*'s production office, as Roddam

⊙ **'I DECIDED I'D BE IN THE HELICOPTER. I THOUGHT IT WOULD BE FUN TO SEE THIS THING COMING TOWARDS YOU WHILE YOU WERE IN THE HELICOPTER.'**
FRANC RODDAM

would recall in 2011. 'The guys had scientifically worked out the physics of it. I decided I'd be in the helicopter. I thought it would be fun to see this thing coming towards you while you were in the helicopter. They worked it all out with a block and tackle to catapult it into the air, and the calculation was wrong, and it literally almost hit the helicopter. Afterwards, I thought it was pretty hilarious.'

As legend would later record, more than one Vespa would be launched off the cliff edge. At sea level, cameraman Brian Tufano was ready to track the descent of the doomed vehicle as it hurtled towards

ABOVE: 'That is Brighton my son!' Running into Eastbourne from Beachy Head, September 1978.

ABOVE: Phil Daniels, moments prior to the scooter's launch into the unknown.

the beach. 'I was underneath following it down, not knowing where it was going to go,' he described to the BBC in 2007. 'You work out the trajectory and everything else, but of course a scooter is a scooter and it is not exactly aerodynamic. So the thing came over and you're standing there thinking, "Is it time to move?"'

Despite those on the beach worrying about where the scooter would end up, one of the Vespas did come to rest in a particularly satisfying way – its landing providing *Quadrophenia* with its memorable finale. The spectacular result was largely guaranteed by Roddam insisting on a wide-angle lens (the specification similar to the one used in much of *Citizen Kane*), which ensured that the descending vehicle was recorded in focus.

The early autumn sunshine blessing the crew with almost perfect conditions, two impromptu sequences were added during filming. The first of these was an extraordinary shot that added further gravitas to Jimmy's addled state of mind. The sun was glinting on the gentle waves at the bottom of the cliff, and it was discovered that if the camera's lens was tweaked slightly, the reflection of the sun on the sea gave the impression of pills bobbing around. The original script alluded to this in overt terms, envisaging 'a polythene bag and a number of blue pills floating on top of the water, drifting away from the scooter'. While this ending would have added weight to Jimmy's rejection of the Mod credo, the organic image was far more poetic.

Another shot came about purely by chance. Challenging and thought-provoking, it would prompt debate amongst the film's devotees for years to come. Pete Townshend's original vision for *Quadrophenia*'s finale had Jimmy purloining a boat and rowing out towards a rock, where he'd meet a destiny of sorts. That ending being deemed too nebulous for cinemagoers to digest, Jimmy's scooter going over the cliff had been an integral part of the script from the offset.

While Beachy Head's poignant reputation as the suicide spot of the world was yet to be publicly recognised, the sequence nonetheless called for a symbolically destructive end. According to Roddam and others, there had been an early plan to invoke elements of the real-life tragedy of Barry Prior, a London Mod who'd fallen off a cliff near to Brighton in May 1964.

Prior's sad demise had hovered over the creation of the *Quadrophenia* script from its inception. During his fastidious research, writer Martin Stellman had come upon coverage of the death in a newspaper archive, the incident having occurred on the morning after the Brighton May Day riots.

Like many teenagers, the 17-year-old had been caught up in the fledgling Mod movement, and with the press whipping up stories of considerable action to be had on the South Coast, he and his Mod cohorts had travelled down from the capital to Brighton to engage in the activities. Rather than risk a night sleeping on the beach or under the piers, the group decided to set up camp around five miles out of town at a location known as Telscombe. Given the late hour, somewhat naïvely, the lads failed to assess the perilous cliff edge that ran alongside the patch of grass they'd earmarked for their camp.

Their night under the stars appeared uneventful, but the following morning an unspeakable horror manifested itself. Shortly after 7 a.m., with Barry missing from his tent, one of his friends spotted him lying motionless at the bottom of the nearby cliff. Initially imagined to be some sort of stunt, the reality was far graver. After the emergency services were called and Prior was pronounced dead, the sheer horror of the accident was processed into harsh truth.

Prior's death hit his family and immediate community hard, and news of his demise and the subsequent inquiry occupied several columns of the press. The family nursed their loss for many

LEFT: 'Is it time to move?' Sting's Vespa meets a dismal fate.

'MOD' FALLS TO DEATH BRIGHTON CLIFF

A group of his friends talk on the c
dead boy's moto

TH E Mods invasion of Brighton ended in disaster in the early hours of today when a 17-year-old trainee accountant plunged 100ft. to his death from the clifftop at Saltdean.

The body of Barry Prior, of Church Crescent, Finchley, was found at 7.30 a.m. today sprawled on the rocks at the foot of the cliffs.

He had ridden to Brighton on his new scarlet scooter with more than 30 London Mods to spend the weekend in Brighton.

Last night they pitched their tents on the clifftop. At 3 a.m. they settled down for the night, and that was the last time Barry Prior was seen alive.

Shortly after 7 a.m. his friends realised he was missing and began a search.

One of the friends, Colin Goulden, aged 17, of Dickens Avenue, Finchley, said: "One of the boys said he was missing and

we started looking for him. Someone looked over the cliff and saw him lying there. He shouted out, but at first we thought he was mucking about, trying to get us all up."

Another of the party, 17-year-old Fred Butler, of Farmilo Road, Leyton, added: "We went over to the houses on the other side of the road to call the police, but they wouldn't open their doors at first. They thought we were out for trouble; you know what it is.

"I don't know what could have happened. There was no trouble or fighting. We came out here to get out of the way. Perhaps he

got up in the night and went for a walk. No one saw anything and there were no screams," he added.

Police and an ambulance were on the spot within minutes.

Ambulance men, assisted by another group of Mods, made the half-mile trek over the rocks at the foot of the cliff to reach the body.

One of the Mods who accompanied the rescue party said afterwards: "It was horrible. He was lying there, wearing a green anorak and socks, but no shoes. He was horribly bashed up."

Several of the Mods who came to Brighton with the boy accompanied the police to the police station.

The rest of the party packed their tents and sleeping-bags and headed back to London.

118

169 Continued   169

the scooter as he wipes the eye make-up from his face in
gestures of finality; for the sight of THE ACE flunkeying
as a Bell-Boy has killed JIMMY's vision of MOD culture, and
his own allegiance to it ...

170 EXT.   ROAD & CLIFFTOPS   DAY   170
         MUSIC OVER: ('I'VE HAD ENOUGH'/'DOCTOR JIMMY')

Heading away from the town, JIMMY careers the scooter off
the coast road leading to Rottingdean, and heads the scooter
along the grassy spaces that separate the road from the clifftops above the sea ...

For a while, JIMMY rides along the cliff edges, dangerously,
playing with life and death, holding us in suspense. Passing
a particularly sheer cliff edge, JIMMY skids the scooter to a
halt with his feet, veers back round and rides up to the edge,
looking down at the sea and the jagged rocks, the seagulls
wheeling around the cliff-face and the pebble beach with a kind
of longing. He turns away from the edge and rides in a straight
line at right angles to it for some fifty yards. Turning the
scooter round again to face the sea, he rides the scooter
straight at the cliff edge ...

As we PAN and TRACK with JIMMY and the scooter hurling towards
the edge, we INTERCUT a rapid tracking shot inside the white,
starkly lit tunnel we have seen in previous scenes but this
time, the tunnel is empty.

171 EXT.   BEACH   DAY   171
         MUSIC OVER: ('DROWNED')

The scooter lies half-submerged at the water's edge with
the incoming sea gently washing over the wreckage of the
machine in an echo of the opening sequence of the film ...
A polythene bag and a number of blue pills float on top of
the water, drifting away from the scooter ...

171A INT.   JIMMY'S BEDROOM   DAY   171A

The bare wall of Jimmy's bedroom, as we last saw it, shorn
of posters, newspaper articles and pictures of The Who;
small pieces of sellotape are still stuck to the wall, some
attached to the torn edges of posters, torn wallpaper,
ripped away by Jimmy with the posters fluttering on the wall
slightly.

A hand and arm come into shot holding a cutting from a
newspaper; the hand, which looks like JIMMY's sticks the

---

years, but to the public at large, Prior's story would be forgotten and preserved only in the files of a newspaper library.

Martin Stellman clearly felt the story echoed with Pete Townshend's original coda – that of Jimmy stealing a boat and heading off to sea – and it appears that aspects of Barry Prior's tragic death might have had some influence on the closing moments of the film adaptation.

Scene 170 of the shooting script clearly listed Rottingdean as the start of Jimmy's clifftop adventure, and with the small town a little under two miles from the location of Prior's death, the final scenes were initially envisaged to be featured there and not at Beachy Head (some eighteen miles further along the coast). What no one knew at the time (or was not imparting) was that a strange synchronicity was linking Barry Prior, Pete Townshend and, ultimately, the fortunes of *Quadrophenia*.

Remarkably, the career path of Barry's brother Tony would see him linked with Pete Townshend, and during the seventies, he ended up working for The Who. In social contact with Townshend and his family, Tony Prior was present when Townshend started work on *Quadrophenia* and when the film started to come together.

Despite these coincidences, there is no documentary proof to suggest that Barry Prior's death inspired *Quadrophenia* in any way. When I presented some news clippings to Pete Townshend in 1999, he was saddened to read of the death, but stated there was no link between the album concept and Prior. However, Franc Roddam begs to differ, claiming Pete had told him he'd written the story after hearing the news of a death that occurred following the Brighton May Day riots in 1964.

After some debate, the filmmakers decided that such a similarly harrowing demise for Jimmy was inappropriate for the atmosphere of *Quadrophenia*. 'When I started,' remembered Roddam, 'I wanted him to die, but I changed my opinion. When I met all these guys and they were so optimistic, I realised that the idea of death was only some kind of morbid thing that Townshend and I had because we were over thirty. I was glad in the end to have him cast off his job, his parents, his girlfriend and end up free of it all… The death of his old life on one level or a true physical death if you wanted to take it that way.'

Nonetheless, with the descending scooter clearly riderless, it would leave a huge question mark as to what actually happened to Jimmy. Initially content to let viewers make up their own minds, the conclusion to three days of glorious shooting atop Beachy Head presented the film crew with a remarkable sunset – a deep orange and crimson orb slowly lowering itself over the English Channel. Everyone was mesmerised by the sight, and it was then that Roddam hit upon an idea to capture a sequence that could act as a more powerful, and oblique, opener to the film.

To offer *Quadrophenia* some immediate lyricism right from the start, Roddam hit upon the idea of Jimmy walking away from the cliff edge to the strains of The Who's overture to *Quadrophenia*, 'I Am The Sea'. Offering nothing other than a suggested hint to the film's conclusion, it gave nothing away to the viewer.

Bathed in an orange glow and with the sun casting long shadows over the sea, Jimmy's retreat from Beachy Head acted as a powerful and poetic entrée to the film. Indeed, not since Robin Hardy's mesmeric cult shocker *The Wicker Man* of 1972 had an autumn sunset been captured with such clarity on film.

Franc Roddam: 'We were sitting on the cliff and there was this beautiful sun, and we decided to film it. And in the end, I put it in the cut, and I guess that caused all the ambiguity about whether he died or not. It's much debated. And if some people think he went over, then they can think that – it's equally valid.'

"I REALISED THAT THE IDEA OF DEATH WAS ONLY SOME KIND OF MORBID THING THAT TOWNSHEND AND I HAD BECAUSE WE WERE OVER THIRTY."
FRANC RODDAM

The Beachy Head material in the can, a short weekend break allowed the rest of the crew to make their way to Brighton and prepare themselves for the following week's shoot. With two weeks allocated to film all the Brighton sequences, a sense of anticipation mixed with anxiety filled the various hotels that had been booked for cast and crew. Many of the production executives were booked into the iconic Grand Hotel on Brighton's seafront; the majority of the cast and frontline crew were booked into fairly understated accommodation, the Salisbury and the Albion just two of the hotels.

Leslie Ash later recalled the sense of adventure and then the harsh reality when she came down to Brighton to prepare for filming the following week, in her memoir. 'We all checked into a hotel the night before filming started. While the executives lorded it up in the Grand, our hotel was like the poor man's relation; it was dirty and full of mice.'

Once everyone had decanted into their various

OPPOSITE TOP:
News clipping regarding Barry Prior's death in May 1964.

OPPOSITE BOTTOM:
An original script page detailing the film's original ending.

ABOVE: Brighton's iconic Grand Hotel.

bedrooms and suites, a roll call was convened in the lobby of Roddam's hotel, to allow everyone to check their times for make-up and other requirements for the following morning.

This was the first time that the actors had seen the full cast list and the daily call sheets – the essential paperwork that was vital to maintaining a sense of order during filming. Having changed for the evening, Sting emerged in the hotel lobby carrying a large ghetto blaster. Settling himself in a corner, he began previewing demos from The Police's first set of recordings. Intrigued, Leslie Ash went over to listen to the songs blasting out of the tape deck. Being coy, Sting didn't let on that The Police were his band and asked Ash for her opinion on some of the songs' merits, in particular, a track entitled 'Message In A Bottle'. 'I don't really think it's chart material,' she replied shyly. Little did Ash know that the song had already been lined up as a single for The Police and would go on to become one of their signature tunes.

Gary Shail was also privy to Sting's enormous talent germinating in the hotel. 'Me and Sting stayed up all night once,' he told the author in 2014. 'He played me "Walking On The Moon". I said, "Y'know what, Sting? That's fucking wicked. You should release that song." I'm sitting in this hotel room with this serious megastar and I was just eighteen.'

Some inadvertent embarrassment surrounded Sting when the call sheets were handed out. Seemingly for the entirety of rehearsals, the cast had happily swallowed his enigmatic moniker without so much as batting an eyelid, but the call sheets revealed his real name: one Gordon Sumner. This discovery caused a large dose of collective hilarity amongst the cast of young actors, most of it directed in the Geordie's direction.

Punk jokester Jilted John's infuriatingly catchy novelty single, 'Gordon Is A Moron' had enlivened the lower end of the charts during the summer of 1978, demonising anyone unfortunate enough to share the name of the song's character, and not surprisingly, the unveiling of Sting's true name afforded the cast a chance to mercilessly tease

the wannabe pop star with the song's refrain. While Sting's reaction to the ribbing has yet to be recorded, to save any further embarrassment all references to Gordon Sumner were swiftly erased from all the film's future paperwork.

While the paperwork was comprehensive in its directions, there was no way that the scriptwriters could have predicted the improvisational moments that would occur when filming got underway. Mark Wingett later recalled a moment from when they were going through their lines the night before. 'I think it was on the Sunday afternoon. Franc got us all in his hotel room to have the script reading. I remember getting halfway through it and Franc saying, "Oh, let's not bother," and closing the book. So he used that script as a basis and most of it we improvised.'

'There was no script,' confirms Gary Shail today. 'Every day we were given a thing called "blue pages" (rewrites). They'd give you the information that you needed in the scene, so we just made it up as it went along.'

Behind the scenes, Roddam and his team of researchers had been minutely plotting the riot scenes. Given that the collaboration of the police and local council was still dependent on watertight scheduling, a vast amount of work had gone into ensuring that these more than lively scenes would not impinge on Brighton's day-to-day activities.

The town's labyrinthine streets and lanes offered the crew a ready-made set that would have proved impossible to replicate in a studio, and like its most famous Brighton-set predecessors – John Boulting's 1947 version of *Brighton Rock* and Henry Cornelius's whimsical *Genevieve* (1953) – *Quadrophenia* would preserve some of the town's architecture on celluloid. More inadvertently than by design, two other films with contemporary music themes had utilised Brighton as a backdrop. The first was Lance Comfort's ephemeral jukebox film *Be My Guest*. Starring David Hemmings and a pre-Small Faces Steve Marriott, this 1965 yarn attempted to place Brighton as the inheritor of the Liverpool sound. Remarkably, the film invoked no frisson whatsoever,

ABOVE: 'Jilted John' AKA Graham Fellows.

despite the riots that had engulfed the town the year before, and it was consigned to the archives. In John Mackenzie's *Made* (1972) Roy Harper's alter ego finds himself down by the seaside in Brighton on a promotional visit, and although it featured the beachside café that would feature in *Quadrophenia*, the film failed to invoke any magic.

After much deliberation, Roddam and his team decided on a modest but visually rich part of Brighton for the film's base. Utilising the promenade from Brighton's Madeira Drive down to the town's historic Grand Hotel, this enclave would contain the entirety of the Brighton locations. Madeira Drive's sweeping expanse and its stone pillars were well positioned to host the Mods' dramatic arrival from London on scooters and required little in the way of period dressing.

Aside from the locations, several other period issues had to be taken into consideration. Due to the continual evolution of British motoring habits, a fleet of vintage cars faithful to the era had to be brought in. Despite a few immoveable reflections of

1978, the camera operators' brief was to steer away from anything too redolent of a latter-day Britain.

High above Madeira Drive, some steep walls were earmarked to recreate an incident that had been played out for real in the sixties. Although the actual event took place a few hundred yards away above the Brighton Aquarium, the imagery of some energetic Mods launching a group of Rockers over the side of a steep wall had long assumed mythic status. These violent events had been captured in photographs and film at the time, the most graphic shot by photographer Colin Jones. Following publication in the *Argus*, they were syndicated around the world. With these genuine artefacts to hand, the production crew were eager to recreate this iconic moment. During the making of *Quadrophenia*, Brighton's skateboarders made use of the site, which they referred to as 'The White Walls', although far more aggressive stunts were scheduled to take place once filming got underway.

Directly underneath the lower promenade lay the Beach Café, a typically low-key seaside eatery that appeared untouched by time. The café was established in 1964, coincidentally around the time of the original Mods and Rockers battles, and over the years it had served the unsophisticated palates of sun lovers and beach dwellers alike. This establishment was the location for the Mods' communal breakfast and, later, for Jimmy's despondent return to the town. Complete with vintage signage, Formica tables, fitted seats and other leftovers from summers past, no re-dressing was required to bring the café's decor in line with the film's timescale. A happy accident discovered while filming was taking place was the reflection of the nearby Palace Pier caught in the Beach Café's windows.

Located directly under the Palace Pier were several storage units, there to house the necessary utilities for pier maintenance and electricity generator ports. One or two were fortuitously vacant in the run-up to shooting and proved ideal as exteriors for the sequence where two of the Mods, Dave and Chalky, find themselves homeless

THE IMAGERY OF SOME ENERGETIC MODS LAUNCHING A GROUP OF ROCKERS OVER THE SIDE OF A STEEP WALL HAD LONG ASSUMED MYTHIC STATUS

of their most amazing gigs. At the base of a stone stairway lay what was once known as the Florida Rooms and more colloquially known as the Aquarium Ballroom (being situated directly next to Brighton's marine centre).

The venue played host to many leading musical luminaries during the sixties, but it was The High Numbers' and, later, The Who's appearances in 1964 and 1965 that earned the venue its celebrity. A grand stone stairway took one down to a sunken area at sea level, that was as much a part of Brighton as its beach, prom and piers. The former exterior of the club was utilised as the front of *Quadrophenia*'s beachside nightclub, bearing witness to Jimmy's forced exit after his dramatic balcony-diving episode.

In another part of the Aquarium complex lay a fortune-teller's kiosk, belonging to one Madame Victoria. A real-life clairvoyant, she kindly loaned her frontage use in the film. To the left of her premises lay a pedestrian tunnel that led directly towards the beach. Ultimately, all these locations would be employed for *Quadrophenia* duties.

Back on the main part of the promenade, another café, this one situated at the junction

for the night. The original script had called for this sequence to be shot in a more salubrious beach hut. However, with Brighton's immediate beaches not hosting any such constructions, these vacant spaces under the pier were more than suitable.

A stone's throw from the pier, another location appeared tailor-made, in this case for the nightclub exterior. The venue chosen was yet another piece of The Who's glorious past and had hosted some

of East Street and Grand Junction Road, was employed for a rather hectic sequence in which it was wrecked by a marauding army of Mods. The small café was part of the Forte chain and was in 1978 known as the East Street Snack Bar. The café was specially dressed to make it suitable for filming these action scenes; in particular, the café's picture window facing East Street was scheduled to have a large table thrown through it.

Flying tables aside, the district in and around East Street shouldered the majority of the Brighton shoot. East Street had a history much in line with *Quadrophenia*'s chaotic moments. Originally known as Great East Street, the site was fortified to foil eleventh-century Norman invaders. Like the town's celebrated Lanes, the area came into its own during the eighteenth century, and while formally a residential area, as the area's popularity increased the street-level properties were turned into shops to meet the demand of Brighton's avaricious consumers.

Situated further down East Street was *Quadrophenia*'s most iconic landmark, the alleyway. Later christened 'Jimmy's Alley' by generations of Mods to come, the tiny cut-through appeared to be tailor-made for Jimmy and Steph's emotional union and the poignant return by the lead towards the end of the film. Narrow, imposing, dark and with just enough room for one person to walk down, the cinematic possibilities were endless.

Obviously, the beach would require no re-dressing for the riot scenes, although the shepherding of late-summer holidaymakers and other revellers was likely to be the most pressing issue. Nonetheless, Roddam and his team were aware that, as in 1964, the onlookers would play just as important a role in events as those battling it out on the beach. With word of the filming out on the Mods and Rockers' grapevine, there would be many characters out to engage with the re-creation with or without invites, and Brighton's residents, many of them having been informed of the filming by the local press and bush network, were also expected to turn out to gawp at the proceedings. Managing an audience of onlookers, potentially numbering many thousands, was always going to be an arduous experience for the director and his crew – as would become all too apparent over the following days. ●

THIS SPREAD, LEFT TO RIGHT: Underneath the Palace Pier, East Street, the riot café and Madeira Drive.

CHAPTER SEVEN

'AS A DIRECTOR, I ALWAYS THOUGHT YOU HAD TO GO AS NEAR TO DESTRUCTION AS POSSIBLE WITHOUT HURTING ANYBODY OR HURTING THE FILM.'

—FRANC RODDAM

'THEY PUT OUT AN ADVERT IN THE PAPER ASKING FOR REAL MODS AND ROCKERS TO TAKE PART AND BRIGHTON WAS SUDDENLY DELUGED WITH THEM. IT SEEMED LIKE AT LEAST 5,000 HAD TURNED UP ON THIS WEEKEND, AND IT GAVE US THE FEELING, WHEN WE WERE SHOOTING, OF NOT KNOWING WHO WAS A MEMBER OF THE PUBLIC AND WHO WAS AN ACTOR.'

—TOYAH WILCOX

Franc Roddam and his team were out early on the morning of September 28th, 1978, finalising the last few details of the Brighton shoot. With cast, crew and a legion of extras to be coordinated around the seafront, the next few days would prove to be the most exhausting of Roddam's directorial life.

For the pivotal riot scenes, three square miles of the town were now in the hands of *Quadrophenia*'s production unit. As a formality, Roddam's team met with the local police. This proved something of a revelation, as many were veterans of the original riots and looking forward to reliving their past glories for a second time. Higher up in rank, others were reportedly viewing the filming as an excellent training opportunity for future riot situations.

Predictably, those wishing to be involved in the film arrived en masse for the first day of filming. Toyah Wilcox recalled the sense of chaos enveloping the city: 'I remember on the day getting up and the production manager saying, "I don't know what to do – I do not know how to get around this. There's five thousand people out there and they all want to be involved."'

While Toyah (or the production manager) might have been slightly exaggerating the numbers, there was no denying that there were hordes of people converging on the town. Scooter clubs from across the UK were arriving and, reportedly, a contingent of Hells Angels was also on the way. While there was the potential for real-life aggression between opposing tribes,

OPPOSITE:
Executive producer Roger Daltrey drops in to check up on filming.

most reported a carnival-like atmosphere as filming started.

So, those charged with shepherding the cast around were faced with the challenging task of determining who had been hired and who was along for the jolly. With an age bar of 18 determined by film agency law, one intrepid youngster had arrived in Brighton the night before the first day of shooting and already collared Franc Roddam for a role. The director described this charming encounter to the authors of *Your Face Here: British Cult Movies Since the Sixties* in 1999: 'I came across one guy, a very small guy, who wanted to be in the film. "You're too young," I told

him. "You can't stay in Brighton because you're underage." One morning I came out of the hotel we were staying at on the beach and I saw this perfect little Mod just standing there, and instead of turning back, I walked across the road to see him. It was this kid. He'd come down dressed as a Mod and had patiently waited outside for me. "Okay," I said. "You can be in the movie."'

While the Mod contingent was well served by the main cast, the front line of the Rocker brigade had to be populated by actors. John Blundell, who'd shared classroom space with Phil Daniels in Anna Scher's acting academy in Islington, was selected as the leader of the Rocker tribe. He had the added kudos of competent motorbike riding and had been practising some complex moves around the streets of his native North London prior to filming.

While Roddam and Co. were checking on the locations prior to shooting, inside the actors' hotel the cast members were having breakfast and preparing for their 8.30 a.m. call on set. Predictably, with a tribe of young actors out on location, there were some high jinks to be had outside working hours.

'The hotel became a den of iniquity,' remembered Toyah Wilcox. 'Certain members of the cast got through other members of the cast

THIS SPREAD:
Rockers, both cast and impromptu members, converge on Brighton.

very quickly. There were stories filtering through of who had who on which night. I think by the end of the film everyone had had each other.'

'It was great,' recalls John Altman. 'You'd be up all night and we'd maybe get a couple of hours' sleep at the most. That wide-eyed look we have on screen was not put on!'

'I don't think we went to bed much,' recalled Phil Davis to the author in 2012. 'We used to stay up all night, smoking dope, drinking and doing all the things you do when you are young. Maybe Phil [Daniels] used to sneak off a bit earlier sometimes because he had more to do the next day.'

'Sting set fire to my shower one morning,' recounts Gary Shail of a particularly eventful start to a day's filming. 'We were in the bathroom and he said, "I need the shower because I have to get my hair done." I said, "You're not the only fucker!"

'YOU'D COME DOWN AT EIGHT IN THE MORNING AND THERE'D BE SOMEONE SINGING, SOMEONE PLAYING PIANO – IT WAS REALLY A BIT CRAZY, BUT VERY ENJOYABLE.'
JOHN BLUNDELL

Anyway, I was in the shower and he set fire to the curtain while I was in it. I still have a burn mark from a piece of burning plastic. That was the kind of thing going on.'

'It wasn't one of the main hotels because they knew with young actors it was going to be a bit of a mess,' John Blundell told the author. 'We took over the whole hotel. You'd come down at eight in the morning and there'd be someone singing, someone playing piano – it was really a bit crazy, but very enjoyable.'

After sharing his bed with a young admirer, Mark Wingett, ever the gentleman, brought his companion down to breakfast the following morning. While the cast were aware of Wingett's punky inclinations and spiky deportment, nothing prepared them for the sight that greeted them across the breakfast table that morning.

'One morning Mark brought this person down to breakfast from his room,' recalled Phil Daniels to the BBC in 2007. 'None of us knew whether it was a girl or boy, or [something] that had come out of the sea. That's what I remember.'

Despite his bullish, precocious exterior, Wingett ran into a few hiccups during his stay in Brighton. Having flummoxed his acting peers with his roommate's otherworldly presence, Wingett's squeeze had left him with an indelible memento of their night together – a large love bite on his neck. Given the actor's neckline would be exposed as far as his Fred Perry top during filming, any mark on his skin would be difficult to conceal. Continuity personnel, fearful that this amorous blemish would present difficulties when the filming transferred to other sequences, alerted associate producer John Peverall who in turn gave Wingett a lengthy kicking-off. And his tardy timekeeping was costing the film dearly. Trevor Laird recalls Peverall telling Wingett, 'Do you realise the film is costing us $15 a second?!'

These admonishments beginning to stack up, Wingett announced his intention to leave the set. Understandably, alarm bells started to ring. High up on the cast list, Wingett's potential absence, especially in the Brighton riot scenes, would effectively scupper the shoot. A walkout like this could easily have stalled the entire production.

'He got a bit carried away when we were on location,' recalled Roddam. 'He turned up in the morning with three big love bites on his neck that we had difficulty hiding. The first assistant told him off rather harshly and he got a bit upset. "Fuck it!" he said. "I'm leaving the film – I can't stand the way people are talking to me."'

Given Wingett's threat, Roddam had to think quickly on his feet. In desperation, he remembered a shirt he'd been given by John Lydon that had once belonged to Sid Vicious. The shirt had an interesting provenance, having been given to Lydon as a peace offering by Vicious following a dispute. During the period that Lydon was being courted for *Quadrophenia*'s lead role, he'd given the old shirt to Roddam as a token of his appreciation. After getting the item sent down

Anyway, this shirt was given to me as a grand prize. I gave it [to Wingett] so that he would stay on the film. Being a punk, that was enough – it was a great bribe and he now has this famous shirt.'

Courtesy of a puke-stained shirt, Wingett was back on board, ensuring that the shooting could continue in earnest. One of the first scenes to be shot in Brighton was at the Beach Café on the lower promenade and it involved the majority of the main cast.

While the production team had mobile caterers set up a food, drink and tea stall on the seafront for cast and crew, everyone took to the Beach Café's simple, uncomplicated fare. As a result, the café ended up supplying the cast with snacks and meals for the duration of the Brighton shoot. Ironically, the café's proprietor, George Wells, was present at the original Mods and Rockers infractions back in 1964, albeit as a Rocker. Putting aside past allegiances, Wells recalled a genial atmosphere for the time that the cast and crew of

to Brighton post-haste, Roddam now had some unique collateral to steer his hot-headed young star back into the fold.

Roddam described the situation in 2005: '[Lydon] got it from Sid Vicious. He'd attacked Sid with an axe and Sid had puked up all over the shirt, and it had safety pins and drawings on it and puke.

Quadrophenia frequented his establishment.

One memorable incident in the café involved Mark Wingett's Dave character having to bite into an underdone egg sandwich. The sequence is excruciating enough for the few seconds it is on screen, but poor Wingett had to endure over twelve runny sandwiches to get the shot just right.

A later scene, where Wingett parks himself on one of the café's tables, emerged from an impromptu moment. George Wells's mother (and then co-owner of the café), Maureen, had been cajoled into acting as a waitress and had instinctively objected to Wingett sitting on one of the tables in no uncertain tones. Wingett's riposte of 'piss off' and Maureen's equally spirited retort was totally ad-libbed and kept in the film. In fact, so taken were the cast with Maureen Wells, they took to calling her 'Mum' for the entirety of the shoot.

Once the communal breakfast scene had been completed, the café was cleared for a less intrusive piece, that of Jimmy's mournful self-reflection there, which came at the end of the film. This heart-rending moment was brilliantly embellished by the reflection of the pier in the café's window.

'In that shot, I could see both Jimmy and the pier,' recalled Roddam years later. 'Shooting into the reflection, I wanted to get both images in the same frame, but also to show Brighton, the solid Brighton. When Jimmy was in Brighton with all his gang, it was all working – the pier was a solid three-dimensional object. But now, when he is in a drug state and he was feeling miserable and suicidal, we put the object in as a reflection and it diminishes his reality.'

Once the café sequences were in the can, things started to get a little more involved as the first riot scenes began. After the Mods' arrival under the stone pillars of Madeira Drive, the cast were filmed walking down the promenade cheering, 'We are the Mods! We are the Mods!' Not referenced in the script, this iconic chant was totally impromptu, owing more to the football terraces than to the landscape of 1964. While it

'SHOOTING INTO THE REFLECTION, I WANTED TO GET BOTH IMAGES IN THE SAME FRAME, BUT ALSO TO SHOW BRIGHTON, THE SOLID BRIGHTON.'
FRANC RODDAM

is a memorable scene, with hindsight it was an uneasy addition, detracting in some ways from the otherwise authentic period feel.

'Improvised,' said Phil Davis to the author on being quizzed as to its derivation. 'Not a sixties thing at all. I was slightly uncomfortable with it. Anachronistic.'

Scriptwriter Martin Stellman has a more detailed answer to the chant's possible provenance and place in the film. He concurs with Davis that it was probably made up on the spot. Improvisation of the moment was wholly welcomed during filming, it was considered valid at the time, and thus it became woven into the narrative of the picture. 'It's likely that Phil [Daniels] and the others – Philip Davis, Mark Wingett et al came up with it spontaneously as they were parading along the front. As anachronistic as it may be, I think it's a great moment. Sometimes reality has to be heightened.'

THIS SPREAD: Normally a fairly sedate coffee bar on the corner of East Street but transformed into one of *Quadrophenia*'s most brutal moments.

'I tend to think it was the first assistant director, Ray Corbett,' remembers John Altman. 'As far as I recall it was him who said, "Why don't you shout 'We are the Mods!'?" I felt uncomfortable about that. It sounded really naff – it really got on my nerves.'

After considerable research, it's now clear that the source for the film's most memorable chant was actor Gary Shail, as he recalled to the author in 2014. 'That's mine,' he confirms. 'We were walking along the promenade, Franc said to me, "When the photographer comes up and starts taking photos you need to do something." I was a Chelsea supporter, along with Phil Daniels and Trevor Laird, and it came from "We are the Blues". And that was it. Everyone went, "Fine, we'll use it."'

As the group advanced along the promenade towards the junction of East Street, the action settled for a brief moment outside a small cinema facing the seafront. In October 1978, the picturehouse (part of the Cannon group) was showing a double bill of the omnipresent musical *Grease* and Warren Beatty's comic yarn, *Heaven Can Wait*. Evidently no approach was made to the cinema to have the advertising re-dressed. Either by design or haste, a bizarre connection between Hollywood's *Heaven Can Wait* and British Modernism was about to be indelibly committed to celluloid. The subject of continuous debate by students of the film, Roddam has been eager to explain the reasons for leaving the signage in the finished product.

'It was such a quick shot,' he recalled in 1999. 'It looked so good with the characters in the foreground. I wanted to put the shot in and said, "To hell with the background." I let that go deliberately.'

> **'I WAS A CHELSEA SUPPORTER, ALONG WITH PHIL DANIELS AND TREVOR LAIRD, AND IT CAME FROM "WE ARE THE BLUES".'**
>
> **GARY SHAIL**

LEFT: 'We'll fight them on the beaches!' Franc Roddam directs the action from East Street to Brighton beach.

Although *Heaven Can Wait* inadvertently stole its way into the first run of *Quadrophenia*'s prints, once a new digital version of the film was made in 2012, all visual references to *Heaven Can Wait* would be squeezed out.

Another impromptu element also made itself known during the filming of this sequence. A Boys' Brigade band appeared unannounced, marching down the middle of the seafront to the beat of their drums. Their uniforms betraying no fixed age provenance, their appearance was wholly fortuitous. This small but welcome addition would make its way into the finished product, adding a greater sense of realism to the Brighton shoot and adding a neat visual link between the conscription era and the new 'army' of Mods taking to the streets.

While the aforementioned innocuous scenes involved minimal setting-up to capture, the rioting would prove far more involved. It would only occupy around ten minutes of screen time, but successfully capturing the action on celluloid took the best part of a week to complete. Aware that real life could easily spill into the pretence of filmmaking, the key cast members were given the services of security men for the entire Brighton riot shoot.

The first confrontation between Mods and Rockers occurs when Jimmy's tribe assault a group of Rockers en masse at a seafront café. The action is shockingly realistic and unnerved many who'd expected something less visceral for filmic purposes. Setting up the shot took a considerable amount of time. 'When we did the big rush out,' remembered Phil Daniels, 'there was this massive traffic jam that stretched for about eight miles, while the coppers just let us tear around and smash up that coffee bar.'

Trevor Laird offered a stark recollection of those crazy scenes playing out over Brighton's

BELOW: The action transfers to Brighton's promenade with police pursuing Mods and Rockers down towards the beach...

seafront, especially the moment when the herd of Mods rounded on the Rockers at a café. 'We came out from the hotel to do the charging scene,' he recalled in 1999. 'What they did was to surround us with stuntmen, so there was a ring around us to protect us from the other Mods and extras when it kicked off. My marker was a Triumph Herald with its hood down that was supposed to drive past. When it appeared it got caught in the melee. I had to jump into the car, over the back seat and out the other side!'

One young man who was clearly not fazed by the action was 20-year-old Paul Curbishley, the younger half-brother of the film's co-producer and Who manager, Bill. Curbishley junior would turn out to be the star of that small vignette, famously throwing a Formica table through the café's glass window. Given the onslaught of scores of crazed individuals trying to pour through the narrow doorway, a cameraman lost a tooth as the violence

erupted in the small venue. Additionally, petite Leslie Ash sustained an injury as the full weight of the action took hold.

'It was pretty scary,' she recalled in 2011. 'They made sure that Phil and I were in front so that we didn't get trampled on. They were all running up the road and then they all turned around and started coming back and, oh my god, it was so frightening. I did actually get knocked to the floor. It was terrifying.'

On closer inspection of the footage, it appears that Miss Ash changed from her natty white stilettos to a pair of flat-soled Hush Puppies for the riot scenes, necessity for running evidently outweighing any on-screen vanity.

There was no let-up as the rioting took a further hold on East Street and in the patchwork of small roads and lanes that fell away from the seafront. It was here that a brief moment of chaos enveloped the production. With a

ABOVE: In the arms of the law; Phil Daniels gets his collar felt.

'THERE WAS SO MANY OF US, YOU COULDN'T ASK ADVICE – YOU COULDN'T ASK, "WHERE DO I NEED TO BE?" WE WERE JUST BEING TOLD, "FIGHT".'

TOYAH WILCOX

few hundred highly charged individuals milling around in a cramped environment, confusion began to take over, not least for the cast. John Altman, in the thick of the Mod frenzy, recalled to the author one crazy moment during the shoot: 'At one point I ducked down this little alley. This little old lady came running into the alley with her little shopping basket shouting, "Oh no! It's happening all over again!"'

Toyah Wilcox was also cutting loose with the main protagonists. She recalled the crazy scene playing out in front of her eyes: 'We were encouraged to be as real as possible. It made things even more realistic in that sense that if you've got 200 people stampeding behind you can't afford to trip up or say "Cut", you've just got to go with the flow…We had occasions when all you knew that a camera was turning was this distant voice shouting "Action!" There was so many of us, you couldn't ask advice – you couldn't ask, "Where do I need to be?" We were just being told, "Fight". I can remember going up to a man dressed as a policeman going, "Excuse me, are you in the film or are you real?" He said, "No, I'm in the film," and I said, "Well, can I hit you?" and he said, "Yes," and *bosh*! I think I shocked him. He said, "We're only acting!"'

Phil Davis wouldn't have time to exchange any pleasantries when it came to determining if any of the policemen were real. He revealed this confusion to the author in 2012. 'There was such a lot of people running up the street saying, "Do this and do that," and then you get there and there's someone in the way, and you can't do it and you jump on a policeman's back and he turns out to be a real policeman and he's keeping people clear of traffic. You don't know where the camera is because it might be a long lens. A lot of it was relatively chaotic. You've got a hundred kids running up the street so anything can happen. There were lots of incidents where we'd arranged some action and you didn't know quite what's going on. At one point, I attacked a real policeman who was holding the crowd back. He said, "No, not me, son. I'm for real. You hit the blokes over there in the old-fashioned bobbies' hats!!'

With chaos breaking out on the streets of Brighton, there were occasions when the craziness had to be reined in. Sting's character was in the thick of the violence, and the script featured two incidents that added greater fire to his incendiary

LEFT AND BELOW: Making up and being led away. More moments from the riots on the beach.

nature. The first was to attack a hotel glass door with a hammer, the other had Ace Face throwing a charity collection box through a window.

'It was part of the disrespect,' Franc Roddam would later reflect on the sequence. 'The older generation was always trying to make you respect things you don't care about. The subtext of the picture to me is very important. All those little details are picked up by the audience subconsciously.'

As undoubtedly powerful as the imagery would have been, the scene stalled. The launching of the charity box – the young child with calipers an omnipresent feature of British high streets during the sixties and seventies – was deemed too controversial by associate producer John Peverall. To assuage delicate sensitivities, an empty plastic beer crate was used instead.

'THE SUBTEXT OF THE PICTURE TO ME IS VERY IMPORTANT. ALL THOSE LITTLE DETAILS ARE PICKED UP BY THE AUDIENCE SUBCONSCIOUSLY.'
FRANC RODDAM

Roddam's expert coordinating of the violence provided a visually exciting close-up concentration of the action. Effectively kettling the action within East Street, it was easy to catch every nuance of the violence on display. Despite just a couple of cameramen on hand to record events, the impact of what was achieved was nothing short of remarkable. Unfortunately the director sustained an injury when a spooked police dog went for one of the cameraman and bit his leg. Turning sharply away, the bulky camera struck Roddam on the head. Toyah, too, sustained an injury to her arm and one of the extras was knocked down by an ambulance.

Present for these crazed sequences was biker Tom Ingram. He'd earned a coveted place in

a police van sequence alongside Sting and Phil Daniels as the riots drew to a close. Elevated above the level of an extra, Ingram was retained for this key scene and had been put up in a local hotel to await his special moment on screen.

'I was in a motorcycle club at a pub called the Eagle's Nest in Kent,' he recalled to *Quadrophenia* archivist Layne Patterson in 2011. 'This guy turned up and said he needed some Rockers to be in a film. I said no problem and offered to help him get more people, which I did… We were in Brighton for over a week, if I remember right. They put us up in local bed and breakfasts. One very big thing I remember was how well all of the Mods and Rockers, who were extras, got on with each other. Everyone seemed to enjoy it. We were

OPPOSITE: Sting and Gary Shail pause for a moment of brief repose during the riot scenes.

ABOVE: The Ace Face resists arrest in East Street.

ABOVE: Led by the Ace Face, a contingent of Mods glide down towards the beach on scooters.

NEXT SPREAD: More moments of scripted chaos endure from the beach sequence.

all trying to figure out who were real Mods and Rockers and who were actors, so that was always the question. Looking back on it now, that showed how well made the film was. The police-van scene was a lot of fun and I think it was five or six takes. I was just standing by the side of the road with everyone else and someone said, "You, can you get in the van?", so I did. I think that took about half a day and I got to chat with Sting a lot. At that time he was basically unknown. He was the complete opposite of his character. I found him very friendly and chatty. When it was time to leave he came over to me to say goodbye, which shows how well we got on. The cigarette case idea was Sting's, I think. It actually cut the top of my finger.'

With word of the action spreading, scores of people desperate to join in were attempting to reach the city. During the rush hour, a three-mile tailback had effectively blocked all the main routes into Brighton, with police vainly attempting to redirect traffic. Inside the heavily secured promenade area, real life and fantasy spookily began to merge into one.

There was no let-up as the action transferred itself to the beach. Improvisation often overriding preparation, a violent confrontation at the water's edge called for some volunteers. John Altman was up for the role and soon found himself knee-deep in the sea. 'I was young and very keen,' he recalled to the author in 2013. 'Kieron Phipps [the second assistant director] said, "Would anyone mind going into the sea?", because it was quite cold for that time of year. So I just grabbed that with open arms. Anything I could do, I was up for it.'

Meanwhile, it was evident to everyone involved in filming that the extras dressed as policemen were not taking the matter of rioting as seriously as they should, with some of them larking around the set. The fact that they'd been briefed in advance that the cast were only going to use fake ammunition had seemingly lulled them into a false sense of security. With word of their levity making its way back to Roddam, he convened a quick conference with his main band of agitators.

◉ 'ANYTHING I COULD DO, I WAS UP FOR IT.'
JOHN ALTMAN

'The police were professional extras,' recalled Roddam to the authors of *Your Face Here: British Cult Movies* in 1999. 'When we did the scene which was quite dangerous – horses jumping over people and the fighting going on and lots of stunts – the policemen, some of them, were being really silly. They were laughing away and wearing their hats back to front. The assistant directors told me this, and I must say I was a bit young at the time and a bit wilder, and before we did take two, just before we said "Action" I ran across to the Mods and I said, "These policemen are screwing up this scene and I want you to attack them for real." What happened was that the policemen had to fight for their lives and I got my scene… I wanted to retain the energy and the integrity of the piece, so when I found out these policemen extras were screwing up the scene, I felt as though they were dispensable. You feel a bit like that when you are a young director – everything for the movie.'

One of these professional 'police' extras was Harry Fielder. He recalled to the author in 2013 the merging between acting and reality during the riot sequence: 'About thirty of us were bussed down to Brighton dressed as policemen. We told all the kids that this was only acting and we would be using rubber bricks and rubber sticks, but I forgot about the latecomers! After two days' filming, we

'If you set a film up in a naturalistic way, and you get your cast in the mood you get them into the reality of the situation,' said Roddam in 1999. 'I was always concerned about English stunts because they always looked as if people were simply bouncing off trampolines. So with the fight on the beach, I disturbed the perfect action by giving it some imperfection. I had these horses coming, police, Mods, Rockers, and we did it in one take and it was fabulous, the editing was sensational.'

Nevertheless, there were times when the violence could have had a disastrous effect. A potentially dangerous moment occurred when the action transferred to the buildings that bordered Brighton's famous Aquarium complex. As outlined in the script, a large plant pot was to be thrown through a fortune-teller's window. Despite Roddam and his crew having thoroughly briefed the woman sitting in the window to look for a youngster dressed in red, confused by the hoards rushing past, she focused on the wrong person. Remaining in situ, the hapless woman was narrowly missed by the missile as it came crashing through the window.

While all the scripted madness was going on, there were several lighter moments that punctuated the seriousness. Two welcome arrivals to Brighton, to witness events and to be of assistance to the crew, were executive producers Roger Daltrey and Pete Townshend. While Townshend journeyed down from London, Daltrey, a relative local, travelled in from his home in nearby Burwash, East Sussex. In addition to witnessing some of the riot scenes, Daltrey and Townshend spent time with Phil Daniels on the beach, talking about filming and the period they were trying to recreate. The meeting evidently had an effect on Quadrophenia's young star, as he recalled to NME at the time: 'I had a really interesting talk to Roger Daltrey one day on the beach in Brighton. He's sayin', "There's a Jimmy in all of us, we're all Jimmy in a way." Like if you

THIS SPREAD: Roger Daltrey certainly made his presence known during the day of the riot scenes, seen here with Phil Davis and Mark Wingett.

all had a few bruises but were well paid for our trouble and headed back to London.'

With the raft of frenzied battles breaking out all over Brighton (both scripted and impromptu), capturing the entirety of the action on film was always going to be problematic. Given Quadrophenia's modest budget, there were only two cameras to document the filming. Aware of the limitations, Roddam had minutely choreographed the key riot scenes. As a result, regardless of the free-ranging movements of cast and extras on the beach, all the cameras had to do was film what was taking place.

ABOVE: 'Once a Rocker…' Roger Daltrey shimmies up with Brighton's Rocker contingent – including chief Rocker girl Linda Regan.

come out of that Mod era, that mum and dad number, you know, the music's too loud.'

As the most eager of The Who to get the period feel right, Daltrey had been concerned that not enough of the extras were wearing white denim, a piece of apparel that he felt defined the Modernists of the sixties. The observation became something of a small issue, but the continuity personnel showed some Polaroids to Daltrey to reassure him that they'd got the dress right. With the press there to capture the celebrity of the moment, Daltrey posed with a group of Rockers above the promenade, the former Mod seamlessly merging with the leather-clad bikers.

The Who's frontman also took time out to talk to Toyah Wilcox during the shoot. During their chat, he candidly revealed some thoughts on her casting. 'Roger Daltrey said that I was the spitting image of his sister. He thought that my image was right on the ball. He confided in me that he would have liked Leslie Ash's role to look a bit more like that, but it would have taken all that attractiveness away from her – because it was almost old-fashioned. At the time that we made the film, it had a sense of being old-fashioned, you couldn't sell the sexuality of Leslie's role if she had the bouffant and everything.'

Amidst the madness, there were quiet moments when the cast took the chance to

Sc 105   Bottom button of Jimmy's jacket
unfastened.
Dave's Parka zipped halfway
up.

Sc 105   Spider

Sc 105 — Steph
White socks, brown suade shoes,
fawn V Sweater, black trousers
beige gloves, black Leather
coat. Goto cross.

Sc 112 — End position holding
parkas + sleeping
bags.

Sc 127/128

Sc 118

repair and relax. The ever watchful Roddam covertly recorded some of these off-guard moments, aware that they would add to the film's realism. His keen eye, schooled through years of documentary making, captured one such impromptu moment during a break from shooting the riot scenes. Instructing Brian Tufano to let the camera run, he caught a brilliant moment of repose from the film's main players, but, despite the subterfuge, Trevor Laird realised that the camera was still rolling. He recalled in 1999 how he 'heard Franc tell the camera operator to switch the camera on. He didn't know I knew this and I thought, "I know what I'll do here. I'll just sneak one in – something that I really feel, with no words." My motivation was, "I like hanging out with these kids, plus they buy my pills but I'm not part of this territorial thing." To me, that shot summed up my character.'

'Trevor shrugs them off,' said Roddam in 1999. 'He's thinking, because he's the dealer and the only black person, as far as he's concerned, they're just a bunch of cunts.'

Laird's cool tug on his jacket lapels, in quiet defiance of his peers, spoke volumes. After the film was processed back at the studio, Roddam informed Laird that this sequence was his favourite of the entire Brighton shoot.

ABOVE: Continuity imagery as captured by Polaroid technology during the Brighton shoot.

Undoubtedly, the scene where Jimmy finally seduces Steph is the most sensitive moment of the film. The original script, while faithful to the love-making sequence, called for the location to be a basement area reached by some steps. Shooting this scene below stairs as another sort of frenzy was carrying on above was a fascinating idea, but no suitable basement area was found. The location scouts got lucky when they chanced upon an alleyway situated just off riot-torn East Street. Nothing more than a rubbish storage area at the rear of Choy's Chinese Restaurant, it was soon to receive its cinematic canonisation, courtesy of *Quadrophenia*.

The two young actors would have to convey unbridled passion under the glare of cameras and lights in a cramped backyard. With just nine lines of direction, considerable effort went into realising the sequence with the conviction it demanded. In the cold print of the script, the sequence was a clever parallel of sex and violence, its passion matched by the outpouring of aggression and liberation happening only a few feet away. The scene was ultimately handled with great delicacy by the filmmakers, but there were several problems, both emotional and otherwise, to overcome before it could be completed.

Shot on the last day of the Brighton shoot, Roddam knew that the scene would be most demanding for Leslie Ash. While she had an attitude and presence that transcended her age, a fairly explicit love-making scene was still a tall order for a young girl in her first film.

Toyah Wilcox: 'I remember her getting really quite pent-up and worried about the quickie scene because everyone wanted to be there.'

As the hours counted down, Ash was in constant contact with her boyfriend, who was naturally anxious about her doing the scene. According to Roddam, the night before the shoot, Ash's partner (35-year-old tour manager Peter Buckland) had rung her up and asked her not to do it. Overwhelmed with anxiety, Ash stalled

128 EXT. BASEMENT AREA DAY MUSIC OVER: ('SEA & SAND') 128
JIMMY and STEPH take refuge from arrest as the sirens arrive ...
wide-eyed, high on the pills and the fights and the adrenalin of the
day, they stand close, regarding each other wordlessly; then STEPH's
arms go round JIMMY's neck and pull him to her in a passionate kiss
... JIMMY, brought out of himself by the events of the day, handles
her boldly, and STEPH shows more than willing ... against the wall
in the cover of the basement area they make love with determinded
abandon as the riot swarms in full cry about them ...

on the morning of filming, informing Roddam that she was not up to performing. The crew and Daniels waited at the location as Roddam's gentle encouragement finally won her over. By the afternoon, Ash was ready.

Emotional worries aside, the logistics of getting a film crew and equipment into the confined space was also going to be problematic. Lighting was also a major consideration. Fitting a large 35mm camera in situ seemed an impossible task. However, the tiny area did have the benefit of a metal fire escape. With platforms on several levels, the opportunity to capture the action from above proved to be yet another happy accident.

Roddam and his team placed a camera on a pulley that swung down as Jimmy and Steph made their hurried entrance. With the cameraman suspended in the air and with a counterweight of

four large bags of sand, a sweeping action was achieved as the couple ran up the alleyway, but, despite the closed-set order, there were around twenty people surrounding the scene, making a genuine transference of emotion in such a congested area even harder.

Both actors were nervous about what might occur once the camera started rolling. Reportedly, rehearsals were done on the set itself. Given that it was only a couple of weeks into the shoot, it had added a degree of anxiety to the two actors' new relationship.

'It was meant to be a closed set,' recalled Daniels to the *Daily Mail* in 2010. 'But there's always someone who shouldn't be there, one of the crew trying every means possible to get a glimpse of the action. Excepting the occasional set-builder with a wandering eye, Roddam was good at keeping people at arm's length.'

THIS SPREAD: 'Love Reign O'er Me': Phi Daniels and Leslie Ash caught betweer takes during the Brighton shoot

Needless to say, the sequence was completed without any graphic display of physicality. Both actors were aware of the intimacy of the piece, and the scene was captured in one take. In a less sensitive director's hands, it could easily have descended into cheap pornography, but Roddam's vision for the scene was sensitive and measured. Predictably, over the years rumours abounded that the consummation between Jimmy and Steph was more real than what was acted on screen. 'There's been a lot of speculation from people saying, "Oh, apparently they really did it,"' recalled Ash in 2011. 'Well, I can honestly say, no, it was all acting. It's just a bit embarrassing to watch. It's the first love scene I've seen that's fully clothed.'

Jimmy and Steph's intimate moment finally committed to celluloid, the last few pieces of Brighton location shooting were ready to be shot. These included a few shots of a lonesome Daniels walking on the beach, a few night-time shots and some cutaways of the sea. While stunt arranger Peter Brayham had to endure sub-zero temperatures portraying an intrepid swimmer (an act for which he nearly caught hypothermia), more unplanned elements such as a lifeboat skimming the edge of the Brighton coastline were welcomed. Given the budget restrictions, it was impossible to light any expansive landscapes, and with any filming on the pier forbidden, there was a lot of head scratching as to how to shoot the night-time sequences. Fortuitously, the illumination from the Palace Pier proved to be a haunting and effective backdrop for Jimmy's nocturnal wander along the edge of the beach.

The final shots included filming at Brighton's opulent Grand Hotel. While the original *Quadrophenia* booklet had included photos from inside the hotel, the film utilised both the interior and exterior to depict the sad revelation Jimmy has on discovering Ace Face's true vocation.

Before the cast and crew could finally pack up their belongings and head off, there were two

OPPOSITE: Phil Daniels cutting a lonely figure on Brighton's beach, September 1978.

ABOVE: Leslie Ash, Sting and Phil Daniels caught between takes on Brighton's Madeira Drive.

⊕ DESPITE THE GRANDEUR OF THE MOMENT CAPTURED ON SCREEN, IN REALITY NO SUCH SWEEPING VIEW OF BRIGHTON EXISTS

key scenes to be captured. The first was the all-important shot of the Mods arriving at the South Coast, a celebratory moment for those recently emancipated from London's stifling environs. Here, Roddam employed a little piece of cinematic licence. Despite the grandeur of the moment captured on screen, in reality no such sweeping view of Brighton exists. The city sits pretty much on one level, so the film crew had to travel back to Beachy Head's more dramatic coastline for a more expansive view. Unlike

Brighton, the run into Eastbourne from Beachy Head has a sweeping panoramic view. *Quadrophenia's* camera focused its lens softly on the coastline as the Mod tribe approached, and few would notice that, unlike Brighton in 1978, Eastbourne only had the benefit of one pier. Aiding the deception, the lens fitted to the camera for this particular shot was incorrect for the dimensions required; this blurred the skyline, and myth assumed reality for a few seconds.

The final South Coast scene took place seven miles from Brighton at Lewes Magistrates Court. A working court, the crew could only get access to the building's interior for filming on a Sunday. The moment when Jimmy faces justice is where real life and filmmaking spookily coincided. Way back in 1964, the courtroom had hosted many of

Sc 130A Stripped pink/blue/White Shirt.

those arrested following the May Bank Holiday riots down the road in Brighton.

Adding even further verisimilitude to the courtroom sequence was the language embedded in the script, especially that concerning the fate of Sting's Ace Face character. The dialogue for the magistrate sentencing Ace Face was swiped verbatim from comments made by Dr George Simpson, the Chairman of Margate Magistrates, who had overseen the sentencing of the May Day rioters in 1964. Magistrate Simpson had slapped an exemplary fine on one young Mod following the ructions at Margate. On sending the recalcitrant youngster down for three months, Simpson concluded his summing-up with a classic line that made its way into Mod folklore and *Quadrophenia*: 'These long-haired, mentally unstable, petty little sawdust Caesars seem to find courage, like rats, by hunting only in packs.'

Another remark that made it into the film was one directed toward the same magistrate. This time it came from a youngster called James Bruton, a 17-year-old bricklayer known (coincidentally) to family and friends as 'Jimmy'. On being fined £75 for his part in the Margate affray, Bruton said, 'I'll pay by cheque.' Bruton's swagger was in fact bluff; the brickie didn't even have a bank account. 'I thought I could make a little joke,' recalled Bruton at the time. 'It didn't work.'

With the Lewes courtroom scenes in the can, there was little respite as cast and crew transported their equipment back to London. While Brighton had been action-packed, in reality they'd only collected what amounted to one third of the film. The London shoot was destined to be even more expansive, and the filmmakers had their work cut out to bring it all in on time. ●

TOP: Sting during his classic moment in court.

ABOVE: Franc Roddam takes control of the action.

CHAPTER EIGHT

'STING WAS A TERRIBLE DANCER.'

—MARK WINGETT

QWith the Brighton and South Coast shoots finally wrapped up, there was still the rest of *Quadrophenia* to commit to celluloid, and importantly, the young band that were to perform at the start of the film still hadn't materialised. Somewhat late in the day, a full-page advert with the headline 'Who Needs You' was placed in *NME* on August 12th, 1978, at the behest of the film's production team, and it was unequivocal in its intention of scoring a band for *Quadrophenia*. 'Fame! Groupies! Polydor Recording Contract! Instant Stardom! Money! Drugs! Speakeasy Membership included!' exclaimed the text, illustrated with a picture of The Who circa 1965.

Needless to say, a mass of eager wannabes responded. Those chosen were duly required to attend auditions at the Electric Ballroom in Camden, London, during the week of 16th to 20th October, 1978. The London shoot was already underway, and the director occupied elsewhere, so auditions were overseen by Roger Daltrey, John Entwistle and others in the production team. Time was now of the essence. 'We're looking for a band to fit into the film in 1964,' said Roger Daltrey to the BBC during auditions. '[An] average high-school hop band, I suppose. A bit above a youth-club band in 1964.'

Despite the overt Mod connotations of *Quadrophenia*, many of the bands who sent tapes in were infused with other styles, many hewn from the punk era or just Who pretenders. Surrey punksters Sham 69 felt moved to record and submit four themed tracks they deemed suitable for the soundtrack. Despite being on the same label as The Who, given their high profile as a proto-skinhead band, they were swiftly dismissed. The Chords, one of the earliest Mod revival bands, seemed a more relevant outfit to submit a tape for consideration, and yet they, too, would be passed over. Others in the fray were just far too polished to be considered believable in the youth-club setting. Most, it appears, were just intoxicated at the thought of being involved in a Who project.

Nonetheless, those granted an audition were extremely competent, if not quite suited for the

OPPOSITE: Pete Townshend shares a traditional dinner with Phil Daniels at A. Cooke's pie and mash shop at 48 Goldhawk Road, Shepherd's Bush.

BELOW: Gary Shail and Phil Daniels cut the groove at the Basement Club in Shelton Street, Covent Garden, October 20th, 1978.

film. One band called The Skunks had already been noticed by Keith Moon and Pete Townshend. Another unit was Straight Eight, a group with a strong fusion of glam and punk. Straight Eight's appearance at the audition certainly turned a few heads, but Roger Daltrey, overseeing these auditions, was unequivocal in his decision not to grant them a place in the film, as he recalled to the BBC during auditions. 'Straight Eight... To change anything they do, it would be stupid to put them in the film. Be like asking to make them worse than they are. They're going to make it anyway.'

Despite their rejection, Pete Townshend recognised their potential and went on to produce their first album, *No Noise From Here*, at his Eel Pie Studios.

After a few hectic days of auditions, coming through with honours were Cross Section, a young R&B band from Kent. Fronted by Vince Martyn and Lawrence Merton, the band previewed an entire set of cover versions. Sensing their instinctive, fresh-faced innocence, Daltrey and Co. were smitten with the band's look and raw approach. Following the audition, and with the band assembled in Camden High Street, Daltrey

approached the band and told them he'd liked what he'd heard, tagging his admiration by asking them if they'd cut their hair. 'Yeah, I'd dye it green,' replied the band's drummer Dene O'Neill.

Elsewhere, the production team were readying the first of the London sequences to be shot. The majority of *Quadrophenia*'s urban filming was to take place in and around West London. The craziness of the Brighton shoot now a memory, the timetable for the London shoot was still going to be frantic. But, with the majority of the cast based in the capital, everyone could easily travel between home and the production base in Wembley.

Proving to be Franc Roddam's nemesis, the securing of locations essential to the authenticity of *Quadrophenia* was proving hugely problematic – Jimmy's family home in particular. Central to so many scenes, remarkably the location scouts had failed to find a property as per the director's instructions, reporting, somewhat dismally, that the blueprint for Jimmy's base didn't exist. Enraged, Roddam personally stalked the West London locale to find his preferred house. During his travels, he discovered a suitable property situated in a largely residential area in Acton.

BELOW: Interior and door exteriors of Jimmy's house at 75 Wells House Road, Acton.

Number 75 Wells House Road sat at the end of a terrace and benefited from an adjoining alleyway with a shed at the rear. Even better, the back garden was adjacent to the railway line that took trains between Willesden Junction and Acton Central – these elements vital to satisfy various points in the storyline.

Situated off a busy road, the location easily accommodated the fleet of vans and large props required for filming. Reportedly, the Wells House Road property was unoccupied during the making of the film and was in need of major restoration. This gave the production team a free rein to do whatever they liked to portray the exact sense of the period. The house required little dressing.

> ⊕ **'I WAS TOLD I WAS BEING DISPENSED WITH BECAUSE I HAD BEEN MISCAST BUT I NEVER BELIEVED THAT WAS THE TRUTH.'**
> **AMANDA BARRIE**

One moment of early poetry within the Wells House Road property was a shot of Jimmy resting on his bed below a portrait of a Mod-attired Pete Townshend. The brief to pay homage to The Who part of the film's original premise, it allowed for several nods to the creator of the concept.

'The shot we did in his bedroom,' remembered Roddam to the author in 1999, 'where we panned off the photograph of Pete on to Phil was deliberate, and for a moment you see the similarity.'

The scripted dialogue in the house was explosive and confrontational, and filming at 75 Wells House Road provoked the first of *Quadrophenia*'s unscheduled upsets. Amanda Barrie, cast as Jimmy's mum, was ushered onto the set for her first days of filming. As mentioned, Barrie arrived beset with personal issues and looking decidedly peaky following a sleepless night. Drained and unprepared, she lasted only a few hours before time was called on her presence in *Quadrophenia*.

'I couldn't keep my eyes open,' recalled Barrie in her memoir. 'I was told I was being dispensed with because I had been miscast but I never believed that was the truth. I really do think it was because I was too exhausted to work properly and was, therefore, very bad. It's a little episode I have always regretted. I believe that I made a complete pig's ear of *Quadrophenia*, largely because of the mess my personal life was in at the time, and lost an opportunity to feature in what became quite a significant cult movie.'

As a matter of the utmost urgency, actress Kate Williams was called in for auditions to replace Barrie. Aged 36, Williams had been a veteran of numerous productions over the years, her most sustained role being that of Eddie Booth's long-suffering wife in the controversial TV comedy

ABOVE: Phil Daniels upstairs at 75 Wells House Road.

Sc 44. 3 buttons of shirt undone.

Sc 44 + wearing pink & white apron
Sc 114 P/S Slippers, no apron.

Sc 44 Reshoot. Dad - 5th button fastened.

Love Thy Neighbour. Aiding her indie credentials, she'd previously featured in Ken Loach's gritty 1968 film, *Poor Cow*. A hastily arranged improvisation for the part took place at the end of a day's filming. Williams was pitched against her onscreen husband-to-be Michael Elphick, and they improvised a scene where they discovered a stash of pills under their son's mattress. Watching events was Franc Roddam.

Kate Williams: 'Franc's directions to us were that he wanted one of those relationship arguments where all the character flaws in the son are laid at the door of the other partner. And all the good qualities are claimed as one's own contribution… I dived in and, so wonderful, Mike just upped and slammed into me like we had been together for years.'

After five minutes of the confrontation, Elphick turned to Roddam to ask if it was enough. Roddam, mightily impressed by what he'd witnessed, gave the part to Williams. Such was the pace, Williams began shooting the following day, filming the sequence where she confronts her son after his eventful weekend in Brighton. Such was Williams' passion, unprompted, she used a newspaper she was carrying to pummel her startled son.

Quadrophenia shot predominately on location, only two studio sets were constructed for the film.

One was the interior of the shelter under the pier that Phil Davis and Mark Wingett inadvertently share with some Rockers in Brighton; the other, the interior of the Kitchener Road party scene.

The exteriors for this lively sequence took cast and crew to 63 Clarendon Gardens in Brent, the area's suburban environs serving as the perfect backdrop. However, the property's modest interior called for a considerably larger space to cope with the lights, camera, crew and thirty cast members partying hard. To this end, a set comprising a kitchen, lounge and upstairs living

OPPOSITE: Kate Williams gets to grips with her errant screen son.

BELOW: Some visual documentation from the London shoot.

Sc.29. Sunglasses in Pete's pocket. Pink Shirt

Sc 107A Claire Stuart Lesley Toeman Turton Dodd

Sc 28

RIGHT: Screen grabs from Franc Roddam's inventive 360-degree camera swoop of the 'Kitchener Road' party house.

quarters was constructed at Lee International Studios, conveniently situated just a few miles from Clarendon Gardens.

The shooting for the party scene was scheduled to last until dawn the following morning. Predictably, the mass of leaping Mod bodies caused an accident in the lounge early on. In this case, it was Mark Wingett's Dave character, who launched himself a little too high while dancing to The Who's 'My Generation'. 'In my enthusiasm,' he recalled in 2011, 'I jumped up, raised my hand and I broke this lamp, and so the film was cut. I went over to Franc and said, "I'm really sorry," expecting another bollocking… I was very clumsy.'

While the choreography of the scene was brilliantly realised, one key moment tested the integrity of the production team. As a lovesick Jimmy engages in a brief episode of mania in the garden, on his scooter, his Mod cohorts are sharing affections with several female partygoers upstairs. Trevor Laird, playing Jamaican drug-dealer Ferdy, found his race called into question for one pivotal moment. Absent from the original script, Laird was scheduled to have an intimate liaison with a white girl at the party. It is evident that the scene emerged from one of the many improvisations that were occurring during filming, although this ran into problems prior to shooting.

'A girl I grew up with called Linda was always shadowing me at the party, to suggest we might get off with each other,' recalled Laird in 1999. 'Just prior to the scene where everybody ends up in bed with each other, someone came up to me and said, "Here, take this bottle of champagne and go back to your dressing room. You're not in the scene." Phil Davis and I sat there drinking it, while I wondered, "What the fuck's going on here?" I started probing, getting a bit lively with people, until John Peverall [assistant producer] told me, "The way things are, we can't have you in the scene. This movie's going to be released in South Africa and we can't have you seen as a black guy getting off with a white girl." Franc Roddam

found out about this later, got very upset, and fought for the scene's inclusion.'

Roddam has his own take on Laird's recollection, which he recounted to the author in 2013. 'I didn't know anything about that until later. I was very angry that they would do such a thing. I think that the South African thing was rubbish, we had a big thing within the industry and we were taking on South Africa. I think that was a bit of old-fashioned racism going on, I really do.'

Roddam had devised some elaborate shots for the party scene, notably a sequence where the camera tracks Jimmy's point of view in a 360-degree sweep. It was imperative to get the set-up absolutely correct. However, with the clock ticking, those concerned with expensive studio time were becoming agitated.

'I was having a lot of difficulty that day, a particularly hard time,' Roddam told the author in 2012. 'The line-producer and I were in a big conflict. I was doing very long elaborate takes and it was taking a very long time to prep it, and they wanted to shoot straight away. It got very antagonistic and at one point me and this guy were going to have a scrap. I said, "Come on then! Outside!" As we walked towards the door, he said, "I can't do this," and he gave me a bear

'I WAS HAVING A LOT OF DIFFICULTY THAT DAY, A PARTICULARLY HARD TIME. THE LINE-PRODUCER AND I WERE IN A BIG CONFLICT.'

FRANC RODDAM

hug and nearly killed me. I found out later that he was a well-known fighter and he was famous for knocking people out with one blow.'

As filming tensions kicked off downstairs, raunchy bedroom action continued unabated upstairs. As engineered, Roddam had ensured that a real-life party was maintained for the cast during these scenes. To that end, he'd ensured that alcohol was on offer during the shoot, including a crate of champagne to loosen up any nerves the actors may have had prior to filming. Mark Wingett had already managed to break a filming with his pogoing antics earlier in the shoot, and in the bedroom scene (according to both Roddam and Daniels) he and a female extra engaged in some real hanky-panky between takes. Others, too, were enjoying a spot of shared affection, which lent further credibility to the sequence.

'It was the best day's work I ever did,' recalls

ABOVE: Mark Wingett and Katharine Rogers during the 'Kitchener Road' party sequence.

John Altman of the party scene, where he was ensconced in a room with a young actress. 'I was put in bed with this girl, and she and I were told to stay there until the camera came around. What a hard job, eh? I must say it was quite pleasurable and then the camera came around at 4 a.m.!'

Like many serious directors, Roddam was eager to imbue his productions with subtle echoes of his past, both professional and otherwise. As mentioned previously, the names 'Cooper' and 'Steph' were based on individuals who'd moved him during his life. Similarly, other personal elements were worked directly into *Quadrophenia*. One oblique reference to Roddam's most recent work was captured during a scene where a despondent Jimmy careers along a towpath on his scooter, nearly colliding with two canoodling lovers under a bridge. The scene, filmed at night alongside the Grand Union Canal in West London, was a fairly simple one. However, what gave the sequence substance for students of Roddam's work, was that the two actors were from his last TV production, the controversial *Dummy*. To emphasise the point, the female character is wearing the leopard-skin coat that Geraldine

ABOVE: A brief moment of repose inside the chemist at Uxbridge Road, West London.

◉ 'IT WAS THE BEST DAY'S WORK I EVER DID. I WAS PUT IN BED WITH THIS GIRL, AND SHE AND I WERE TOLD TO STAY THERE UNTIL THE CAMERA CAME AROUND.'

JOHN ALTMAN

James' hapless character, Sandra, wore in *Dummy*.

Night shoots formed a large part of the schedule, so there were some important considerations to be taken into account. Analogue film stock in 1978 was not as receptive as twenty-first-century digital photography (and post-production at that point was equally basic), so cameraman Brian Tufano had to employ a mass of equipment to ensure that the action was sufficiently lit. This often required placing massive lights suspended from cherry pickers and, on occasion, lamps situated far back in the landscape to illuminate key scenes.

Other elements came about purely by chance. Roddam's early career in advertising largely inspired the working environment Jimmy find himself in. To facilitate this, a real-life advertising

agency on Eastbourne Terrace, Paddington, West London, was utilised for filming all of Jimmy's office-based sequences. Roddam had links with the agency, and much of the building's layout was similar to that in the director's formative days in the media.

The shooting of a scene in a chemist's (the object of which was to relieve the premises of its amphetamine stock) drew on elements from the activities of Roddam's early associates – the more nefarious of whom had used the same tactics to break in to similar premises. Filming for this sequence took place at a genuine chemist's in Uxbridge Road, West London. An amusing aside cooked up on the night of the shoot saw Phil Davis deciding to steal some talcum powder, an improvisation that was further embellished with Davis's comic remark that it was for his mum!

Such was the heavy shooting schedule, there was little time for any distractions for *Quadrophenia*'s main cast, professional or otherwise. For Sting, his acting career was running swiftly in tandem with his burgeoning musical aspirations. With filming on *Quadrophenia* consuming everyone, Sting requested – and was granted – an afternoon off filming to appear with The Police on the BBC's flagship contemporary music show, *The Old Grey Whistle Test*. He was flown from London to Manchester to perform on the programme. Filming had taken its toll on Sting, as had the demands of keeping his barnet in shape. On the day of The Police's *Whistle Test* appearance, Sting sustained an injury to his eye while dying his hair with peroxide. The strong astringent inflamed the skin on his face, and he arrived for the recording looking well below par. The show regularly pulled in an audience of a few million viewers, and Sting found himself in a predicament. With conventional spectacles revealing his distressed profile, he opted for a hilariously oversized pair of tinted sunglasses to cover his embarrassment – handed to him by drummer Stewart Copeland.

ABOVE: Sting keeps time at the Royalty Ballroom, Southgate, North London, October 19th, 1978.

Over the years, rumours persisted that Sting's face had been injured in some of the more frenzied action during the making of *Quadrophenia*. The truth was somewhat more mundane…

Surprisingly, Sting's emerging celebrity in no way drove a wedge between members of the frontline cast. In reality, they were more than happy to support their colleague as he took his first steps on the music ladder. An important gig in London on September 14th, 1978, bore witness to this solidarity, as Gary Shail recalls: 'All of us were supportive of Sting. We went to the Rock Garden in Covent Garden for The Police's first major gig. We knew this was an important gig for him and there were eight people there, and it was us.'

After his peroxide-related incapacity, Sting's face recovered in time for the important shooting of the Brighton club scene. To facilitate this, the Royalty Ballroom, a popular nightclub in Southgate, North London, was chosen to host the energetic sequence. The venue had been popular with clubbers and concert-goers for decades. During the mid-seventies the Royalty had hosted some formative punk nights, drawing in North London's new wave brigade to party and pogo. As punk fizzled out in 1978, the ballroom gained a less wild reputation hosting rockabilly bands. In later years it would give way to changing tastes, ultimately becoming a gym in the late nineties.

Despite the venue's disparate allegiances in the mid-seventies, what made it particularly appropriate for *Quadrophenia*'s purposes was the balcony that encircled the dance floor. With Jimmy's airborne dive from the higher reaches aimed at catching Steph's attention, it was perfect. As archive photographs prove, leaping off the Royalty's balcony was not exclusive to *Quadrophenia*; it had become a bit of a cult activity for attendees of the North London club. During the ballroom's flirtation with punk, Roddam had read about the balcony diving in his local newspaper. After visiting the club and witnessing the aeronautics himself, Roddam incorporated just such a spectacular moment into the script, alerting the location scouts that the venue was the perfect spot for Jimmy's leap.

The nightclub shoot was to be held over an entire day; cast and crew were to take possession of the club early on the morning of Thursday, October 19th, 1978. To give the production some advance publicity, the producers had contacted Capital Radio – London's primary music station – and invited any Mods with time on their hands to sign up for a day in Southgate to mingle with the stars and earn a few quid. Ultimately, fifty-five extras showed up for the 8.45 a.m. set call; the main cast had arrived two hours earlier. In addition to the 'Boy Mod' and 'Girl Mod' extras, the call sheet would call for '1 girl beatnik' to play a character who would draw Garry Cooper's Pete character's attention away from Steph.

Shadowing the cast's dance steps was Jeff Dexter. As previously mentioned, Dexter was a key part of the authenticity team required to tutor the cast in all things Mod, especially the dancing. In the midst of the action on the Royalty Ballroom's dance floor, Dexter guided the moves of the lead characters.

'We'd discussed everything,' recalled Dexter in between takes to the BBC. 'All the attitudes of each individual person. What would he be into? Would he be a sweet dancer? Would she be aggressive? Everyone has their particular kind of dance that they do and it gives some idea of what their character is.'

By all accounts, the day at the ballroom was arduous. For the first time, the cast's dance skills would be closely examined by the camera – not least Sting, the star of the sequence. Described variously as 'rather good' or 'swinging his arms from side to side in a rough approximation of dancing', Sting's presence on the ballroom's floor was evidently memorable. Despite having scores of dancers to tutor, Dexter's prime concern was with Sting's moves.

OPPOSITE: Sting getting down to 'Green Onions' at the Royalty Ballroom, October 19th, 1978.

ABOVE: Midnight at Alfredo's, Essex Road, Islington, as captured by Dave Worrell's lens.

'The hardest one is Ace Face,' he recalled to the BBC. 'He has to be very, very cool. Up until Sunday, he was all over the place, and it didn't fit his character. Now he's very trim and has neat, tight footwork which goes with the way he dresses.'

Despite the goodwill on display, an important piece of Sting's apparel – his silver tonic jacket – went missing during a break in shooting. Most productions in *Quadrophenia*'s league would have had several sets of identical clothes for their lead cast, but on this occasion Sting would be afforded no back-up. The suit had cost £500 to tailor, and a spare would have been an expensive luxury.

After a few urgent announcements over the sound system, a reward was offered to encourage the culprit to hand back the jacket so that filming could continue. The item was surreptitiously returned during a lunch break and the cameras were able to roll again.

And roll again they did, time after time; the club scene lasted little more than two minutes of screen time but required numerous takes. 'I got sick and tired of hearing "Green Onions",' recalls John Altman today. 'While I quite like the song, I remember I must have heard it around fifty times that day.'

Once filming was over, the cast and some of the extras were bussed to Covent Garden in Central London for another, less populated club scene. In contrast to the frenetic ballroom sequences, a quieter moment was being recorded by a second unit in a room adjacent to the ballroom. This

involved a typical news broadcast circa 1964, and the redoubtable BBC and ITN reporter Tim Brinton had been chosen. The 48-year-old had recently eschewed reading the news for a career in politics. His entire *Quadrophenia* sequence would be cut, but he did score a more memorable high when he was elected as a Tory MP for Gravesend the following year.

Brighton's cafés had proven fortuitous in presenting a ready-made environment for filming, and the base for the Mods' preferred London hangout was another timely find. Seemingly caught in a time warp, Alfredo's Café at 4–6 Essex Road, Islington, was perfect for *Quadrophenia*. A dream location, the café's frontage sported original hoardings and aged livery from its opening in 1920,

and inside were unique examples of art deco opaque glass. There was little need to dress the café.

With two major scenes and exterior cutaways to be captured outside Alfredo's, three night shoots were built in to the schedule. These sessions were particularly long, starting at dusk and, on some occasions, taking the cast into the early morning.

Until the late nineties, Alfredo's had been in the hands of the de-Ritis family, an association that had been maintained for over seventy years. While the family had seen plenty of activity during their tenure, *Quadrophenia*'s brief stopover was something altogether different.

'They filled the place with charcoal and incense, to make a smoky atmosphere,' recalled proprietor Vincent de-Ritis in 1999. 'Consequently, when they

ABOVE: Inside Alfredo's by Dave Worrell.

ABOVE: 'These rolls have got scabs on!' Leaving Alfredo's in October 1978 and (below) in early 2000.

left, my shop stank. We washed the ceilings, the walls and thought, "That's the end of that – we won't see them no more." Two weeks later they returned. My poor old dad was alive – he lived upstairs keeping an eye on the place. At about five in the morning, a customer came in and asked him for a packet of fags. He paid for them, took his change and left. Those cigarettes were dummies, props for the film. And he never came back.'

The shoot in Islington a fairly sustained one, cast and crew were enlivened by a visit from Roger Daltrey and John Entwistle one evening to check on progress. Elsewhere, the crew shuttled around London at breakneck speed, documenting Jimmy and his cohorts' home turf. As a result, a host of genuine London locations were utilised to great effect. Despite the hideous incursions into traditional architecture during the late sixties and seventies, there remained numerous examples of traditional buildings and businesses that were more than suitable for *Quadrophenia*'s purposes – Dave Wax Tailors in Hammersmith and a gentleman's barbers in Islington were just two timeless interiors.

Presumably more through design than accident, many of the backdrops were faithful to The Who's old stomping ground in Shepherd's Bush. Goldhawk Road was one example and, despite the seventies cars and advertising hoardings, the location didn't appear to compromise the period the film was attempting to recreate. Jimmy and Steph's scooter ride down Goldhawk Road wasn't too out of kilter with the time span, although, to the purist, Daniels' scooter-riding abilities

ABOVE: John Entwistle and Roger Daltrey pay a late-night visit to Alfredo's to check up on filming.

DRIED FRUIT   COOKING OIL

2 15   3rd button only buttoned.

ABOVE: Jimmy
drops in on Steph
at Ashken's store on
the Goldhawk Road,
Shepherd's Bush.

appeared a little uncoordinated.

Other, less familiar places in Hammersmith also made it into the film. A supermarket then called Ashken's on Goldhawk Road and a side road at Bamborough Gardens in Shepherd's Bush both played a part in hosting Jimmy's determined wooing of Steph.

While it may have appeared absurd to the younger audiences of 1978, there were occasions where the film had to reflect some of the coarser practicalities of sixties working-class life. For many, home bathing during that time was still in a zinc bath in front of a coal fire once a week. For Mods, keeping clean was an absolute necessity. For those denied conventional utilities at home, there were several places where a bath could be acquired for a few pennies. In one scene Jimmy finds himself at a public (or 'slipper') bath where he is reunited with school friend turned Rocker, Kevin Herriot, played by Ray Winstone. The location scouts had found one of the last surviving public baths at the Porchester Centre in Queensway, Westminster (still a popular leisure centre today). Preserving a unique slice of local history, *Quadrophenia* captured the atmosphere of the establishment and the only visual record of its interior before its closure shortly after filming.

On a brief venture over to the other side of the Thames, the Alma Public House at 499 Old York Road in Wandsworth hosted the scene of a pub gathering prior to the party in Kitchener Road.

With the production team centring their activity mainly in West London, it was obvious that at some point the traditional haunts of The Who and their original entourage would be revisited. The café A. Cooke & Son at 48 Goldhawk Road was one such

landmark that welcomed *Quadrophenia*'s roving crew for a key scene. The eatery had been a mainstay of the local community, providing sustenance for workers, locals and entertainers alike for over ninety years. The Who often popped along to the place in their early days, as would the scores of Mods who'd often meet up there to savour pie and mash covered in a unique pea-green 'liquor' flavoured with parsley. A sequence in which Jimmy required sustenance after his bath called for a traditional pie-and-mash shop, and Cooke's proved ideal. With no dressing required, the café's time-defying setting couldn't help but drip onto the film stock. With budgetary restrictions in everyone's mind, the occasional merging of real-life customers and the actors proved hugely memorable. Pete Townshend was present for the cafe shoot and was pictured tucking into a traditional dinner with Phil Daniels in between takes.

Alongside Cooke's café lay Shepherd's Bush Market, established since 1914. During the day a

ABOVE: Roger momentarily escapes auditions for *Quadrophenia*'s house band to *parlez* with Gary Shail and some of the extras present for the basement club scene in Shelton Street, Covent Garden.

LEFT: A. Cooke's pie and mash shop shortly before its closure.

scene of hectic activity, at night the place took on an almost alien feel, with its cobblestones, vacant stalls and barrows betraying no particular era. A tea bar that had long been the haunt of BBC staffers from nearby Lime Grove Studios, was put into use – its lengthy opening hours convenient for *Quadrophenia*'s purposes.

A key scene where Jimmy witnesses his school friend Kevin (Ray Winstone) being beaten up by his Mod cohorts was filmed mostly along Wells Road at the junction of Shepherd's Bush tube, its glistening cobbled streets proving ideal for the night scene. To give the location greater texture, the streets around the market were sprayed with water, enhancing the existing light with a greater texture. Winstone had recently taken possession of a motorbike and was quite competent in handling any mechanical beast. Remarkable for a production of the stature of *Quadrophenia*, Roddam let Winstone perform the stunt of driving into a wall of boxes – an act that could have proved problematic if things had got out of hand, but the seemingly fearless Winstone was keen to oblige.

While Winstone's fake crash was perfectly executed, elsewhere real life nearly derailed the rest of the sequence. In what was an involved scene, it was vital to the continuity that much of what occurred was captured in one shot. In the midst of an emotional whirl, Daniels' scooter decided to stall, resulting in the actor having to furiously kick-start the machine. The camera still rolling, Jimmy's getaway was dramatic, although to the keen eye the focus of the lens picked out the bank of lights illuminating the sequence. Cinematographer Tufano asked for a retake, and the sequence was filmed again, but it missed the spontaneous energy captured on the first take. As a result, the original was left in.

As well as all the authentic locations and venues, there were several occasions where the film had to deceive to achieve. By 1978 the Goldhawk Club, one of The Who's earliest residential venues, retained little of the energy from its mid-sixties heyday. In an act of homage, a re-creation of its exterior was mocked up on a property on Shelton Street, a road cutting through West London's Covent Garden district. Ironically, across the road in Langley Street (a road that Jimmy drives through on his scooter) was the site of the London Film School, Franc Roddam's former college. With the addition of a few neon lights and a mocked-up sign, the site assumed some of the frisson that had accompanied the Goldhawk's early days. With the addition of a

OPPOSITE: Phil Daniels and Pete Townshend attend a photo-call at A. Cooke's pie and mash shop.

ABOVE: Shepherd's Bush Market and Jimmy checking out the vinyl.

posse of scooters outside, it served its purpose for the opening scene where Jimmy first meets up with his Mod compatriots.

For the 'Goldhawk' interior, just a few paces along at 29 Shelton Street, the crew used a real club known as the Basement Youth Club. It had the benefit of a large downstairs area and a stairwell that were perfect for filming. On the night of October 19th, 1978, immediately following the Royalty Ballroom scene, the Basement Youth Club was transformed into a sixties look for *Quadrophenia*. Given the mass of Mod extras hired for the Royalty 'Brighton' Ballroom scene in Southgate, once filming had concluded there, some were bussed over to the Basement Club. For the rest of the night, they danced around to the sounds of The Cross Section and a few other linking pieces. Such is the patchwork of filming…

Elsewhere on their odyssey around town, the cast and crew visited Notting Hill Gate, West London, for a triad of scenes: one outside a pub where the hapless Spider and his girlfriend are ambushed by Rockers, another, a fruitless attempt to locate Ferdy, and a sequence where Jimmy visits a scrapyard in search of pills. The location scouts had done their stuff well in the district; they'd found a pub – the Bramley Arms – at the junction of Bramley Road and Freston Road, and an active scrapyard just a few metres away on Latimer Road in North Kensington. As well as some television exteriors, the pub had been used for *The Lavender Hill Mob* back in 1951.

While the twenty-first century has gentrified Notting Hill beyond recognition, during the

THE LOCATION SCOUTS HAD DONE THEIR STUFF WELL IN THE DISTRICT; THEY'D FOUND A PUB – THE BRAMLEY ARMS

seventies the area earmarked for *Quadrophenia* filming formed part of Frestonia, a highly idiosyncratic experiment in community squatting. Influenced by sixties hippie idealism, a largely anarchistic group had commandeered a swathe of derelict Notting Hill property in the early seventies. Once ensconced, they assumed their own 'principality' – the Free and Independent Republic of Frestonia – whose aims were largely based on the *Passport to Pimlico* school of self-governance. Frestonian protocol required that the cast and crew be issued with special visas before filming could commence. Ironically, Frestonia's headquarters was the Bramley Arms, which would become one of *Quadrophenia*'s landmark sites.

While the Bramley Arms acted as a backdrop for Spider's beating by Rockers, the scrapyard scene was more involved. The sequence features car-breaker Peter Fenton (Garry Cooper), who receives a visit from Jimmy, who is looking for a connection to acquire some pills for the imminent Brighton trip. The vicious barking dogs that greet Jimmy's entrance into the scrapyard were indeed the resident's dogs, as were the piles of old vehicles. A casualty of the area's gentrification, the yard closed down in 2001.

Fiction was soon to merge with real-life criminality when John Bindon arrived on set. Bindon – sometime actor, sometime socialite – was best known as a shady character who dipped in and out of the fringes of dodgy dealings. Adding to his charisma, Bindon's edgy presence had already enlivened three bona fide cult classics: *Poor Cow*, *Performance* and *Get Carter*. He'd also had a quieter moment in Stanley Kubrick's *Barry Lyndon*, as well as notching up several appearances in the likes of *Special Branch*, *Softly, Softly* and *Love Thy Neighbour*. Outside his drama roster, he'd also acted as security for one of Led Zeppelin's tours.

Bindon's lifestyle was already well known to those who monitored the gossip pages of Britain's tabloids. An alleged

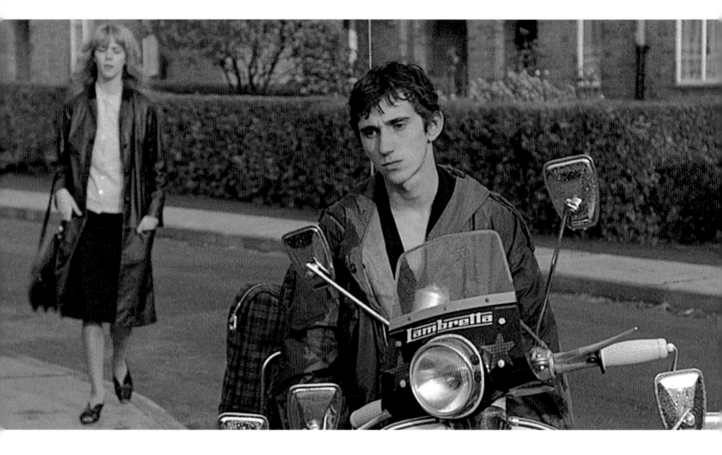

ABOVE:
Confrontation
imminent; Jimmy
awaits Steph after
his troublesome
night, Orchid
Street, Acton, West
London.

consort of Princess Margaret, and on speaking terms with a raft of celebrities both famous and infamous, Bindon's inclusion brought a dose of stark realism to the production.

Bindon played Harry North in *Quadrophenia*, a contact of Mod Peter Fenton and someone with connections to the narcotics trade. With Jimmy on a mission to acquire enough amphetamine sustenance for his gang's Brighton caper, he encounters Bindon in the back room of a pub that doubles as a boxing gym. It's here that the underworld of sixties London criminality collides with young working-class Mods such as Jimmy.

The Wellington pub in Highgate, North London – one of the few boxing pubs that existed at the end of the seventies – played host to the sequence. Its famous alumni included the likes of Frank Bruno and John Conteh. As was his style, Bindon brought an entourage – all on a major buzz at the prospect of being in a feature film.

Also present was former Kray twins' associate, Bobby Ramsey, who'd find himself refereeing the boxing match inside the pub. His name had cropped up frequently on the London call sheets, principally as security coordinator on set. Several characters brought along by Bindon added some true gangster gravitas to the proceedings. While director Roddam welcomed the spontaneity and edge, things soon got out of hand. When one sequence required several retakes, the atmosphere grew tense.

'Johnny Bindon I considered an actor, not a gangster,' Roddam recalled to the author in 2012. 'These night shoots go on, and when it gets to about 2 a.m., they begin to fade – and get short-tempered and irritated with the lighting or waiting for things to happen, and this was not a good group of people to be irritating. I looked at Bindon for support and I hoped he'd help me deal with this, but he did the opposite and played to the gang.

So I suddenly found that I had forty irate gangsters getting impatient with me.'

Just weeks after filming, Bindon found himself in an altercation with one John Drake, a small-time crook who frequented the same West London haunts as Bindon. Following a vicious spat during which Drake was stabbed, Bindon found himself standing in the dock at London's Old Bailey on a murder charge. The allegation was later found unstable and thrown out, but Bindon's notoriety would continue to stymie future film work, and he found a more consistent audience in the pubs and clubs of South West London. *Quadrophenia* proved to be his last appearance on celluloid. A taste for hedonism running in tandem with his illicit activities, John Bindon would succumb to an AIDS-related illness in 1993.

Meanwhile, less charged scenes in West London were bearing witness to Jimmy's emotional breakdown with Steph. The sequence had its roots long before the production, having formed the basis for Phil Daniels' screen test. The setting for this dramatic confrontation between the pair was the social housing environs of Acton, the terraced Orchid Street acting as a perfect backdrop. Like many of the film's key scenes, it drew heavily on improvisation. Before the camera rolled, Roddam

got Daniels and Ash to go through the scene and invited them to add a few impromptu profanities to the dialogue to heighten its impact.

A few streets away from Orchid Street, at the junction of Sawley Road and Galloway Road, Jimmy's trauma was to deepen, following a collision with a Royal Mail van. The scene required a stunt double to take Jimmy's scooter under the vehicle, but the emotion on display from Phil Daniels was startlingly real. Aware that the driver and his assistant may well be shocked having to deal with such an outburst, Roddam primed Daniels to express the agony of having his prized Lambretta mullahed. On cue, the young actor turned in an emotional tour de force.

'The stuntmen were really shocked at the language and were shocked at the tirade at anger directed at them,' reported Roddam in 1999. 'The main guy started saying, "I'm sorry, I'm sorry". If you watch, you can see the look of shock on the guy's face. He wasn't ready for the emotion.'

Elsewhere, some establishing scenes for important sequences were required. Jimmy's fateful trip down to the South Coast would obviously tie in with the *Quadrophenia* album's landmark song '5:15'. Facilitating this sequence, the crew took over Paddington Station in West London for an afternoon's shooting. More involved filming took place on a specially chartered train commissioned to travel up and down a stretch of a South London railway line, for the important scenes of Jimmy's miserable return to Brighton.

There were a few occasions when London was not expansive enough to contain some of the larger scenes, especially those involving bikes, such as the Mods' exodus from London to Brighton and their inadvertent engagement with a group of Rockers. On paper, the scene appeared straightforward, but the production team met with a potentially devastating scenario that no one had predicted. Initially, some cutaways were filmed at the Defence Evaluation and Research Agency (DERA) test track in Chertsey, Surrey. Mainly used for the motor industry, the two-mile track had previously featured in the first part of *The Omen* trilogy, as well as the TV sitcom *George and Mildred* and several television dramas. For *Quadrophenia*'s purposes, the private track allowed for shots of both Rockers and Mods to ride around without helmets and for a sequence that was later edited out of the film. However, for a more complex episode, the crew had to hit the open road. Permission denied by the police for filming without helmets, a snap decision was made to go ahead regardless.

This sequence took the scooter and bike-riding cast out to Denham, Buckinghamshire. The area was fairly rural but conveniently close to where *Quadrophenia*'s precious negatives and rushes were developed. Once there, vintage scooters and Rocker's bikes were scheduled to converge at the junction of Southlands Road and Willett's Lane for a mouthy exchange that would lead to a carefully coordinated stunt with Phil Davis bearing the brunt. However, real life intervened and upstaged the action destined for the screen.

According to members of the cast and crew, local travellers based in the Denham area were upset at the large filming contingent taking over the stretch of road that ran alongside their encampment. Reportedly demanding money to allow the shoot to go ahead unhindered, their advances were flatly rejected by the film crew. In a fit of pique (and unbeknownst to the production), an old car was pushed into the road as the caravan of Mods and Rockers negotiated a sharp bend. The result was nothing less than mayhem.

'We had a big accident here,' recalled Roddam in 2008. 'A car pulled out and all the bikes piled up, all of these antique bikes – it was a huge mess and we had three ambulances to take them all to hospital, but we were lucky, we only had one broken limb.'

Phil Davis was at the head of the caravan that day, although his dexterity allowed him to leap off his scooter before he hit the vehicle. John Blundell, the head Rocker in the staged confrontation, also managed to steer his bike to safety alongside the roadside hedge. Blundell's task was considerable as he had actress Linda Regan riding as pillion.

'We all came off our bikes,' recalled Phil Davis to the author in 2012. 'I came off and I managed to dodge all the Rockers who were trying not to run me over. Franc said I was like "an electric rabbit waiting to dive into a hedge". And we all went up to the hospital and there were all these Rockers with lots of cuts and just one solitary Mod.'

Stuntman Gareth Milne wasn't as lucky as Davis; he'd taken the full weight of the collision. With a dozen or so scooters and bikes in his slipstream, Milne came off worst, sustaining a severe leg injury. The damage to Milne's limb was deemed so serious, he was airlifted to hospital. Before police could fully survey the damage, production personnel, aware that no one had been wearing headgear, called for an immediate cache of helmets to be delivered. These were then placed strategically alongside the road just in case any embarrassing questions were asked later on.

Such is the indestructibility of stuntmen, Milne was back on set two days later to reshoot the same sequence at the location – earning the nickname 'Legend' as a result. The derelict car that had prompted the debacle was still visible at the roadside. With no time to remove it, it was left in shot as an oblique homage to the grisly scenario it had caused the previous week.

Filming outside Jimmy's West London home on Thursday, October 25th, 1978, allowed for a brief hiatus to let Phil Daniels celebrate his 20th birthday. The schedule was far too involved to allow time for a full-scale party, but a large cake adorned with a model scooter and attendant Mod was brought over to the set. This allowed Daniels to share his special day with the other cast members and pose for a few celebratory photographs.

November 1979 saw filming draw to a close, although there was still the need for a title sequence for the opening credits to run over. A series of scattershot images were captured by a modest camera crew tracking Phil Daniels and several other scooter riders around South West London at night, with exteriors of Lots Road Power Station in Chelsea, the nearby ornate Albert Bridge and other fleeting glimpses of Hammersmith and Acton. The majority of the funding now drained from the filming budget, some major improvisational work was required to light these sequences.

'The title sequence was the last thing we did, some considerable time later,' cinematographer Brian Tufano explained in 2012. 'We had no money, so I spent night after night looking for streets that had enough light to give me something of an exposure… I just had one battery light to shoot the whole sequence.'

The cessation of filming allowed cast and crew a well-earned breather. After sixty days of almost continuous shooting, with 16-hour days not uncommon, an even longer period of editing and post-production was about to start. With a summer 1979 date scheduled for *Quadrophenia*'s release, beyond the editing and dubbing suites, the burgeoning Mod revival was already starting to mirror the action that had been contrived for the film. ●

LEFT: Last coming first; *Quadrophenia*'s title sequence, ironically the final sequence to be filmed.

He pins the article to the wall, admires it for a second, then
dumps himself on the bed fully clothed, the wrong way up, feet
at the headboard end, admiring the whole wall in comfort.
Outside, the sound of DAD shuffling along the corridor in
slippers en route to the toilet.

FATHER (V.O.)
How many times have I told you
to turn the hall light off behind
you?

JIMMY
(under his breath, dreamily)
Hundreds of times, thousands of ...

FATHER
(locking himself in
the toilet)
At least a hundred times!

JIMMY gazes upwards, listening to the sound of DAD slashing,
the clank of the chain, the rush of the cistern.

8   INT. TUNNEL   NIGHT   8

Dressed in a t-shirt and jeans, JIMMY walks alone through a
seemingly endless white tunnel, under a white glare of
light from the regularly-spaced bulbs above him. The image
is stark, yet surreal ... Over it, the rush of the cistern in
the previous scene MIXES to become 'the muted underwater'
sounds in the next scene ...

9   INT. PUBLIC BATHS   DAY   9

In a bath cubicle, with his clothes heaped on a small wooden
chair, JIMMY lies almost totally submerged in the enormous
old bath, gazing at the skylights above him ... the muted,
underwater sounds that reach him rise from almost total
silence to a noise something like the sea in the pre-titles
sequence ...

Lifting his head, JIMMY becomes aware that the bath in the
adjacent cubicle is filling, producing the sound he has heard..

ATTENDANT (V.O.)
How's that?

BOY (V.O.)
That's alright ...

CHAPTER NINE

'A LOT OF OUR BEST MOMENTS ENDED UP ON THE CUTTING-ROOM FLOOR.'

—TOYAH WILCOX

'ART IS NEVER FINISHED, ONLY ABANDONED.'

—LEONARDO DA VINCI

With the majority of the script now committed to celluloid, only minor edits were required to maintain the continuity and pace of the picture. As a result, very few scenes would be cut from the finished version of the film. However, on scrutiny of the shooting script, it's apparent that several key sequences remained unfilmed. For students of *Quadrophenia* it is important to document these omissions, which were likely the result of time and budget constraints, or simply a wish to keep up the pace. Others, as we shall see, are contentious and would perhaps have proved challenging to the sensibilities of a 1979 film audience.

One thematic element that maintained some continuity throughout the script concerned Jimmy and an attractive blonde model. In the finished version, she is in the stills that Jimmy steals for his own private purposes, but there were other moments where the girl was to feature, albeit in an ambient manner. Production photographs bear witness to one scene which features Jimmy, clearly in awe of this woman's beauty, sharing a lift with her at the agency. A more sustained moment later on was one of Jimmy hiding from an advancing phalanx of Rockers behind a large advertising hoarding featuring a large poster of the same model. Although both scenes were filmed, they were cut from the finished product.

It has also been suggested that several scenes featuring Ace Face talking were jettisoned to maintain his enigma, but there is no proof of this. Equally, some have cited seeing Jimmy in a tin bath attempting to shrink his Levi's in an early cut of the film, although no photos of this sequence have ever surfaced.

Other scenes in the script not supported by production stills are presumed not to have been shot at all. While much of the detail lost is negligible, some of the omissions, deletions and additional scenes embedded in the original script are revelatory.

Perhaps the biggest revelation is that the original opening scene (Scene 1) was designed to present a wholly different scenario to that seen in the finished version. While Jimmy's mournful trudge from the cliff's edge was committed to film, this scene would perhaps have offered just a bit too much foreshadowing of the ending.

OPPOSITE: A deleted scene from the shooting script.

1 EXT BEACH DAY
CLOSE SHOT of a Mod's scooter, lying
half-submerged in a misty sea. The
incoming tide is gently swallowing the
machine. The noise of the sea builds
to the music over - 'I Am The Sea' -
until the volume is enormous.

The scene would then cut to the familiar strains
of 'The Real Me' and the familiar shots of Jimmy
riding around London.

Another early sequence explored Jimmy's
fatigue and detachment following a heavy
weekend's partying and took on a far greater
significance than the final realisation. Following a
mind-numbing day at work and clearly hungover,
Jimmy attempts to make his way home on public
transport. The following dialogue and attendant
direction are taken verbatim from the original
script. While it offers a fuller picture of Jimmy's
alienation and detachment, it also hints strongly
at the metaphor of the sea.

SCENE 40:
INTERIOR. TUBE TRAIN. EVENING
JIMMY is amongst the passengers
on the crowded tube... Seated, the
excesses of the weekend catch up with
him and his head lolls sideways,
coming to rest on the shoulder of a
WOMAN seated next to him... With a
grimace, she attempts to move away;
JIMMY merely lolls further, dead to
the world.

SCENE 41:
INTERIOR. TUBE TRAIN. EVENING
JIMMY is still in the same seat, fast
asleep; making a forlorn figure now
with the carriage empty all around
him. The tube rolls on and an eerie
noise, like a far-off sea, begins to
grow in volume...

JIMMY wakes, blank-faced and
frightened, as the tube passes through
the enormous cleaning apparatus
at Neasden's depot... He gets up
unsteadily, trying to orientate
himself in this alien situation.

The train halts; beyond the window,
the depot at Neasden looms huge and
empty of life... empty trains rattle
by on the criss-cross of tracks that
stretch away on all sides.

SCENE 42:
EXTERIOR. NEASDEN DEPOT. EVENING
JIMMY manages to escape from the
stationary train using the emergency
doors at the end of the carriage, and
finds himself utterly alone in this
bizarre conglomeration of enormous
buildings and machinery... even the
lights blazing here and there add to
the sense of lifelessness all around
him. He crosses the tracks towards
the high fences in the distance,
making a small figure in an unknown
landscape... Awkwardly, he manages to
climb the fence...

(LEADING TO)

SCENE 43:
EXTERIOR. STREETS. EVENING
... to find himself on a wide,
deserted road, a street to nowhere...
Lost, he looks about him for a
moment before trudging off along the
desolate street.

Ultimately, the viewer only sees Jimmy arriving
back at home to announce to his parents that he
ended up in 'bloody Neasden'. While it's unclear
why this remarkable vignette was removed prior to

filming, screenwriter Martin Stellman has offered a valid reason for its removal: 'The schedule was tight. London Transport was not exactly helpful in those days when it came to filming. In fact, I'm pretty sure that was the issue.'

Scene 65 features the club where Jimmy's gang are enjoying a dance while Spider and his girlfriend are being beaten up by Rockers outside. In the original script, a live band was to entertain those present. Named explicitly in the script are Geno Washington and the Ram Jam Band, While Washington was still very active in 1978, for reasons presumably due to budget the live band were replaced by a DJ playing The Crystals' 'Da Doo Ron Ron'.

◎ JIMMY SITS ALONE AT A TABLE, WITH A CUP OF TEA BEFORE HIM AND A BREAKFAST WHICH HE IS TAKING NO JOY IN EATING...

Further on, there's another echo from the *Quadrophenia* booklet that serves to emphasise Jimmy's alienation. The film depicts the moment where Jimmy tells his mum he's too sick to go to work, but it fails to recreate a sequence later that day where Jimmy finds himself alone at his and his cohorts' preferred café, which, again, is another nod to the imagery within the original booklet.

SCENE 70:
EXTERIOR. CAFE. MORNING
JIMMY's scooter stands alone, with a couple of parked lorries where the ranks of scooters are generally to be seen...

SCENE 71:
INTERIOR. CAFE. MORNING
Inside, the cafe is likewise changed, with the juke-box and the pinball machines silent... and a couple

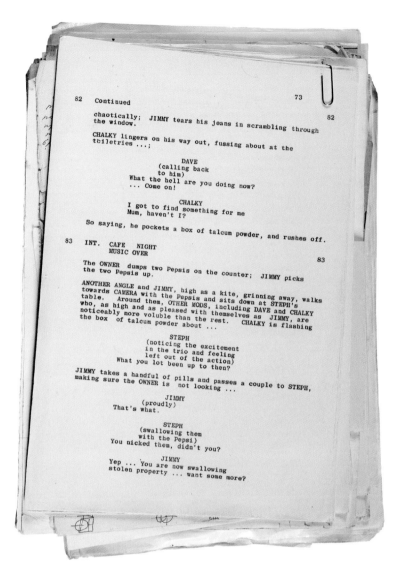

of DRIVERS sit at the counter in desultory conversation with the OWNER. JIMMY sits alone at a table, with a cup of tea before him and a breakfast which he is taking no joy in eating...

A few pages later, another deleted sequence reveals the confusion that Jimmy feels after seeing his old schoolmate, the hapless Rocker Kevin, being pummelled by his Mod friends. The finished film duly reflected Jimmy's distress at the scene, but the sequence that was cut digs deeper into Jimmy's confusion over split loyalties in a discussion with fellow Mod traveller Dave.

ABOVE: Excised scenes from the finished product.

```
140A  EXT.   LOCAL CAFE    NIGHT                          140A

        Several scooters parked in front of the cafe.  It is raining.
        Through the window of the cafe, we see that things are very
        much as we left them before Brighton - MODS whiling their time
        away, crowding around the pinball machines, horsing around, etc.

        The sound of a scooter off-screen, and, JIMMY, in a
        strangely cowed way, walks into the cafe.

141   INT.   CAFE    NIGHT                                141

        All the mob are there: FERDY and DAVE at the pinball machines,
        CHALKY and STEPH sitting opposite each other at a table close to
        the pinball machine, FINGER propped up at the counter, MONKEY
        sitting at another table with another group of MODS.   As
        JIMMY, wet through, walks in, there is a surprising lack of
        response to his arrival.  It is only MONKEY, following him
        with her eyes who regards him with any real concern.

                            DAVE
                  (glancing round briefly,
                  then returning his attention
                  to the pinball machine)
            Look who it isn't ...

                            FERDY
                  (at least looking up)
            Hey, man, we thought you would be locked
            up in a cell in The Scrubs by now.

        JIMMY goes up to the counter and orders a tea, turning to look
        at his friends - in the foreground, CHALKY sitting, FERDY at
        the pinball machine;  in the midground, DAVE and STEPH and in
        the background, MONKEY.  But JIMMY's eyes cannot help but drift
        in the direction of STEPH ...

                            JIMMY
            No, got fined, didn't I? ... Fifty
            quid ...

        FERDY lets out a whistle of amazement ...

                            FERDY
                  (still at his game)
            Another good customer hits the
            dust.

                            DAVE
                  (still at his game)
            Yeah ... sorry we couldn't hang
            around for you, like, but, you know,
            we had to get back for work and that ...

        The OWNER dumps the tea on the counter.
```

SCENE 74:

EXTERIOR. STREET. DAY

JIMMY drives aimlessly through the deserted streets on his scooter... At one point, he realises he is at the cross-roads which was the scene of Kevin's beating the night before. In the road, bits of glass and a piece of headlamp are visible, as is a dark stain on the pavement... JIMMY rides on...

ABOVE: A page detailing the final London café scene.

Moments later, Jimmy meets his mate Dave at work on the dustcarts, and he engages in a spot of mutual banter, mostly concerning what occurred after the altercation the previous night.

DAVE: Where d'you get to after the barney then?

JIMMY: Nowhere, really... I went home... (Guiltily) Why?

DAVE: Oh nothing... You seemed a bit upset about something. The way you were looking at the bastard. I thought he was a friend of yours for a minute...

JIMMY: What a bleeding rocker? You must be joking... I couldn't get in there, that's all...

DAVE: Anyway, I bet that cunt won't get out of bed for a while... and he'll think twice about getting back on that bike when he does... serves him fucking right and all...

JIMMY: Yeah, right...

The vital acquisition of amphetamines for the Brighton trip dominated many pages of the Quadrophenia script. The trip to the scrapyard, subsequent drug burn and raid on the chemist's were filmed; several other scenes relating to buying drugs did not make the cut.

Following the fruitless trip to Ferdy's North Kensington flat, a far more involved scene prolongs the quest to acquire drugs. This sequence, covering nearly three pages, mines the police corruption that was prevalent in London during the mid-sixties. Scene 78C takes place at Notting Hill's Colville Pub, situated on the district's popular Portobello Road.

SCENE 78C:
EXTERIOR: PORTOBELLO ROAD
'THE COLVILLE PUB' NIGHT

A WIDE-ISH SHOT, with, in the
foreground, scooters their mounts-
CHALKY, and DAVE - PARKED AT THE
KERBSIDE.
Ahead of them, JIMMY is approaching a
BLACK MAN, one of several BLACK MEN,
most of them obviously with something
to sell, standing on the street
corner outside the pub...

◎ THE PANDA CAR REVS OFF UP THE STREET TOWARDS THE MODS AND SKIDS TO A HALT RIGHT OUTSIDE CHALKY AND DAVE

This scene appears fairly well set up for a drug
deal, but the emergence of the police takes the
scenario into far darker realms.

The 2ND BLACK MAN shows JIMMY
something wrapped in silver foil.
JIMMY shakes his head just as a
police car approaches the street
corner... The POLICE CAR slows to a
halt directly outside the pub... The
2ND BLACK MAN makes a gesture as if
to say 'stay there a minute' and goes
over to the car, as a policeman leans
out of the window... At the car, the
2ND BLACK MAN takes out what looks
suspiciously like a wad of notes and
hands them to the POLICEMAN.

DAVE: Feck me, he's only given him
          a backhander, hasn't he.
CHALKY: How d'you know? Could have
          passed him a few hot tips for

the 2.30 at Newmarket.

The panda car revs off up the street
towards the Mods and skids to a
halt right outside Chalky and Dave,
obscuring his - and our - line of
vision to the street corner. Alarm
from the Mods but a tight-lipped
attempt to look calm and collected. A
POLICEMAN winds down the window and
leans out.

POLICEMAN: Evening lads.

The 'lads' don't reply, just a half-
hearted, paranoid nod from CHALKY.

THE POLICEMAN screws them hard for a
few seconds, silently and sullenly,
as if deliberately holding the Mods
in suspense, then...

POLICEMAN: I wouldn't stay there for
           too long if I was you. Double
           yellow lines.

The POLICE CAR revs off up the road.

CHALKY: (doing a 'V' sign) Horrible
        bastards!

Meanwhile... JIMMY is attempting
to get back to the scooters but is
having his sleeve tugged by the 2ND
BLACK MAN trying desperately to get
JIMMY to buy his wares... JIMMY
finally shrugs him off and makes his
way over to the scooters.

JIMMY: Nothing Hash, that's all
       they got. Couldn't get rid of
       the cunt, kept trying to sell
       me some.

CHALKY: 'Ash. What out the fire?

DAVE: No, out the crematorium,
         ashes of dead bodies, gets
         you right out of your brain,
         haven't you heard?

Later on, ostensibly on the night prior to the Mods' mass exodus to Brighton, there's a deleted scene set outside London's famed Marquee Club, a sequence which served to highlight the heavy drug dealing prevalent in the Mod scene at the time.

SCENE 97:
EXTERIOR. MARQUEE CLUB. NIGHT
A couple of sharply-dressed BLACK
MEN, somewhat older than their
customers, move amongst the small
groups of MODS dealing pills;
their eyes roaming the street for
any sign of trouble... Pound notes
and polystyrene bags change hands
smoothly here and there.

Nestled in between these narcotic shenanigans, a more involved scene includes dialogue shot earlier, featuring the newsreader Tim Brinton. The scene was committed to celluloid the day of Jimmy's spectacular balcony aeronautics, and was seemingly destined to run before the sequence where Jimmy watches The Who on *Ready Steady Go!*.

SCENE 92A:
JIMMY'S HOUSE SITTING ROOM. EVENING
JIMMY moves into the room with the
bundles of newspapers and the towel,
making for the T.V set. He switches
on the T.V set and, although the
picture takes a while to warm up,
the sound comes on straight away -
the news:

NEWSCASTER: After today's session
            at the Conference, the
            Colonial Secretary spoke to
            newsmen and commented that
            he was hopeful for a speedy
            transition to independence
            in Aden, 'within the year'.
            (pause)

The Bank Holiday starts
in earnest this evening as
thousands of holidaymakers
take advantage of the fine
weather and head towards
the South Coast resorts. A
spokesman for the Automobile
Association commented this
evening that traffic is heavy
on the A127 Southend road and
that there are traffic jams
on the Southbound sections
of the M1, causing severe
delays. Motorists are advised
to take alternative routes.
Shopkeepers in the Brighton
area fearing a recurrence
of the disturbance caused
by rival gangs of youths in
other seaside resorts...

Later on, when the action has moved fully to Brighton, a short scene details the scale of the Mods' descent into the city. While the scene was presumably never filmed because of the logistics involved, it would have added further impact to the sheer numbers of Mods pouring into Brighton that Bank Holiday weekend – and not just on scooters. For whatever reason, the music that was to play over this chaotic scene was scheduled to be The Who's 'Doctor Jimmy' – a strange choice in that it doesn't quite tally with the action on screen.

SCENE 119:
BRIGHTON STATION. DAY
MUSIC OVER: (DOCTOR JIMMY)

A head-on view of a train pulling
into a stop at Brighton Terminus...
Even before it does so, the doors
are opening and swarms of MODS are
leaping from the train and pouring
down the platform, forcing the
barriers open and scattering across
the concourse, heading for the
streets.

The riot scenes filmed are largely faithful to what
was in the script, but an extension to the later
courtroom sequence adds a further sense of
drama to Jimmy's reversal of fortunes.

SCENE 130A:
INTERIOR. COURTROOM. DAY

A POLICEMAN walks over to JIMMY and
accompanies him to the dock. To JIMMY
it seems like a long walk... As JIMMY
takes his place finally in the dock,
the CLERK OF THE COURT reads out the
charges.

CLERK OF THE COURT: James Michael
        Haines, you are charged
        that on August 31st of this
        year you did use threatening
        behaviour likely to cause a
        breach of the peace and were
        in possession of an offensive
        weapon. How do you plead?

JIMMY: (in disbelief at the charge)
        Not guilty...

A BOY POLICEMAN starts to walk
towards the witness box...

CLERK OF THE COURT: (informing the
        magistrates) Police Constable
        Adrian Chandler...

JIMMY   (as the boy policeman takes
        his place, to the Magistrates
        angrily) Excuse me sir, but
        he wasn't the one that nicked
        me...

MAGISTRATE:You will not interrupt the
        proceedings... you'll have a
        chance to put your case in a
        moment.

We hold on JIMMY's dismayed and
bewildered face, as the BOY POLICEMAN
swears himself in.

Back from Brighton, freshly unemployed and not
welcome at home, a lengthy scene was excluded
from the finished product. While filmgoers saw
Jimmy angrily driving away from the family home,
a lengthy scene was devised to detail where he
spent the night before retreating to the shed in
his parents' garden. If the scene had survived,
some comic relief would have been injected into
Jimmy's downfall.

SCENE 146:
EXTERIOR. STREET. NIGHT
Beyond caring, JIMMY rides through
the night streets of West London,
cruising in perfect Mod style on his
beloved scooter, riding just for the
feel of it...

SCENE 147:
EXTERIOR. WAREHOUSE. NIGHT
Some distance away, a figure squats
over a small fire... JIMMY approaches
and makes out the TRAMP seated there,
boiling water in a battered kettle...

The TRAMP looks up, and grins at
JIMMY toothlessly, his eyes gleaming
in the firelight...

JIMMY: Hello.

The TRAMP's reply is a soft,
high cackle... JIMMY smiles a little
uncertainly and squats near the
fire.

JIMMY: I just left home, see...
        couldn't think of nowhere
        else to come but here.

Taking a tea-bag from his pocket,
the TRAMP pours water from the kettle
into a tin mug, dunks the bag for a
moment before carefully retrieving it
and proffers the brew to JIMMY; who
takes it, and in return offers some
pills to the TRAMP.

SCENE 148:
WAREHOUSE. NIGHT
(MUSIC OVER: THE WHO'S 1966 SINGLE -
HAPPY JACK)

JIMMY is curled up, sleeping
fitfully... whilst the TRAMP is wide
awake on pills...

SCENE 149:
INTERIOR. WAREHOUSE. MORNING
JIMMY wakes, cramped and bewildered,
to the noise of the morning traffic
all around him... in the cold light
of morning, the TRAMP sleeping next
to him, is an unsavoury bundle of
rags; and JIMMY's reaction is one
of distaste at the sight... he gets
up stiffly and moves away to his
scooter...

The film was faithful to Jimmy's emotional return
to Brighton, except for one scene, which extended
his dismal tenure on the South Coast to over two
days. The following moment is a clear reflection of
the *Quadrophenia* booklet, with Jimmy alone on
the Palace Pier late on the evening of his return.
For obvious reasons, given Brighton's refusal to
allow either of the piers to be used for filming, this
was going to be an impossible scene to realise.

SCENE 161:
PALACE PIER. HALL OF MIRRORS. EVENING
Mirror reflection of JIMMY changing
and flowing. Another angle and we see
JIMMY moving amongst the illusions of
the mirrors. He stands at last before
the mirror that he is apparently most
at home with... its reflection splits
him into four separate images before
his eyes.

SCENE 161A:
EXTERIOR. PALACE PIER
BRIGHTON. EVENING
The pier is almost deserted; JIMMY
leaves the Hall of Mirrors and
wanders along the pier with the
Regency backdrop of the town bathed
in evening sunlight behind him.

SCENE 162:
EXTERIOR. PALACE PIER. NIGHT
... Alone on the pier, standing out in
the black water from the night façade
of the town, JIMMY lies sleeping in a
deck-chair, his parka over him... as
the music fades, nothing remains but
the noise of the moving sea around him.

The following morning, before Jimmy catches
sight of Ace Face's scooter, there's a small scene
that invokes the atmosphere within Brighton
following the riots.

SCENE 164: EXTERIOR. BRIGHTON. DAY

JIMMY wanders around the seaside
town, now oblivious and indifferent
to the lone MOD [sic]... the
deckchairs stand once more in their
neat rows along the promenade... shop
windows have been replaced, and new
signs and hoardings hang in place
of the previous wreckage of the bank
holiday... holidaymakers doze on the
beaches; once the scene of running
battles and stone-throwing mobs... an
air of quiet calm pervades the town,
as if the riots have never been...

The final clifftop sequence remained largely
unchanged from the scripted version; the original
visualisation carried with it a unique lasting image
from the demise of Ace Face's scooter at the
bottom of Beachy Head.

SCENE 171:
EXTERIOR. BEACH. DAY

The scooter lies half-submerged at
the water's edge, with the incoming
sea gently washing over the wreckage
of the machine in an echo of the
opening sequence of the film... a
polythene bag and a number of blue
pills float on top of the water,
drifting away from the scooter.

While cinemagoers would stay with the final
shot of the scooter's descent and subsequent
destruction, a small addition failed to make it to
the screen. This was more than likely an echo of

the tragic story of Barry Prior who'd fallen off a cliff
near Brighton. This dénouement would probably
have raised more questions than answers.

SCENE 171(A):
INTERIOR. JIMMY'S BEDROOM. DAY

The bare wall of Jimmy's bedroom,
as we last saw it, shorn of posters,
newspaper articles and pictures of
The Who; small pieces of sellotape
are still stuck to the wall; some
attached to the torn edges of
posters, torn wallpaper ripped away
by Jimmy with the posters fluttering
on the wall slightly.

A hand and arm come into shot holding
a cutting from a newspaper; the hand,
which looks like JIMMY's, sticks
the newspaper to the wall and on the
newspaper we read;

'MYSTERY OF MOD'S DEATH DIVE'

We ZOOM further into the newspaper,
as far as the smallest of the small
print in the corner of the article
which reads

'1964'

The image then fades to black, allowing a
montage of black-and-white footage of the
original Mods and Rockers' riots to run over the
closing titles. ●

Proizvodnja:
POLYTEL FILM

THE WHO
Režija:
FRANC RODDAM

Distribucija:
VESNA FILM

QUADROPHENIA

PHIL DANIELS   **LESLIE ASH**   **MARK WINGETT**

Ljudska pravica, Ljubljana

CHAPTER TEN

'WHEN WE FIRST STARTED THE FILM WE HAD NO IDEA THAT THERE MIGHT BE A MOD REVIVAL. WE HOPED THAT WE WOULD CREATE ONE, STYLISTICALLY, AND WE HOPED THAT THERE MIGHT BE LOTS OF LITTLE MODS WANDERING AROUND THE STREETS, AND THAT WOULD OBVIOUSLY INCREASE THE INTEREST OF THE FILM. I THINK OUR INTEREST WAS RIGHT ACROSS THE BOARD – BUT THE MOST OPTIMISTIC WAS THAT WE STARTED THE MOD CULT AGAIN, WHICH WE THOUGHT WOULD BE GREAT FOR THE FILM. THE OTHER PART WAS THAT WE THOUGHT THEY MIGHT BE FIGHTING ON THE BEACH AGAIN – I DON'T THINK ANYBODY REALLY WANTED THAT TO HAPPEN – BUT IT DID OCCUR TO US.'

—FRANC RODDAM

With filming completed, *Quadrophenia*'s precious negatives were safely transported back to the studio to allow the editing process to begin. It had taken under three months to complete *Quadrophenia*, but the post-production work would take the best part of seven months to prepare it for cinema screens.

For a story that relied on its frenetic pace, cohesive editing was vital to secure the film's continuity. Mike Taylor, an editor with a lengthy television CV, was brought in to cut the film. Despite best intentions, Taylor's take on the film wasn't in line with what *Quadrophenia* was trying to achieve.

'He was putting the material together and it was looking terrible,' explained Franc Roddam

to the author in 2012. 'It just wasn't working out. He didn't like the kids – he didn't like the violence or the lusting after the girls. Then I realised two things: one was he didn't like young people because he'd been mugged recently, and he just hated the whole group; he couldn't understand what was going on. He didn't have teenage retro passion in his history. He was cutting all the wrong things. I thought, "This guy's got to go. I'm shooting this great material but he doesn't know how to cut it." So, I would have to recut it. After about two weeks, I had to ask him to leave.'

Clock ticking, Roddam had a chance meeting with *Quadrophenia*'s first scriptwriter, Dave Humphries, and mentioned his dilemma with Taylor. Humphries recommended an editor friend of his named Sean

OPPOSITE: One of a multitude of *Quadrophenia* themed posters.

Barton. Requesting a meeting that night, Roddam was duly impressed with Barton's cutting style and employed him on the spot to assemble the picture. Barton, who'd previously been editing commercials, was in tune with what *Quadrophenia* was aiming for. Working alongside Roddam, the rest of the editing process was smooth. (Despite his minuscule involvement, Mike Taylor would end up receiving a co-editing credit.)

The not unimportant task of putting together the title and end credits became an issue. Ultimately – and purely for financial reasons – some bog-standard yellow typography was used. It served the purpose, but for a film of *Quadrophenia*'s stature, it was a disappointing choice.

'We didn't know much about titling in those days,' reflects Roddam. 'It just looked plain and unsophisticated.'

In contrast, the editing process allowed for a breathtaking piece of synchronicity, a moment where the setting sun at Beachy Head seamlessly morphed into Jimmy's scooter headlight. A detail lost on most who see the picture, but something Roddam would be most proud of. Likewise, a few inconsequential sequences and cutaways were removed, their omission seemingly doing little to hamper the film's continuity. However, others more intimately involved with the film would beg to differ…

As a courtesy, the cast were allowed to see the film as it approached completion. On her first viewing of *Quadrophenia* at a press screening at the Plaza One in Lower Regent Street, Toyah Wilcox claimed that a substantial amount of material had been cut from the finished version. 'I went to see the final cut at the press showing with Sting and

BELOW: The standard UK quad poster.

OPPOSITE: The Japan/Asian variation.

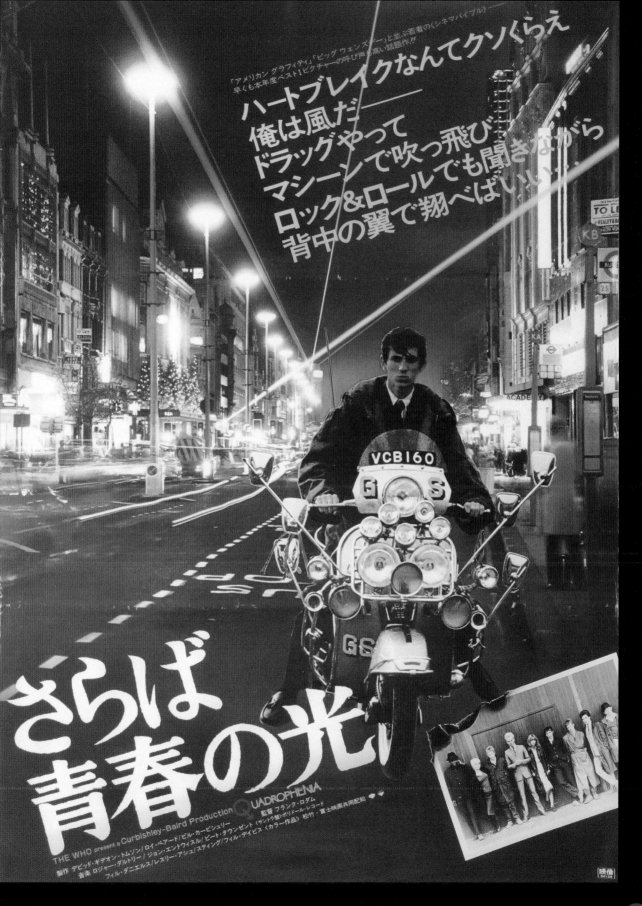

「アメリカン グラフィティ」「ビッグ ウェンズデー」と並ぶ若者の《シネマバイブル》
早くも本年度ベスト1ピクチャーの呼び声も高い話題作!!

ハートブレイクなんてクソくらえ
俺は風だ——
ドラッグやって
マシーンで吹っ飛び
ロック&ロールでも聞きながら
背中の翼で翔べばいい……

さらば
青春の光

QUADROPHENIA

THE WHO present a Curbishley-Baird Production

監督 フランク・ロダム
製作 デビッド・ギデオン・トムソン/ロイ・ベアード/ビル・カービシュリー
音楽 ロジャー・ダルトリー/ジョン・エントウィスル/スティング/フィル・デイビス 〈カラー作品〉 松竹・富士映画共同配給
フィル・ダニエルス/レスリー・アシュ (サントラ盤)ポリドール・レコード

considerable thought. While The Who's original album acted as a more than suitable backdrop, there were moments when nothing from the original score fitted the moving imagery. To this end, Pete Townshend furnished the soundtrack with three new songs: 'Four Faces', 'Get Out And Stay Out' and 'Joker James'. Ultimately, only 'Get Out And Stay Out' featured in the film, although some extra instrumental pieces were included on the soundtrack. Sessions for those new compositions were historic in the story of The Who, featuring as they did new drummer, ex-Small Faces Kenney Jones.

These new tracks were obviously going to enhance the soundtrack album. The Who's original album was still on Polydor's back catalogue, so it was decided to present a brand new collection that reflected the film's content. Over two discs, the release comprised the majority of the music featured in the film, pitching the likes of The Kingsmen's 'Louie Louie'; Booker T. & The M.G.'s 'Green Onions' and The Crystals' 'Da Doo Ron Ron' with *Quadrophenia* tracks (both old and new) by The Who. Initially promised the inclusion of four tracks, The Cross Section (the film's club band) saw only 'Hi-Heel Sneakers' included in the package.

For reasons best known to The Who, it was decided to remix some of the original music and add some new instrumentalism to several tracks. To this end, 'The Real Me' and 'Love, Reign O'er Me' were thoroughly remixed by John Entwistle; 'The Real Me' included a new bass line while 'Love, Reign O'er Me' had a flute playing over the beginning. While Who purists might conclude that these reworkings did little to enhance to the originals, they did serve to distinguish the new release from the 1973 album.

Equally, the presentation of the soundtrack's cover was markedly different to the original album. It featured a colour production shot of a parka-clad Phil Daniels standing at the entrance of the now-iconic Brighton alleyway. Inside, a host of stunning photographs from the film were reproduced on

Gary Shail,' she recalled later, 'and we realised that a lot of our best moments ended up on the cutting-room floor. I was very disappointed. We actually walked out of the cinema halfway through.'

Sadly, with the preservation of seventies film stock being expensive and cumbersome, none of *Quadrophenia*'s edited moments or outtakes would survive the ravages of time. These and other ephemera connected with the film were stored in Elstree Studios for a period of time before a decision to rationalise the property led to the storage material being unceremoniously dumped in skips and landfill. Along with material from many other films, the entirety of *Quadrophenia*'s outtakes, bloopers and off-duty moments were lost for ever. Equally disappointing, John Lydon's original screen test was discarded early on, denying students of popular culture a rare glimpse of the punk icon's first foray into mainstream cinema.

In terms of the synchronisation of the music with the film, the brief was not to make the soundtrack too invasive, so the musical interludes required

the gatefold sleeve and internal packaging. As the spirit of *Quadrophenia* was seemingly tended by the spirit of Pete Meaden, a quote of his – 'Mod living is an aphorism for clean living under difficult circumstances' – was printed on the rear sleeve. In a further tribute to the recently departed Meaden's strong influence on *Quadrophenia*, his two contributions to The High Numbers' oeuvre, the Mod-centric 'I'm The Face' and 'Zoot Suit' were also given space on the soundtrack album.

As furious activity was taking place in the cutting-room suites, Phil Daniels and Ray Winstone found themselves briefly reunited in the cinema version of *Scum*, a film that had gone into production immediately following the *Quadrophenia* shoot, and it would go on to accrue a similar cult following. Within a year, both films were part of a cinema

'MOD LIVING IS AN APHORISM FOR CLEAN LIVING UNDER DIFFICULT CIRCUMSTANCES.'

PETE MEADEN

package: *Quadrophenia* with 'Way of Life' as a tagline; *Scum* with the subtitle 'A Fact of Life'.

A host of associated promotional material was created for *Quadrophenia* with front-of-house stills, posters, press books and a fairly predictable trailer being previewed around the country before the film's release. Elsewhere, some promotional radio spots were produced. One of these featured Alan Lake, husband of Diana Dors. Advertising agent Bertie Nicholas was in charge of coordinating some

ABOVE: By association; *Quadrophenia* and *Scum* make for a powerful double bill in 1979.

ABOVE: The revamped UK soundtrack album.

OPPOSITE: Leslie Ash and Phil Davis display a *Quadrophenia* themed line of attire during late 1979.

of the promotional material. He recently recalled a comical incident in a Covent Garden recording studio: 'We needed a flat, Cockney-attitude voice. Because he was known as an East End character, we brought Alan Lake in. But he was incapable of saying "Quadrophenia" without saying it in an Italian accent. It was incredible, he just couldn't be himself. We just couldn't use him. We ended up getting a guy who was sitting outside the studio to do it.'

Even before the film was ready for its first screening, the synchronicity occurring between *Quadrophenia* and the Mod revival of 1979 was gathering apace. The seeds of this resurgence, which first emerged at the time of *Quadrophenia*'s pre-production, were now starting to germinate on the streets of Britain. The punks were splintering into undefined and fragmentary directions, to be replaced by sharp suits and neat haircuts, and it was obvious that the original protagonists would be forced to take notice. For some it was an embarrassment to revisit their formative days; for others it served to revive long-forgotten careers.

Record companies were quick to jump on the bandwagon and archives were filleted for old photographs and promotional films to accompany re-releases from the Small Faces, The Kinks and the early part of The Who's career. Other bands that had merely flirted with the original Mod scene back in the sixties such as The Creation and The Action were now back in vogue with a late seventies audience.

Similarly, the original Mods' interest in soul, blue beat and ska was now gaining a huge ascendancy. What had been cultish pursuits of the original scene were swiftly carving out a large niche within the Mod's all-encompassing revival. Soon, ska-driven bands such as The Specials, The Beat, The Bodysnatchers, The Selecter and UB40 were fronting their own movement.

Predictably, those eager to make a fast buck were quick to get in on the action. Punk's DIY approach had given freeloaders little scope, but Mod's more conservative wardrobe was ripe for exploitation. Soon shops were stocking a large range of Mod uniforms, of varying degrees of quality. Just months after the punk fashions had fallen out of favour, parkas, button-down shirts, tonic suits and other pieces of apparel were being shipped out to youngsters desperate to buy in to the craze. Whereas the original movement had placed great store in acquiring finely tailored and unique pieces of clothing, the tastes of the new Mods on the block were less particular. Badges – an accessory the original Mods would have royally rejected – were now in. Similarly, cloth patches – many of them crudely boasting the names of their favourite Mod bands – were omnipresent. Additionally, the Union Jack was adopted as a crude fashion accessory for the neophyte and the uninformed. The parka, a utilitarian piece of clothing designed to protect expensive suits from the detritus of scooter riding, was now elevated to a primary fashion accessory. With a large green canvas available to daub any manner of Mod-related graffiti on, the parka's rear was now viewed as an advertising opportunity.

ABOVE: 'Where d'you get those new blue jeans?' Levi's buys in on the *Quadrophenia* buzz.

London's Carnaby Street, long since disavowed of its Swinging Sixties tag, was also caught up in the Mod whirlwind. With no other recognisable landmark in the capital to symbolise the revival, the narrow West London street underwent a heavy resurgence and teemed with Mods from all over Britain – all seemingly on a frenzied mission to gear themselves up with the latest fashions. To mop up this rush of interest, shops such as Carnaby Cavern, Sherries, Merc and Melandi began selling predominately Mod uniforms. Other shops, not carrying the vintage or reputation of the better-known operations, were similarly churning out poorly made costumes that did little more than incur hilarity once they were unwrapped. From the

eye of the hurricane in 1979, it would appear that the whole country had gone Mod crazy.

With the buzz from the streets already causing considerable interest, there were a few tie-ins to help the film along. Levi Jeans had already signed a merchandising deal with the filmmakers and, in advance of the film, had prepared a clutch of promotional adverts advertising their jeans in tandem with the film's release. Utilising imagery of a Levi's-clad Phil Daniels astride his scooter, the adverts would be accompanied by the banner text of 'Quality Never Goes Out Of Style'.

With *Quadrophenia* seemingly a marketable brand, The Who's management went to considerable lengths to protect the reputation of the film from inevitable exploitation. Many were champing at the bit to adorn all manner of items with the film's iconography, so an alliance was made with a top design company to preserve the integrity of *Quadrophenia*. Furthermore, a statement claimed that a line of clothing inspired by the film was about to be produced. 'There's a difference between protecting one's interests and blatantly exploiting the same,' reported a Who Films spokesman in 1979. Despite the announcement and a lavish feature in the *Daily Mirror* featuring Phil Davis and Leslie Ash in Mod gear, only a few heavily priced items surfaced. A fashion show with a *Quadrophenia* theme at London's Lyceum Ballroom did little to advance the clothing range and the project was quietly shelved.

As if the impending release of *Quadrophenia* wasn't enough, The Who's re-emergence into touring during the Spring of 1979 ignited the interest of latter-day Mods, many of them desperate to see first-hand the elder statesmen of the movement. Outside the band's first concert at London's Rainbow Arena on May 2nd, 1979, a sea of green parkas worked its way around the venue.

Off stage, the group were having some unexpectedly personal interactions with their new audience. For The Who's bassist, John Entwistle, this came as something of a shock. Having only briefly flirted with the Modernist lifestyle, he had a lively encounter with a group of parka-clad youths outside his front door in 1979. 'The Mod revival came along and kids were driving around with parkas on scooters,' he recalled in 2002. 'In the meantime, I'd gravitated to a chauffeur-driven Rolls-Royce. I was just about to pull in to the driveway to my house and I couldn't. I'd turned off the road and there was a bunch of Mods sitting on scooters. So my chauffeur beeped his horn a couple of times and they all turned around and went 'fuck off!'… In the end, they moved out of the way as we edged forward. As I was driving past they were screaming abuse at me [saying], 'Fucking old bastard'. A couple of them had Who signs on the back of their jackets. I guess they never found out who I was. All I was doing was trying to get in my bloody driveway.'

Quadrophenia's creator, Pete Townshend, was fairly objective about it all, although he was acutely aware of how central he and The Who were in relation to the re-emergence of the scene. 'I don't think that The Who have got much to do with the Mod revival,' he pointed out to the *Daily Mirror* in 1979. 'I've heard a few of the new Mod bands and they're quite good. They have to be careful not to stand still. We've moved on from what we were doing in the sixties. If you stand in one spot then you're really going backwards as everyone moves on.'

In tandem with The Who's sensational re-emergence, the film's post-production had finally been completed, allowing the first precious print to be struck from the negative. Ironically, for a film that was so embedded in working-class culture, *Quadrophenia*'s first public screening was in Cannes, at the glitzy international film festival. Global deals were vital to the film's extended success and it was given a large platform. Cannes in 1979 had a strong Who theme, with both *Quadrophenia* and the Roger Daltrey-led *McVicar* completed and awaiting distribution. The band and their entourage flew in from their UK tour to put in an impromptu performance on the Côte

d'Azur – their presence propelling the world's press to pay serious attention to The Who's film wing.

Back in the more mundane setting of Britain, the ever-growing Mod community was eagerly awaiting *Quadrophenia*'s release. With marketing then as essential as it is today for selling the product, those responsible for publicity began generating teaser advertisements to promote the film. Press and publicity shots from *Quadrophenia* were already circulating within the national media and music press, and expectations of what to expect were at fever pitch.

◉ 'WE'VE MOVED ON FROM WHAT WE WERE DOING IN THE SIXTIES. IF YOU STAND IN ONE SPOT THEN YOU'RE REALLY GOING BACKWARDS AS EVERYONE MOVES ON.'
PETE TOWNSHEND

The London Weekend Show, a popular youth magazine programme broadcasting to London and the South East, took a look at the burgeoning Mod scene, with *Quadrophenia* at its core. To this end, the show's presenter, Janet Street-Porter, canvassed (mixed) opinion from Mods gathered in Carnaby Street. The view wasn't entirely positive, although it was generally agreed that the synchronicity of *Quadrophenia*'s arrival was quite fortuitous. For some, with the revival dependent on the movement's exclusivity, there were fears that *Quadrophenia* would nationalise what had been up to then a lifestyle shared by a select few.

'*Quadrophenia*'s going to end all that,' complained one Mod to Street-Porter. 'I'm dying to go and see it but it's going to end it all, and we all know it. They're gonna go and see it, come out, buy new parkas, try and get a scooter if they can and end up on pushbikes and end it all.'

Elsewhere, to gauge the all-important opinions of the main protagonists of the Mod revival, several

When the bitterness of youth ends in terror

QUADROPHENIA (Plaza, "X", 115 minutes) puts you eyeball to eyeball with the Mods and Rockers of Britain in 1964.

They were the teenagers, you will remember, whose idea of getting a kick out of life was to put the boot in against each other.

You may think such a subject is not for you, but the film is a magnificent achievement in current British cinema, shatteringly honest in intent and stunningly photographed.

Its theme comes from Pete Townshend and The Who's album, *Quadrophenia*, and here is no nostalgic remembrance of times past but a painfully accurate case history of frustrated adolescence.

The story concerns Jimmy, from a dismal terraced home in London's Shepherd's Bush, who has absolutely nothing in common with the sophisticates of the advertising agency where he works as post-boy and who feels he is living only when he is popping pills and burning up the streets at night on his chromium-plated scooter with his trendily dressed Mod chums.

Being a Mod gives him a sense of identity, even purpose, but it does not please his father who, when not asleep in front of the telly, sneers at him for wanting to shrink his jeans and watch *Ready Steady Go.* His parents are not totally unsympathetic to him : it is just one of those families in which nobody is capable of throwing a bridge across the generation gap.

Jimmy is a kid under increasing pressure.

FILMS

by Richard Barkley

ATTRACTIVE

Around the coffee bars and dance halls there is a girl (Toyah Wilcox) who would gladly be his, but he wants attractive Steph (Leslie Ash) and is suffering feelings of inferiority because he cannot make her interested in him. His best friend Kevin (Raymond Winstone) has become a leather-clad Rocker, and such is the antipathy between the two groups, Jimmy dare not be seen talking to Kevin.

When some Rockers on motorbikes stop to beat up a Mod whose scooter has broken down, the other Mods take revenge by pursuing a lone Rocker who turns out to be Kevin. As they set about him, Jimmy stands back, upset but powerless to help Kevin.

There is more aggression to come, on the seafront at Brighton where Mods and Rockers clash in a riot that spills over amongst the crowds peacefully deck-chaired on the beach, until the police move in and some at least of the rioters pay the penalty of a stiff court fine.

There is nothing commendable about the way these kids live for instant gratification, be it from pep pills, sex, or violence. And the film never tries to say there is.

Under the direction of Franc Roddam, and through Brian Tufano's photography, what you get is the simple statement : there were teenagers like this and this is how it would have looked if you were there. It is like *cinéma verité.* You watch as if an eye-witness to actual events, and it is a chastening experience, a powerful antidote to the sloppy, sentimental movies about the 1960s that are proliferating.

The young cast are superbly natural with Phil Daniels particularly excellent as Jimmy, who finally reaches a point of despair about the way his life is going, a moment when he will either ride his scooter over a cliff, or grow up to become a great big star like Pete Townshend.

* * * * *

Leslie Ash . . . a leading role in Quadrophenia.

private screenings were convened just before the film went on general release. As recounted in Graham Lentz's excellent retrospective of the Modernist scene, *The Influential Factor*, one of these screenings brought together all the new Mod musical entities under one roof. Brian Betteridge, a singer with Mod revivalist band Back To Zero, was one of the lucky few to be handed a ticket to the advance screening. 'At the time in London, the attitude was "It's going to finish the scene, we're doomed",' he commented to Lentz. 'I thought it was a bit "precious" and that any fresh interest is always good, and people might have got into a whole lifetime's worth of stuff just because of that film. We were invited to see it at a special preview in Wardour Street two weeks before it came out. This was quite amusing because The Jam were sitting in front of us and Secret Affair were there. Ian Page and Paul Weller couldn't stand each other and they were studiously trying to avoid each other around the sandwiches before the film.'

Brett 'Buddy' Ascott, drummer with The Chords, was also present at one of these select screenings. 'That was the day The Chords signed to Polydor,' he recalled to the author. 'We got some champagne and [got] really pissed. We went down to the Bijou Cinema Club in Wardour Street and as I wrote in my diary, "Fucking great film. Is it the best I have ever seen?" I thought it was fantastic. Later that day we went back to the Bijou to see if it was on again.'

With the *Quadrophenia* and *The Kids Are Alright* soundtracks already in the shops by the summer of 1979, The Who were on an enormous revival of fortunes, a welcome turnaround given the dark vortex that had followed Keith Moon's death. While the broader, more music-based approach of *The Kids Are Alright* anthology would appeal to numerous territories, the parochial content embedded in *Quadrophenia* would be a harder sell, especially in America where the idiosyncrasies and realism of the film might have challenged Stateside sensibilities. Under the microscope, it was

clear that only Britain could lay claim to an intimate understanding of the Mod lifestyle and yet, for the film to truly succeed commercially, it had to make an impact on America.

As was the literary fashion of the time, a novelisation of *Quadrophenia* was a predictable by-product. The adaptation was written by original Mod Alan Fletcher, the fan who'd originally prompted the film's production and had been signed on as a story consultant. While Fletcher didn't have the benefit of seeing the film, he was given a shooting script to work from, and thus shaped the novel from the original document. 'You will have noticed that in the novel Jimmy rides a Vespa GS but is on a Lambretta Li 150 in the film,' he reported to *Quadrophenia* fan Alan Shine. 'I had in mind the line out of one of Pete's original songs on the album ("I've Had Enough")… "I ride a GS Scooter with my hair cut neat…" so a Vespa it was in the novel.'

OPPOSITE: Mixed messages from the *London Evening News*' Richard Barkley.

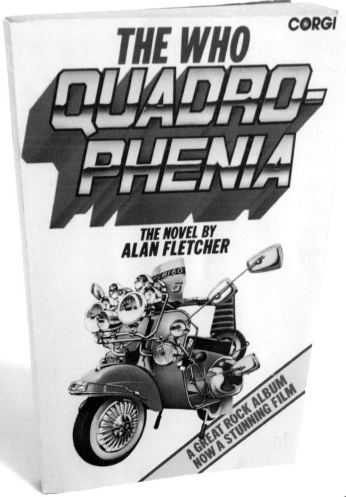

CORGI

THE WHO QUADRO-PHENIA

THE NOVEL BY ALAN FLETCHER

A GREAT ROCK ALBUM NOW A STUNNING FILM

SIXTIESPHENIA – but

THE FILM

Reviewed by Felix Barker

JUST about everything I dislike is to be found in Quadrophenia (X, Plaza 1). The music is so loud and raucous that there should be a free issue of ear-plugs with every ticket.

The film reeks with mindless violence. Without any meaning in their lives, the characters constantly take refuge in noisy vulgarity.

The first word spoken consists of four letters starting with "f", and if all the times the word is used were expurgated, the film would be about half its length.

Sex is treated as cattle market traffic, with an explicit scene of a pair of teenagers coupling standing up in a Brighton alley.

In the face of all this, why do I consider Quadrophenia one of the best films to have been made in Britain for a very long time?

Quite simply because it is utterly realistic — an uncompromisingly honest picture of a way of life that existed in the early 1960s.

In the age of Mods and the Rockers, and of London Wild Ones on scooters

'It reeks with mindless violence but is utterly realistic about 60s life'

festooned with pennants and headlamps, the story puts on celluloid once and for all the mood of a frustrated younger generation.

The young director and part-author, Franc Roddam, has dug back into the recent past to re-create a time when, gulping down "blues," hepped - up, young people created riots for lack of anything better to do.

Values

For this to have any values, you can't wear kid gloves. Roddam puts on knuckle-dusters.

His hero — or rather, anti-hero—is an ingratiating weazie-faced kid (Phil Daniels) who has drifted listlessly into a job of office dogsbody in an advertising agency.

Like all his fellow layabouts, his interests are confined to Mod-ish snazzy clothes, roaring scooters, and violent punch-ups with their rival leather-clad Rockers.

Sex is something to be taken and performed without affection like the pep pills. Immediate gratification is the only antidote to boredom.

Parties

It is a terrible picture, and we see its manifestations in middle-class suburban parties wrecked by surly gatecrashers, and a mass Mods v Rockers clash at Brighton which recreates the actual events of the period.

Except for Daniels, who is absolutely frustrated, the camera does not stay long on anyone but the smooth, faintly sinister good-looker, seen sitting emerges from the woodwork.

So does pretty Leslie Ash as the boy-swapping girl she is so pure... that her anguished... It seems as if ...things is going back...

Realism

The genesis of Quadrophenia (named after The Who's double album of the same name) is as strange as the title.

Based on the 1972 album by rock group, the film uses about seven of the "concept" numbers and uses them as background "commentaries" on the action scenes.

It's an odd way to achieve realism, but it works.

British films with cockney accents rarely take off in America but I gather this one has overcome Transatlantic prejudice and is to be widely shown there.

So apart from anything else are going to make money out of washing yesterday's dirty linen in public

---

Despite its formulaic cover and cheesy back-cover blurb, Fletcher's novel expanded well beyond the boundaries of the script, examining much of what is merely glimpsed at in the film. What gave the novel a solid credibility was the involvement of Pete Townshend, who personally assisted Fletcher with several passages in the novel, sections that he'd later regret were not in the film – not least Jimmy's schizophrenia and mood swings. In Fletcher's book, these elements assumed a much deeper reality than in the film.

The free hand employed in the novel gave a greater prominence to several themes denied a place in the film. The sequence below, from the tail end of the story, describes Jimmy falling off the cliff, a scenario that, according to Franc Roddam, was to form the original ending of the film.

THIS SPREAD AND NEXT: *Quadrophenia* was reviewed in all of Britain's newspapers.

'At first it was just the release of pressure beneath my feet, my tired weary feet, then it was the actual weight of my legs hanging from my waist somehow. I moved to the edge and the ribbon of white chalk close to the edge suddenly widened and I went over. I was slow, falling slowly, dropping down the side of the chalk cliff, nearer to the sea and its sound. It changed colour as I fell. There was no noise. No sound at all, anywhere. But I knew it was real. I was falling in the thin rain, moving towards the sea. It felt warm. Comforting deep, folding me in, closing over me. I sank in its greenness, and then rose, slowly still, breaking the surface and back in the light and the gentle rain. I saw something glinting and strange in the distance, through the mist, and I was swimming towards it. The scooter. It floated on the water, on its side, one chrome breast washed by the waves. I touched it, feeling along the lines, rubbing the chrome with my fingers. Then the tide swelled and took it away, into the mist. I lost sight of it.'

WHAT AN EAR-BASHING AGGRO SHOW

NEW FILMS by Arthur Thirkell

BACK in the swinging Sixties the mindless, moronic activities of teenage gangs called Mods and Rockers polluted Britain.

The Mods dressed nattily and drove around on customised scooters. The Rockers wore leather gear, and roared about on motor bikes.

On Bank Holidays they confronted each other in pitched battles at seaside resorts.

QUADROPHENIA (X, Plaza I) is a romanticised view of the pimply teara-ways. It is a far from pleasant film, filled with a collection of characters so grotty they made me itch.

The music of The Who provides the raucous background. The simplistic moralising of Pete Townshend, their leader, is everywhere.

It was Townshend, you may remember, who composed the rock opera "Tommy", the tale of a deaf, dumb and blind boy, who became a genius.

The main character in "Quadrophenia" also doesn't have much sense.

To use the vernacular of the film, Jimmy (Phil Daniels) didn't have a chance in life, did he?

What with rotten bosses and dozy parents what else is there in life but tatty birds, bikes, drugs and punch-ups?

You just gotta kick a geezer in the 'ead before he puts the boot in you.

The film, distinguished by brilliant photography, comes perilously close to glorifying the foul-mouthed punks.

Depressing, innit?

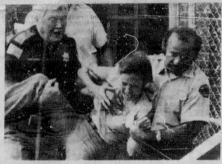

new films   by virginia dignam

Dark vision of raw youth

BASED ON Peter Townshend's original idea. Quadrophenia (X, Plaza I) with The Who, centres around confrontation between mods and rockers, in the early 60s.

Like the Capulets and the Montagues of old, mods and rockers are sworn enemies, their rigid codes of behaviour, modes of dress and style so different that when they meet they clash.

We follow Jimmy (Phil Daniels) a young mod in his late teens.

By day Jimmy is a post boy at a large advertising agency, by night he is a mod and a pill-head swallowing "uppers, downers, French-blues," anything he can either buy or steal to make him feel good.

Frustrated and inarticulate, caught between the sharp practices at work and the family where his inner needs are answered with blows, Jimmy prefers the volatile world of the mods.

Musical directors John Ent-whistle, Pete Townshend and Roger Daltrey have added many new numbers to the original Quadrophenia album made in 1973, numbers which they say will communicate, especially to young audiences, a vibrant sense of identification.

There are some raw edges and raw language in "Quadrophenia" as well as anger despair and violence, so that it says much for the central performance of Phil Daniels that he evokes sympathy and compassion with his volcanic and destructive out-bursts.

Is he victim or victimiser, predator or prey? Director Franc Roddam without getting either frenetic or sentimental allows Jimmy's internal struggle to

dominate even scenes of murderous confrontation, but this is still a dark, nihilistic vision of youth.

A vision of turmoil and disintegration, where the rituals, practical jokes and horseplay have deteriorated into crippling brutality and hostility.

During a battle for unionisation at a textile plant, Norma Rae (SALLY FIELD) feels the force of "law and order."

Despite the differences in approach, Fletcher's novelised version of the film went on to sell over 90,000 copies as a Corgi paperback. Nonetheless, despite the sales figures, the book did not survive to reprint, ensuring that only rarely do original copies come up for sale, and then at a hefty price.

With everything in place, a date was finally set for the film's general release. *Quadrophenia* was one of forty-nine British films made in 1978, a time when cinema was a hugely disparate landscape. Homespun films with an overtly British theme had few highlights: *Monty Python's Life of Brian*, *Yanks* and *Yesterday's Hero* were barely representative of the country that spawned them. Alan Clarke's long-delayed film version of *Scum* finally receive a cinema release in September 1979 and, along with *Quadrophenia*, became one of the most pertinent pictures of the year.

While the media had had their first exposure to *Quadrophenia* back in Cannes and at other specially appointed venues during the summer of 1979, the all-important world premiere was scheduled to take place at the Plaza 1 cinema complex on Lower Regent Street, situated just off London's Piccadilly Circus on Thursday, August 16th, 1979 ('7.15 p.m. for 8.00 p.m.').

While the Plaza was some distance from the more usual Leicester Square film-premiere location, the film was nonetheless afforded the red-carpet treatment. Aiding the atmosphere, a contingent from the Scooter Club of Great Britain arrived on scooters, forming a protective phalanx to usher in the guests (and effectively blocking off the street).

The entire cast turned up, along with members of The Who and their entourage, and everyone was afforded a chance to don their glad rags for

'Mods' Return As 'Quadrophenia' Spotlights Britain's Youth Cults

Old Mods

Ted Whitehead

Quadrophenia (Plaza 1)

Quadrophenia (X) is a splendid wallow in ferocious nostalgia: 1963 teenagers stuck in dead-end jobs, lumbered with beaten parents, and trapped in the suffocating British class structure; relieve their frustrations and escape their political identity by assuming the roles of Mods or Rockers, and beat each other up on Brighton beach. The general atmosphere of the early Sixties is accurately established, apart from a few prochronisms designed presumably to avoid alienating the contemporary youth audiences. The political consciousness is nonexistent, but then the political ignorance of the youth of the time was one of the major problems (if you like democracy). That problem is still with us. So is sex.

It's an odd thing that most analysts of the mass youth culture will constantly harp on bad environment, boring jobs and dull parents, but fastidiously avoid the problem of sex. Yet sex lurks in almost every frame of *Quadrophenia*. It's the propelling force of the narrative. The interesting thing is that it's the men who, for all their brash and violent chauvinism, cling to the concepts of True Love and Monogamy, while it's the girls who want a quick bang in the back alley and, goodbye forever.

Parents are quickly defined as hypocritical champions of a sterile morality. Mother (Kim Neve) pleads with Father (Michael Elphick) for a bit of sex, and then screams hysterically at her son (Phil Daniels) for his ritual escape to Brighton at the week end. The Son, Jimmy, is in love – whatever that means – with Stephanie (Leslie Ash, well-cast for her look of virginal innocence). They are perfectly matched, as he is the mailboy in an advertising agency while she is the checkout girl in a supermarket. There should be no problem for these two young servants of capitalism. Except that this is the early Sixties.

Jimmy is a Mod, worshipping the style and mood personified by the music of The Who, deeply sceptical about the superiority of his superiors. His life centres around the Brighton confrontations with the nasty greasy Rockers, and his pursuit of Stephanie. There are some splendidly orchestrated scenes of violence in the streets and on the Beach as the rivals collide, intercut with flashes of Jimmy and Stephanie at it in a back alley. But when Jimmy is later arrested, Stephanie transfers her affections to another member of the gang; and when Jimmy complains, she says: 'We had it off together but it doesn't mean anything, does it?' Instantly the young romantic contemplates suicide.

Punks will be curious about these early gestures towards anarchism. So, I imagine, will be the more conventional young who are still struggling with the strictures of monogamy and all that. The film is directed with a beautifully detailed naturalism by Franc Roddam, considerably helped by the satirical chorus of songs from The Who. Patsy Pollock has cast the film with lots of exciting and unfamiliar British actors who deserve to become very familiar. The treatment of nudity is unduly coy – penises peeping through bathwater – but the dialogue is rich in authentic obscenities. This Who film is as abrasive as most of the Who music. I hope it has the same kind of success.

London, Aug. 21.

History may or may not be repeating, but suddenly the media are alive again with stories of latter-day "Mods," "Rockers," and "Teddy boys" whose forerunners symbolized mindless violence in the 1950s and '60s.

Coincidental with the apparent revival was last week's London world premiere of "Quadrophenia," based on an album by The Who rock band, which harks back to the mod-rocker English subculture of the '60s. Local critics hailed its "realism" and a few rated it a landmark of British filmmaking.

What must be pondered in and out of the trade is whether, as "Quadrophenia" release fans out, pic may prove as provocative around Britain as Paramount's "Warriors" seemingly was in the US.

"Quadrophenia's" preem performance Thursday night (16) apparently had an overrun of the new "Mods," whose presence, as noted by one tabloid, "was proof that the Mod youth cult is back in business."

If by that is meant the real terrifying article, there appears to be some evidence on the basis of recent, prominently-played assaults on innocent bystanders by "vicious" youths. In one such, a man was fatally injured from repeated kicks to the head. In another, two teenagers were in critical condition from switchblade knife wounds perpetrated by what the papers described as "teddy boys." Both latenight incidents occurred on the London subway.

Postwar youth cults in England seem to emerge periodically, the last having been the recent and colorful Punks with their way-out hairstyles and costuming, a contrived effect that smacked of violent aggression. Instead, the Punks proved relatively tame.

The Teddies (or Teds) of the '50s sported drainpipe trousers and sleek, Tony Curtis hairdos. The later Mods of the early '60s affected a similar style, while the Rockers wheeled around on motorbikes dressed in leather.

Mod-Rocker clashes, apparently over nothing more disputatious than differing life styles, terrorized many a seaside resort over long holiday weekends. That short but notorious period is what "Quadrophenia" vividly recalls. The film has been acquired for U.S. playoff by World-Northal.

what was labelled a 'World Gala Premiere'. Some of the other stardust present that night were Boomtown Rats' star Bob Geldof and his wife Paula Yates, and the former British heavyweight boxer Billy Walker, who arrived with Anna Bergman, the 29-year-old daughter of Swedish film director, Ingmar Bergman. One amusing story concerned Pete Townshend, whose casual attire caused one crusty commissionaire to query his attendance at the VIP event.

Commanding the fashion stakes in a cream silk tuxedo and matching scarf she'd bought in King's Road, Leslie Ash caught the interest of the photographers camped outside the cinema. Phil Daniels was similarly of interest to the camera lens, although he'd decided to appear in non-Mod gear. Furthermore, his hair had grown several inches from the carefully styled bangs that accompanied his passage through the film. Part-way through filming the equally cultish *Breaking Glass* with Hazel O'Connor and *Quadrophenia* co-star Mark Wingett, Daniels was already outgrowing any typecasting *Quadrophenia* may have suggested.

At last, the cast could view the finished product – for some, their first exposure to the film. With a hugely partisan audience present, each cast member was brought to the stage. While it was exciting to see their profiles blown up on the big screen, some found the experience difficult to process. Despite her intimate scene with Phil Daniels in the alleyway being captured in one, relatively brief take, Leslie Ash found the viewing excruciating. 'I know it's my work and I had to do it,' she explained to the *Daily Mirror*. 'But when I saw the film in the cinema I could not watch that scene.'

The press had been afforded several private screenings of the film and timed their responses in tandem with the premiere. The media then as opinionated as it is today, there was always a risk that some journalists might base their reviews on *Quadrophenia*'s more challenging scenes, rather than its overall merits. The Britain of 1979, still reeling from the effects of strikes and disharmony, and

Rocking along with the mods

with a predominantly right-wing media, was out to avenge anything deemed to be anti-establishment. Dissent and rioting were polarising the nation, and to the cynical and ignorant, *Quadrophenia* may well have appeared apologetic to these elements.

Of all the popular media, one would have expected the *Daily Mirror*, the so-called mouthpiece of the British working class, to have championed the film. However, their (unknown) critic was decidedly lukewarm: '*Quadrophenia* takes a long time to say very little about the Mods and Rockers of 1964,' ran the review. 'It will mainly appeal to past and present members of those rival youth gangs.'

So, it was with some surprise, that the right-leaning *Daily Express* positively gushed. Under the headline 'Mods and Rockers – It's Musical Mayhem', the *Express*'s review screamed: 'A brilliant exposition of the Mods and Rockers phenomenon of the sixties. Directed with a sharp eye for detail by Franc Roddam, it examines the lifestyles of the youths in dead-end jobs who find a release from their frustrations by joining one of the factions that tear about either on motorbikes or scooters and beating up any member of the other lot they come across.'

The *Express*'s Sunday edition was equally ecstatic: 'When the bitterness of youth ends in terror, *Quadrophenia* puts you eyeball to eyeball

with the Mods and Rockers of Britain in 1964. It's a chastening experience, a powerful antidote to the sloppy sentimental movies about the sixties that are proliferating.'

In contrast, the *London Evening News* disliked the film. Its critic, 51-year-old Felix Barker, was clearly out of touch with the film's aims. 'It reeks with mindless violence but is utterly realistic about sixties life,' he spat. 'Just about everything I dislike is to be found in *Quadrophenia*... It is a terrible picture, and we see its manifestation in a middle-class suburban party wrecked by surly gatecrashers.'

The *Financial Times*, its fiscally-minded readership not normally disposed to the fortunes of British cult movements, was surprisingly optimistic about the film's ambitions: 'One of the most exultantly off-beat British films I can remember,' wrote cinema critic Nigel Andrews. '*Quadrophenia* reaches out a grimy hand and hauls you inside the characters' minds and culture. It's fairly squalid in there, but it's also funny and unpredictable and insidiously intoxicating.' Satirical magazine *The Spectator* was also unequivocal in its praise, describing it as 'a splendid wallow in ferocious nostalgia'.

The film received welcome media exposure with a feature on the BBC's film-related show, *Talking Pictures*. The programme-makers had been granted rare access to the *Quadrophenia* film set the previous year and devoted a large part of their first edition on September 2nd, 1979, to discuss the film with cast and crew.

Predictably, the street-wise music papers were far more in touch with the ambitions of the film. Both the hugely influential *Melody Maker* and *NME* devoted significant column space to heap praise on the film. *NME*'s Neil Spencer was effusive: 'Like a Mod on speed, let's not hang about: *Quadrophenia* is not simply the best film of '79, but probably the best British rock film ever… It is simply brilliant.' *Sounds*, another popular music paper of the period, was perhaps the most enthusiastic, allowing the larger-than-life reporter Garry Bushell a full-page to gush lovingly about the film.

'Brighton '64 and a proud, rowdy mob dominate the sea-front revelling in a white riot, a riot of their own… That's just one of the amazing authentic scenes from *Quadrophenia* OUT NOW. A celluloid slice of a week in the life of West London Mods way back when; their sex, drugs, fights, clothes, transport and lifestyle – and in particular one Mod, Jimmy for whom the Brighton riots are a turning point in his fast-developing, drug-fuelled identity crisis… Director Franc Roddam has captured the spirit of the era. Phil Daniels is cast perfectly as the anti-hero. His scene with Steph (Leslie Ash) will stain sheets for years to come… The film of the year for the movement of the moment.'

The media interest gave *Quadrophenia* a huge push around its initial release. Taking in a cool £36,000 in its first week, by the end of the year it had become the UK's eighth most successful picture – no mean feat given that its X-rating excluded a large chunk of its target audience.

Of course, it was clear that, despite the positive reaction at street level to the film in the UK, it was in America where the serious money could be made. The Who's American tour was already selling out huge stadiums and arenas, and manager Bill Curbishley had hit upon a brilliant piece of synchronicity by previewing a trailer of *Quadrophenia* prior to The Who's Stateside performances that summer. The tour, which included a five-night residency at New York's cavernous Madison Square Garden in September, ensured that *Quadrophenia* received the highest possible level of advance publicity.

Once the film hit the screens, the bulk of the US media, perhaps more hard-nosed than their British cousins, appeared to like the film. In particular, the heavyweight *New York Times* appeared upbeat about the film. 'This is a dramatic film,' ran the review. 'One that's gritty and ragged and sometimes quite beautiful. It happens to incorporate rock songs, and to be saddled with a silly title. Though it's by no means a movie for everyone, *Quadrophenia* is something very special. It demands – and deserves – some special allowances. But Mr. Roddam is as concerned with the general experience of adolescence as he is with these particular groups of people. And he is able, in recreating the seaside riots between these rival gangs, to capture a fierce, dizzying excitement that epitomizes a kind of youthful extreme. Jimmy, who is so electrified by his new identity as a Mod that he makes a quick, thrilling sexual conquest while the fighting is going on, may never again feel so fully at the height of his powers. *Quadrophenia* fills the moment with equal elements of regret and celebration.'

Back in the UK, a more uniform response was occurring where it really mattered – on the streets. Thousands and thousands of youngsters, some not even born when the events took place in 1964, were flocking to cinemas around Britain to thrill in this remarkable Mod odyssey. Others were desperate to replicate much of what they saw in the film. They'd soon get the chance. ●

OPPOSITE: An American poster for *Quadrophenia*.

QUADROPHENIA THE MOVIE   ...a trip that will wake you up and shake you up

QUADROPHENIA THE MOVIE   ...a pocketfull of dreams was their way of life

QUADROPHENIA THE MOVIE   ...a condition of today

QUADROPHENIA THE MOVIE   ...produced by 'The Who'

QUADROPHENIA

THE WHO FILMS Present A CURBISHLEY BAIRD PRODUCTION QUADROPHENIA
Musical Directors ROGER DALTREY • JOHN ENTWISTLE • PETE TOWNSHEND
Screenplay by DAVE HUMPHRIES • MARTIN STELLMAN • FRANC RODDAM • Produced by ROY BAIRD & BILL CURBISHLEY
Directed by FRANC RODDAM • A POLYTEL FILM • DOLBY STEREO ™

RELEASED BY W RLD NORTHAL CORPORATION

MUSIC FROM THE SOUNDTRACK AVAILABLE ON POLYDOR RECORDS AND TAPES

STYLE A   QUADROPHENIA

Here by the sea and sand

A symposium on the album and film

QUADROPHENIA

Sponsored by the Centre for Modernist Studies, University of Sussex Co-sponsored by the Centre for Visual Fields and the Centre for Research into Childhood and Youth, University of Sussex

University of Sussex ◉ 10–11 July 2014

Keynote Speaker: **James Wood** (Harvard University, The New Yorker)

With the participation of **Franc Roddam** (Director, Quadrophenia)

US
University of Sussex

More information on registration and programme available at
herebytheseaandsand.wordpress.com
or email quadrophenia.symposium@gmail.com

CHAPTER ELEVEN

'"MOD" IS A SHORTER WORD FOR "YOUNG, BEAUTIFUL AND STUPID" – WE'VE ALL BEEN THERE.'

—PETE TOWNSHEND

QFollowing months of feverish expectation, *Quadrophenia* began its journey around the country. Exploding over the nation's screens in a blizzard of publicity, the adventures of Jimmy and his companions sent the Mod revival into overdrive. More than any other factor, *Quadrophenia* served to nationalise the Mod message. With the revival at its peak, even the heavyweight Sunday press got involved, with the *Observer*'s magazine of September 2nd, 1979, devoting its front cover and main feature to the resurgence.

While punk had been restricted to mainly urban areas, Mod was igniting interest in places not normally receptive to revivalist movements. By the autumn of 1979, it appeared that the whole country had gone Mod crazy.

'It was massive,' reflects Michael W. Salter, author of *Punks on Scooters: The Bristol Mod Revival, 1979–1985*. 'In Bristol, you'd walk into the city centre at weekends and there'd be a sea of green parkas everywhere. Even the punks were wearing them over their punk gear. For us it was the holy trinity; the scooters, the music and the fashion. We were looking for the next thing to come along, and we were only too happy that the thing that came along had scooters as transport.'

With clothes and music caught up in the revival, interest in scooters was similarly elevated by the Mod resurgence. Following the tempestuous years of the mid-sixties, scooter clubs across the UK were largely the torch carriers for the movement. Dorset's Modrapheniacs scooter club was one of the few organisations operating in the South of England before the revival took hold. The club had provided scooters and extras for *Quadrophenia*'s filming in September 1978, but nothing prepared them for the reaction the film generated.

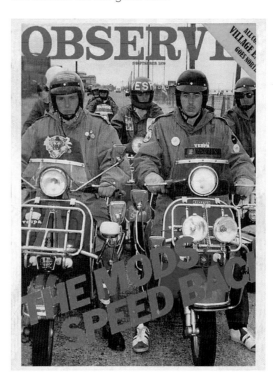

OPPOSITE: *Quadrophenia* goes to college; the film gets the symposium treatment at Sussex University in 2014.

LEFT: The heavyweight media gets serious on the Mod revival, *The Observer*, September 2nd, 1979.

THE JAM

JAM PACT
SPRING TOUR 1979

OFFICIAL BOOKLET

Tour Dates

Coventry, 1978
Pic: Denis O'Regan

4th May, 1979	SHEFFIELD	University
5th	SHEFFIELD	University
6th	NEWCASTLE	City Hall
8th	SALFORD	University
10th	LONDON	Rainbow
11th	LONDON	Rainbow
12th	LOUGHBOROUGH	Auditorium
14th	EXETER	University
15th	LIVERPOOL	University
16th	LIVERPOOL	University
18th	GLASGOW	Strathclyde University
19th	GLASGOW	Strathclyde University
21st	BRISTOL	Coulston Hall
22nd	BIRMINGHAM	Odeon
24th	PORTSMOUTH	Guildhall

BEAT SURRENDER '82

ABOVE: Jam on it: *Quadrophenia*'s success was helped no end by the success of Paul Weller and The Jam during the late seventies/early eighties.

'Prior to *Quadrophenia* coming out, we were a very isolated group in Dorset,' says club founder Rob Williams. 'We would probably get a maximum of about twenty on a Sunday ride-out, and that was from across the county; that was as many as we could muster. Once the film was released, the club swelled to over a hundred members. It just went nuts after that. In fact, there were so many people trying to join the club it got out of hand, and quite a few other clubs sprang up as a result.'

Sitting uneasily at the head of this revitalised movement was Paul Weller and The Jam, during 1979 on a major high with their *Setting Sons* album. Their nationwide success had dovetailed with *Quadrophenia*'s release and they were swiftly anointed (whether they liked it or not) as kings of the Mod revival. Despite a clutch of Top 20 singles that had more than hinted at their sixties influences, it was the group's late 1978 album *All Mod Cons* that sharply demarked the band's Modernist leanings, above and beyond any new wave posturing.

Relentless touring around the UK had transported the Jam's Mod-infused sound (and sartorial style) to the four corners of Britain, sweeping up thousands of disaffected youth in its wake. With Mod an attractive alternative to dismal seventies British culture, many were eager to emulate Weller and Co.'s dress sense and abrasive personas. Fused with the ferocity of punk, Weller's lyrics were drawn from the harsh landscape of an austere Britain, one that was eternally bleak, poor and without hope. The Winter of Discontent was soon to morph into Margaret Thatcher's reign, and music was one of the few beacons of light around.

Although Weller would never have admitted it, the landscape that underpinned Jimmy's tale of woe in *Quadrophenia* resonated sharply with much of what the singer was writing about. But, ever the individualist, Paul Weller had little interest in aligning himself with the wave of nostalgia that was breaking out over the country. While clearly in awe of the original movement, Weller wasn't entirely in tune with the craze status of the Mod revival, nor the uniformity of a large part of his audience. 'I used to be on stage singing all these songs about being an individual,' Weller would reflect many years later. 'All I could see in front of me was a sea of green parkas.'

Regardless that The Jam had absolutely no involvement with *Quadrophenia* and that Weller was lukewarm about its authenticity, the similarities they appeared to share meant they were lumped together. Weller's sensibility, honed by years of sharp dedication to the Mod ethic, found *Quadrophenia*'s broader manifesto a difficult pill to swallow. Never comfortable name-checking the film, when I pushed him for an opinion on the picture's merits in 1999, he dismissed it curtly as 'awful', principally on account of its 'lack of detail' – an obsessive quality that was essential to a purist such as Weller.

Others, too, would start to pick holes in *Quadrophenia* as the years passed, but not just in its stylistic contrasts. Because of the mania the film generated, it was evident that, with many studiously examining every frame of the picture, some inconsistencies were bound to come to the surface. No one, not least the filmmakers, expected the film to be put under such a powerful microscope, and a quirky little movement soon gathered momentum in which fans (and critics) were swift to cite the continuity errors. In reality, very few cult films escape some level of compulsive examination, and although most of these minor inconsistencies shoot past in the blink of an eye, they have formed the basis of some lively conversation over the years – DVD technology only serving to fuel this obsession further.

Perversely, these inconsequential bloopers are an oblique testament to the film's enduring popularity. Listed below are several of the continuity errors that, to this day, provoke eyebrows to raise high above the anorak hood when they are mentioned. For the rest of us? Well, we just try to enjoy the film…

- When Jimmy gives Steph a lift along the Goldhawk Road, they pass a Mk3 Ford Cortina. These were not produced until the mid-seventies. In addition, Jimmy's gear changing of his scooter was heavily out of kilter with what was normally expected on a straight road in traffic (but hey, he was on the back of a film trailer!).

- When Jimmy greets Steph in her supermarket workplace, she holds up a tin of Cadbury's Drinking Chocolate – of the seventies variety.

- During the Kitchener Road party scene, Jimmy puts on the record of 'My Generation' on a radiogram. Above is a copy of The Who's US compilation album containing the LPs *A Quick One* and *The Who Sell Out*. This album wasn't released until years after the riots of 1964. It has also been argued that 'My Generation' was out of kilter, given that it was released in October 1965.

- The Mods' pursuance of the Rockers after the beating-up of the hapless Spider and his girlfriend mysteriously finds John Altman's character on the back of a scooter leaving the club. Moments later, he is seen dancing at the premises he's just left.

- When Jimmy visits the scrapyard to obtain the necessary information on where to purchase some drugs, some of the cars rotting away in the yard are seventies models.

- When Jimmy emerges from his parent's shed, a high-speed train rushes past – these were not in operation until the seventies.

- Similarly, eagle-eyed trainspotters who recognised Paddington station as the site for Jimmy's departure to Brighton would note that no train leaves the West London station for the South Coast.

- Jimmy's clifftop ride: apart from the aforementioned tyre tracks seared into the early morning dew, his scooter initially sports a fly screen, then it momentarily disappears, and then it returns a few seconds later. Furthermore, when the scooter flies off the cliff you can see the shadow of the helicopter filming the scene.

There are other minor inconsistencies, but only those with a maniacal attention to detail appear keen to dig even further. For Franc Roddam, these rather trifling issues prompt a mixture of hilarity and frustration. 'When I did my first ever talk at the Lincoln Center in Manhattan,' he told the website heyuguys.co.uk, 'there were 600 people in the audience. They saw the film and afterwards I was waiting for the questions, wondering if someone was going to say something wonderful to me. One guy says to me, "So I noticed there were two yellow lines on the side of the road but yellow lines didn't come out until 1965, but this is supposed to be '64." So I was thinking, "This is supposed to be my moment," so out of the blue the line came into my head: "What are you, some kind of fucking traffic warden?"'

If these observations were an example of people taking things a little too far, others were inspired to re-enact some of the action in the film for real. Predictably, the confrontational aspect of *Quadrophenia* served to lure many who were eager to act out some of the riot scenes for their own gratification. The 1980 Spring Bank Holiday certainly managed to upstage the rioting in the film, especially in Brighton, where many local residents were totally unprepared for the scenes of violence that returned to their city for the first time since 1964.

ABOVE: Demand was such that Mod uniforms as worn in *Quadrophenia* were readily available in the Mod citadel, Carnaby Street.

'THE ONLY REASON THEY COME HERE IS BECAUSE OF THAT FILM *QUADROPHENIA*.'
'FRIX – THE SOUTHERN SKIN'

The following year saw events escalate even higher. The May Bank Holiday of 1981 saw over 300 Mods engaged in a pitched battle on Brighton seafront, not with Rockers, but with their nemesis, the newly reactivated skinheads who'd decreed that the new breed of Mods was fair game. Tensions had been bubbling for some months between the two tribes, and, while the Mod revival had slowly begun to lose some of its craze status, there were still many who dutifully followed the May Day trail to Brighton, geared up for a weekend of chaos.

'Word is out that a load of Mods from Scarborough are coming down here,' reported 'Frix – the Southern Skin' to the *Argus* newspaper's evening edition. 'The only reason they come here is because of that film *Quadrophenia*. All these young kids just copied it to follow the trend. They

DAILY STAR

BOOT GOES IN FOR EASTER

TUESDAY, APRIL 8th, 1980   8p   (10p C.I.s, Eire)   Printed in London

Carter breaks it off with Iran

UNITED STATES President Jimmy Carter last night broke off diplomatic relations with Iran.

And he ordered all 35 Iranian diplomats in the United States to be kicked out.

And Carter's get-tough move in the hostages crisis didn't end there.

He said the States would also be bringing in biting economic sanctions against the Teheran government. This meant a near-complete end to any trading with Iran.

His bombshell decisions came after Iran's Ayatollah Khomeni announced that militant Moslems would retain control of the 50 remaining American hostages in Teheran.

Links

President Carter reached his tough verdicts after day-long meetings with his foreign-policy experts.

He decided the crisis had gone on long enough.

So out went his orders to break all diplomatic links, and to boot out Iranian diplomats by 5 a.m. tomorrow.

State officials said many diplomats had already left the country, but eight requested political asylum.

The President said Iran was guilty of "continued and outrageous illegal holding of the hostages."

He also said Iranian assets, frozen in the United States soon after the hostages were seized on November 4, would be examined with the aim of possibly paying off hostages' claims against the Iranian Government.

And President Carter warned: "Other action may be necessary if these steps do not produce the prompt release of the hostages."

Hostages' plight — Page 4.

Ugly face of Easter at Southend . . . a youth gets a kicking   Picture MARK BOURDILLON

MODS AND WRECKERS!

by HUGH WHITTOW

THE BOOT went in all around Britain yesterday as skinheads, Mods and Rockers went on a seaside Bank Holiday rampage.

Ugly scenes like this sent holidaymakers scattering in terror at a string of resorts.

At Southend over 1,000 skinheads ran amok after foiling a police plan to run them out of town.

Beaten up

They were herded on to two special trains back to London—but jumped off just outside the resort after the train drivers refused to carry on.

Within an hour hundreds were marauding along the seafront again spreading violence and terror.

Two Press photographers were beaten up and thrown in the sea—one losing cameras worth £2,000.

Millwall football fans in town for their team's match with Southend had to be escorted to their trains by police with dogs to prevent clashes with skinheads.

One skinhead, who had cut off the top of his finger when he jumped off a train, said: "I'm bleeding bad

Turn to Page 4

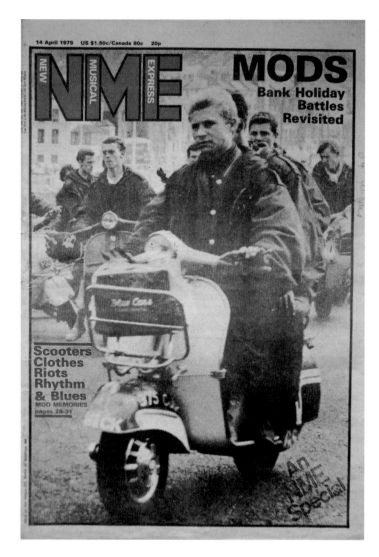

ABOVE: While cautious of the Mod revival, Britain's most prickly music paper, the *NME*, gave the movement blanket coverage in their April 14th, 1979 edition.

and then set fire to Brighton's Volks Electric Railway station (the miniature railway ran along the seafront and was a popular family spot).

This act of vandalism prompted a baton charge by police, sending over 300 Mods running back along the length of Madeira Drive to a grassed area where a barricade had been set up. Effectively hemmed in, police shouted orders through a megaphone that the Mods were to remove their shoes and jackets before lying face down on the grass in rows; the rows stretching almost a hundred metres in some cases. They were then ordered to remain silent for the entire night as police with spot lamps watched over them. 'No one is to move or talk,' barked an officer through a megaphone. 'You might as well go to sleep.'

Naturally, these acts of violence made front-page headlines, many commentators gleefully reviving a link with the scenes from the past, an issue Sussex Police were eager to play down. 'I think the Mods and Rocker clashes in the sixties were much worse than we have now,' said a police spokesperson to the media. 'The difference today is that the targets are police and property, which is different from the days when the trouble was confined to the seafront. The clashes on Sunday night only lasted a couple of hours and the vast majority of young people were pretty reasonable.'

Others in remote areas were eager to make a connection with the rioting that was taking place in inner-city areas such as Brixton and Toxteth. Sociologist Professor Stanley Cohen, author of the classic 'Mods and Rockers' case study *Folk Devils and Moral Panics* (1972), witnessed the rioting and felt moved to comment. 'The issue is a massively deep one,' he reported, 'stretching into unemployment and urban tension of the kind that helped cause the Toxteth and Brixton riots… I can fully understand people in Brighton being worried about their tourist reputations and I don't blame them for getting upset, but it's simply no good calling for the reintroduction of magical charms like prison and flogging. There is very little prospect

go around with their scooters and tonic trousers like something out of *Quadrophenia* and they have the nerve to take the rise out of us. We hate everyone of course, but we hate the Mods and soul boys the most, – 'cos they're flash. I reckon there's going to be a lot of trouble down here in the summer 'cos that's what skins are all about. Skinheads never really went out of fashion. Sham 69 started them up again and they've just come back.'

Coincidentally, the flashpoint for the worst of the violence occurred on Madeira Drive, where *Quadrophenia*'s Brighton sequences opened. Tensions were running high from an assortment of issues during the day and a pack of youths wrecked

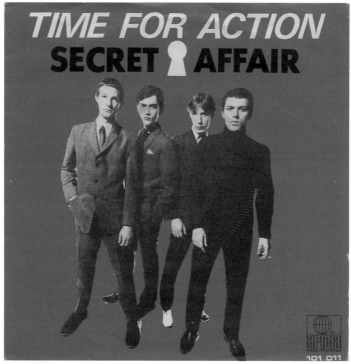

of dealing with problems that way. I feel we shall see these clashes get worse and a solution can't be found by the police changing their methods like this. That just makes matters worse.'

However, the authorities were taking no chances for the following Bank Holiday – Monday, August 31st, 1981. With The Chords playing at the Brighton Corn Exchange, they were primed for any possibility.

'I remember we did the sound check,' recalls Chords drummer Brett 'Buddy' Ascott today. 'We then walked along the seafront to the hotel. For a Bank Holiday, there was a dearth of scooters or anything Mod-related. We heard that the police had put a complete roadblock around Brighton and were also turning people away at the station. Nevertheless, there were rumours of fights breaking out all day between Mods, Rockers and skinheads.'

Quadrophenia's first cycle started to wind down as the eighties took a greater hold. The Jam, the neo-

Mod scene's primary emissaries, controversially split up at the Brighton Conference Centre on December 11th, 1982, a few yards away from where Jimmy has his sad epiphany on witnessing the Ace Face's real life. With emotions running high, Weller was interviewed by *NME* the day before the band's last hurrah – cheekily suggesting that he'd

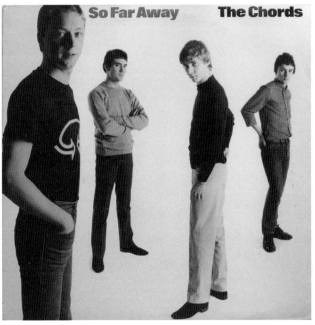

ABOVE: The Merton Parkas and The Chords, just two of the bands who rode high on the Mod revival.

◎ WITH RAVE CULTURE EXCITING MOST OF THE EIGHTIES GENERATION IN A HAZE OF ECSTASY AND ALL-NIGHTERS, THE APPEAL OF THE STYLISED MONOCHROME IMAGERY OF MODERNISM TOOK A SHARP DIP

originally envisaged taking the band's equipment up to Beachy Head and throwing it off the cliffs in an oblique homage to *Quadrophenia*. It was, of course, ironic that The Jam bade their farewells in Brighton, its connection to Modernism stronger than anywhere else on the planet.

As the eighties advanced, the British youth were turning towards brighter subcultures: New Romanticism, casuals, soul boys and, later, rave culture, all of which offered more contemporary and colourful themes than those found on the Modernist trail. Nonetheless, *Quadrophenia* proved it still had the power to enchant and enrage as the years moved on. Although the film had to wait several years to transfer to home video, the primitive machinations of the fledgling video industry saw

several key scenes cut for *Quadrophenia*'s first domestic release on the Betamax format, which left many who'd seen the film at the cinema feeling cheated at the extortionate price of the tape (somewhere in the range of £90 – around £200 in today's money).

Quadrophenia's first broadcast on national television, on November 26th, 1988, was nothing short of a disaster; the film had been crassly censored, with the deletion of most of the profanities in the first half of the film, which prompted more laughter than tears from most viewers but left a sour taste in the mouth. Presumably as a result of the numerous complaints, the film would never be shown again in such a butchered state.

With rave culture exciting most of the eighties generation in a haze of ecstasy and all-nighters, the appeal of the stylised monochrome imagery of Modernism took a sharp dip, and newcomers to the Mod lifestyle were rare. Yet, on the cusp of the era of Britpop, *Quadrophenia* started to be referenced on a regular basis across all medias, with magazines such as *Loaded* and *FHM* paying due deference to its cool youth chic. Indie band Flowered Up sampled pieces of dialogue from the film in their

1992 single 'Weekender', and elsewhere others were starting to seriously reassess the film. Blur were making direct references to the film, not least through their collaboration with Phil Daniels for their 1994 'Parklife' single. With Paul Weller still mining the Mod ethic, there was never going to be a better time to take a fresh look at the film. Attitudes, too, were being reassessed, and with the film's original X-rating now replaced with a more liberal 15, it was time for *Quadrophenia* to meet a new audience.

Video had carried *Quadrophenia* through the eighties and nineties, and now DVD technology would rightfully restore the film to its proper length, with a quality not seen since its original screenings. As is the way with such releases, the DVDs contained a multitude of extras over the years to satisfy the film's legions of devotees. In 2012 the film received its long overdue release on Blu-ray, giving home viewers the finest representation of the film to date. The move was timely. With reportedly only two usable prints of the film still in existence, it was vital to preserve *Quadrophenia* for future generations.

Large screen outings were rare and often modestly publicised, although independent cinemas such as London's Scala had access to coveted 35mm prints. In 2004 Stella Artois successfully linked *Quadrophenia*'s cult credentials with its product. Under the banner of Screen Tour, several large-scale outdoor events took place. Films such as *Get Carter* and *Withnail and I* courted interest during the campaign's run, but it was the screenings of *Quadrophenia* on Brighton beach and in Battersea Park that outstripped all expectations; the London event drew a remarkable 16,000 revellers.

'It's a great movie with a great soundtrack,' recalled Stella Artois' Jeremy Winton on the Battersea event. 'It hadn't been shown on TV for a long time, and it was a good location. We got all the Mod clubs down with their scooters; we promoted that.'

During the nineties, when Britpop reignited interest in the film, a *Quadrophenia* Walking Tour

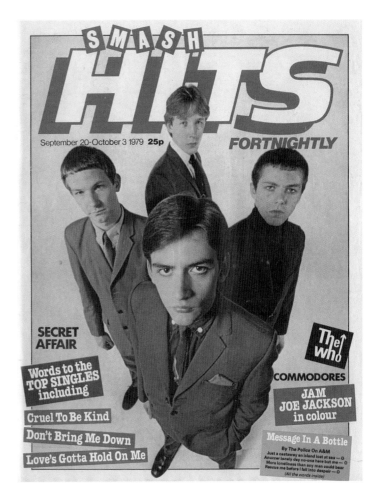

was established. Run by Blue Badge guide Glenda Clarke, the tour takes in the entirety of the Brighton locations and reveals many of the secrets of the 1978 shoot. Not surprisingly, the scene where Jimmy and Steph consummated their passion is the highpoint of the tour, with many devotees from abroad visibly moved as they venture up the narrow alleyway to pay homage to one of the film's most affecting moments.

Its celebrity increased by the tour, Jimmy's Alley remains as it always has been. With just enough room for one person to pass through, it's a dank voyage; sunlight barely creeps through the high walled buildings that surround it. Without *Quadrophenia*, its presence would be strictly utilitarian, nothing more than a quick short cut or a pit stop for those with weak bladders.

ABOVE: The teen bible of the late seventies, *Smash Hits*, gives Mod band Secret Affair a cover splash.

Can You feel
The Real ME!
Can YA "

Oii Oii
Keep the faith
Mody & Dawn

LOS AGGROTONES
Hammond LOVERS

WE ARE THE MOD
WE ARE THE MOD
WE ARE WE ARE
WE ARE THE MOD!

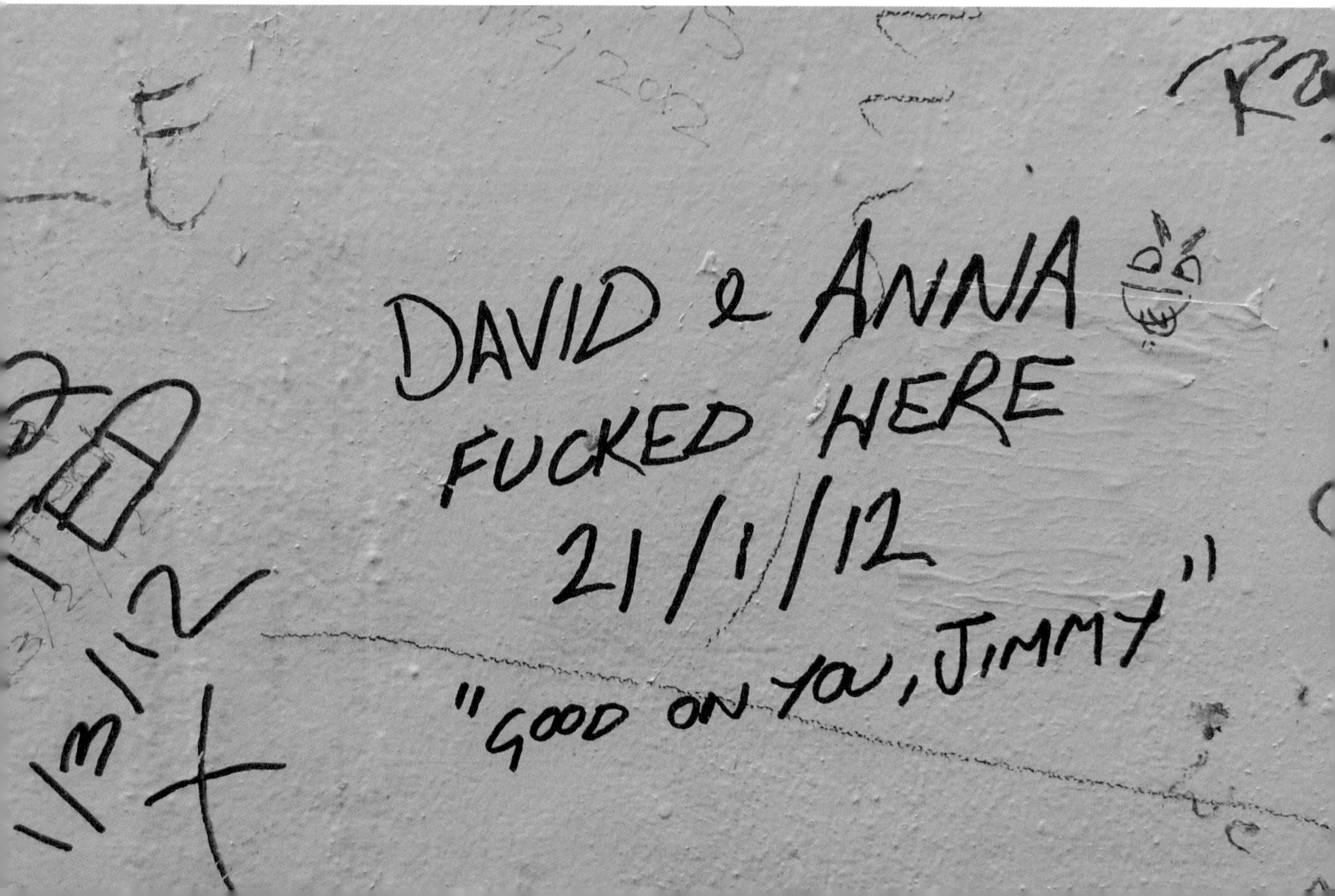

MODS RU

QUADROPHENIA

MODS RULE

DAVID & ANNA
FUCKED HERE
21/1/12
"GOOD ON YA, JIMMY"

The restaurant Rasa ('an award-winning chain of restaurants bringing the taste of authentic, home-cooked southern Indian food to the UK') currently plays unwitting hosts to *Quadrophenia*'s most durable location. The rear of their premises is still an area for waste bins awaiting collection. With barbed wire and broken glass cemented into the top of the backyard wall, they are fully aware that some of *Quadrophenia*'s more spirited fans might attempt to recreate Jimmy and Steph's most intimate encounter. Given some of the graffiti present, it seems that more than a few have tried over the years. (The graffiti – in many languages – undergoes a paint job every so often.)

During one unscheduled Mod convergence in Brighton in the nineties, a mass invasion of Jimmy's Alley resulted in the back door to Choy's Chinese restaurant being broken down, allowing some a free run to enjoy a communal moment of shared affection. Terrified staff called the police and the alley was sealed off, while those involved in the impromptu re-enactment were swiftly removed.

Even in the twenty-first century, the alley retains much of the residual energy that spun off *Quadrophenia*. Without setting foot in Brighton, you can take a virtual tour of the alleyway via YouTube, where a dozen or so home movies take a meander down Mod's most hallowed piece of ground.

The filmmakers remain amazed that their afternoon's work in this Brighton back alley has had such enduring appeal over three decades. 'I always have a quick look in the alleyway, whenever I'm up there,' said Roddam in 1999. 'I know Mods from Holland go there, and it's a shrine for so many fans, but it makes me laugh.' (Roddam may be underestimating the film's global appeal; looking at the graffiti today there are messages left from across the world, many from the United States and South America.)

Ultimately, more than anywhere else on the film's dial, the alley is *Quadrophenia*'s emotional centre. While there are plenty of other sites that fans could have earmarked for their appreciation, Jimmy's Alley

will remain as *Quadrophenia*'s enduring symbol of a young Mod's hopes, dreams and ultimate downfall. As long as the brickwork endures, the alley's relevance will last well beyond the lifetimes of those who engineered its celebrity.

More recently, and in lieu of any official livery, Bone Clothing, a Mod emporium, has taken possession of the store closest to the alley's entrance and placed a sign there reading 'Quadrophenia Alley', which acts as a guidepost for the uninformed or curious.

Sadly, after four decades in business, the Beach Café closed in the early 2000s. Despite some opposition over the years, it had had some modest makeovers, but it didn't deter hardy *Quadrophenia* fans soaking up the residual energy. Over the years, members of the cast have paid the odd return visit to the café, including Phil Daniels, who it is said resumed his seat by the window and stared out to

THIS SPREAD: *Quadrophenia*'s Mecca, 'Jimmy's Alley'.

ABOVE: Graffiti from fans of the film continually litter the alley's walls.

punk rocker. But everybody loved the film – whether you were a Rocker, a Mod, punk – it had that youth culture appeal. The museum is really popular. We have quite a lot of scooter ride-outs to the museum, people from Japan and all over the world.'

At the time of writing, there are plans to relocate the museum to Brighton, although there's been some initial local authority hostility to the idea. Surely it's obvious that Brighton should have a permanent memorial to its most celebrated screen reflection.

London locations particular to *Quadrophenia* receive some modest interest, although not as much as their Brighton relations. A. Cooke's pie and mash shop in Shepherd's Bush hit the headlines recently as developers, in their relentless gentrification of the area, were planning to raze the site. With support from the likes of Pete Townshend, there was some hope that it may escape demolition, but sadly it closed in July 2015. Jimmy's house in Acton receives less attention but witnesses the occasional visitor. The address, freely available online, ensures that there are always a few curious onlookers heading down Wells House Road. The property has changed hands a few times since filming completed in 1978, although as legend informs, one *Quadrophenia* obsessive did make off with the lounge's fireplace during a refurbishment in the early nineties. In 2017 it was reported that a large swathe of Wells House Road was due for demolition to make way for the HS2 rail link. Despite considerable local opposition, it appears that Jimmy's home may well succumb to the incursions of twenty-first-century redevelopment.

Several themed *Quadrophenia* events, with appearances from members of the original cast, have taken place in the first decade of the new millennium. Despite some reservations in the past, most of the cast appear happy to chat, pose for photographs and sign film memorabilia. These events have acted as a rare gathering point for fans, many of whom were not even born when the film

sea. At the time of writing, after a short spell as a Turkish shisha bar, the property is unoccupied.

A more permanent fixture, some 200 miles from Brighton, at Littledean in Gloucestershire, is the *Quadrophenia* museum. Set in a former jail, the collection is a veritable treasure trove of memorabilia relating to the film, housing film scripts, signed film stills and other paraphernalia – the highlight being Sting's Vespa scooter. The museum's curator (and ex-punk bassist) Andy Jones is an unashamed fan of the film and is keen to expand on its collection.

'I saw it when it first came out,' he recalled to the author in 2013. 'My brother was a Mod and I was a was first released. While posters, front-of-house stills and all sorts of memorabilia are hugely sought after, anything that featured directly in the film, however inconsequential, commands huge prices these days.

Not surprisingly, examples of Jimmy's and Ace Face's scooters command enormous prices when they surface. Once filming ceased, one of Jimmy's vehicles was sold to Portsmouth-based scooter dealers, Rafferty Newman. It made its way through several owners on the South Coast before ending up in Bonhams auction house in London, where it sold for a staggering £36,000 in 2008.

Carrying the spirit of the film into the twenty-first century currently lies with Drew Stansall's *Quadrophenia* club nights. Stansall, an accomplished saxophonist who has played with The Specials, is an unrepentant first generation fan of the film, and in 2012 he decided that there was still enough interest to tour the film around the country as a basis for themed nights.

'I JUST WANTED TO WALK INTO THAT ROOM. I WANTED TO PUT IT BACK TOGETHER AGAIN. I WANTED TO MAKE IT HAPPEN.'
DREW STANSALL

Drew Stansall: 'The inspiration for the nights came from the scene at the beginning of the film where Jimmy goes down into the club and the band play "Hi-Heel Sneakers", and everyone is dressed up in their Mod gear and they're dancing. It was that scene that inspired me. I just wanted to walk into that room. I wanted to put it back together again. I wanted to make it happen.'

Stansall's concept has found enormous favour with *Quadrophenia*'s devotees, selling out venues normally reserved for popular bands of the moment. With the film acting as the backdrop, Mod and northern soul acts entertain the audience from the stage, ensuring that the atmosphere is successfully

recreated. With stars from the film occasionally gracing these special nights, its future popularity seems assured.

While *Quadrophenia* aficionados spent years poring over every frame of the film, the cast of the film moved swiftly on to other projects, although, in some cases, *Quadrophenia*'s popularity often eclipsed much of their future work. For some of the associate members on the cast list, their modest involvement came to serve as a dining-out anecdote for years to come. For others, the bright, youthful imagery embedded in the film's imagery made it difficult for them to shake off their *Quadrophenia* alter egos.

Carrying the weight of this reputation was, predictably, Phil Daniels. The enormous promise he displayed in *Quadrophenia* made the character of Jimmy hard to dissociate from. Initially, Daniels had little interest in maintaining his connection with such a defining role. Despite *Quadrophenia*'s majestic, global influence, for a young actor barely in his twenties, Daniels was eager to distance himself from the iconic role of Jimmy lest it become an albatross around his neck. A subsequent part in *Breaking Glass* (1980) expanded Daniels' acting chops well beyond *Quadrophenia*'s crazed manifesto and other challenging projects would come his way to stretch his immense talent. In 1983 Daniels featured in another cult classic, Mike Leigh's *Meantime* (1984) – a role that won him numerous plaudits and introduced him to a new audience. The following year, Daniels reunited with Sting, Gary Shail and Timothy Spall to play the role of Bela in Franc Roddam's *The Bride*.

He continued to work prolifically on stage and in television, notably in *The Pickwick Papers* (1985), *Holding On* (1997), *Time Gentleman Please* (2000) and *The Long Firm* (2004). In 1990 he played the role of Alex in the Royal Shakespeare Company's version of Anthony Burgess's *A Clockwork Orange*. The part garnered copious space in the news media, with the youth and gang elements in Burgess's work raising the spectre of *Quadrophenia* again. In the

ABOVE: Phil Daniels as 'Mark Pollock' in the cult movie, *Meantime*.

nineties, the first era to seriously assess the impact of the sixties, Blur courted Daniels for dialogue in their 1994 chart-topping single 'Parklife'. The band were flirting with Modernism, and the alliance was seen as daring.

In 1995 Daniels firmly realigned himself with his *Quadrophenia* roots, this time courtesy of The Who. While Pete Townshend had attempted to distance himself from much of his Who past during the eighties, at the behest of the Prince's Trust, he convened a star-studded revival of *Quadrophenia* at London's Hyde Park. The request had gone out from Townshend to Daniels to reassume the role of Jimmy for the stage and, surprisingly, he acceded. Sitting in what appeared to be a messianic throne at the rear of the gigantic Hyde Park stage, Daniels delivered a monologue between the songs. With clips from the film of *Quadrophenia* playing on the massive screens behind the stage, Daniels had

successfully morphed his Mod past into the present.

Not surprisingly, the concert was an enormous success. The resulting accolades kick-started The Who into reviving the album and taking the show across the world. For Daniels, the experience was something of a turning point; he had evidently come to accept that his association with *Quadrophenia* was inescapable. His role in the popular soap *EastEnders* in 1996 displayed his talents to a wider audience, but it was his role in *Quadrophenia* that was one of the most defining moments of his career. In 2008 Daniels wrote his memoir *Class Actor*, in which he went a long way to dispel many of the myths surrounding his time on the film. Forty years on from his first audition for the part of Jimmy, Daniels appears at peace with *Quadrophenia*'s generous legacy: 'I'm proud of the film immensely, but it's caught me somewhere that I can't kind of climb out of. There was a time when I'd just had enough of it. But in the end I went with the adage "If you can't beat 'em, join 'em".'

The film's love interest, Leslie Ash, would move swiftly on from *Quadrophenia* and into sustained work across the performing field. While her intimate scene in the film eclipsed the entirety of her contribution to the film, it was obvious that her career would take off in numerous directions. Still only 19 on the film's release, she enjoyed considerable success on television, first as a presenter on the music show *The Tube*, and then on the long-running sitcom *Men Behaving Badly*. In 1984 she had a *Quadrophenia* reunion (of sorts) when she appeared with Toyah Wilcox and Roger Daltrey in the film, *Murder: Ultimate Grounds for Divorce*. In 2007 Ash broke a long-standing reticence to discuss her time on *Quadrophenia* in her biography, *My Life Behaving Badly*, and the following year she offered some brief commentary for a DVD release of the film. While her words were brief and cautious, it would be her most sustained account of the film.

Mark Wingett, unforgettable as Jimmy's sidekick Dave, was quick to build on his success in *Quadrophenia*. Denied a role in the screen version of *Scum* (director Alan Clarke was eager not to include too many *Quadrophenia* ex-pats on the film), he found himself in a role alongside Phil Daniels and Hazel O'Connor in the rock musical *Breaking Glass*. In tandem with his film roles, he continued his stage work and joined Birmingham Rep for a season of plays. Not surprisingly, his time spent on *Quadrophenia* was never that far behind. 'In 1981 I was doing a production of *Chips with Everything* at the Birmingham Rep,' he reflects today. 'I was dressed up as an Air Force man conscript. I had gone to the stage door to have a cigarette and this group of Mods went past on these bikes, and the guy screeched to a halt, ran towards me and he was dressed like Dave – the exact replica... He came up to me and said, "Mark, Mark, I based my life on you!"'

Wingett's most sustained role, post-*Quadrophenia*, was that of the popular policeman DC Carver in ITV's long-running drama *The Bill*. Several decades on from trundling into Brighton as a 17-year-old, he cuts a less combative presence these days and occasionally turns out at *Quadrophenia*-themed events. His time on the film is still a major highlight, as he recalled in 2012: 'It was all exciting and it was all great. Films have got their own lives – you do a film and you forget about it. It gave me a false impression of what the business was about, because I was young and so impressionable, so to go into something which was an extraordinary experience and survive it, really was something you had to grow through. I was very young and stayed very young for a very long time. I think *Quadrophenia* held me in that place for quite a while.'

Phil Davis would build on his performance in *Quadrophenia* with celebrated appearances in Mike Leigh's *High Hopes* and *Vera Drake*. In 1988 he scored a memorable part in Alan Clarke's gritty drama *The Firm*, a film that owed much to the frenetic energy of *Quadrophenia*. Highly respected, Davis's acting skills now run in tandem with directing – a move that has won him considerable plaudits.

Frontline cast members Gary Shail, Trevor Laird and Garry Cooper all recall their time spent on the film as a landmark in their respective careers. In 1981 Trevor Laird starred in another cult classic, *Babylon*, a film written by *Quadrophenia's* scriptwriter Martin Stellman and a brilliant exposition of black working-class culture in South London. Laird found consistent work through the years, a large part of it played out on stage. Garry Cooper carved out a respected niche in acting across all dramatic mediums including choice cameos in *1984* (1984), *My Beautiful Laundrette* (1985) and *London Kills Me* (1991). Gary Shail, his acrobatic stunts noted on *Quadrophenia*, was signed on as a stunt actor soon after filming – a talent that would illuminate his acting skills alongside such luminaries as Michael Caine (in the 1988 TV mini-series *Jack the Ripper*). Shail also featured on children's television in the Micky Dolenz-directed *Metal Mickey*, which regularly pulled in thirteen million viewers at the beginning of the eighties. Music running a close second to acting, Shail formed the band The Actors with fellow *Quadrophenia* star Gary Holton before diversifying in the Los Angeles music scene as a songwriter, working with the likes of Smokey Robinson.

Toyah Wilcox's acting promise also ran in tandem with her music; she took off in the early eighties as part of the New Romantic scene – garnering several hits and a large fan base. After marriage to Robert Fripp in 1986, she settled into a not unsuccessful career in presenting, punctuated with the occasional spell of acting, and is still performing live.

Despite his performance dividing opinion, Sting's presence in *Quadrophenia* would prove to be no obstacle to his stratospheric rise to fame. Sting would lead The Police to phenomenal success during the eighties, before embarking on a similarly celebrated solo career. Sting's acting career included roles in the BBC's *Brimstone and Treacle* (1982) and the David Lynch film *Dune* (1984).

Ray Winstone's memorable appearance in *Quadrophenia* only hinted at his incredible talent. With frequent appearances across all dramatic mediums throughout the years, he has become one of Britain's leading actors, commanding enormous attention on every level (notably for his outstanding performance in Jonathan Glazer's *Sexy Beast* in 2000).

Other actors such as Timothy Spall, John Altman, Daniel Peacock and John Blundell would find acclaim elsewhere as the years advanced, but their time spent on the film would prove memorable. '*Quadrophenia* encompasses something,' says John Altman. 'As long as there are restless teenagers who have had enough of their parents and they just want to get away and do their own thing. It's a time when you head out into the world; it's that coming of age, it's what people identify with always and it's stood the test of time.'

A strong kinship has endured between the cast members since the film was first shown. 'I guarantee you won't get a Rizla paper between us,' says Gary Shail on their bond. 'We've had births, deaths, marriages, divorces and bankruptcies, but all of us have got one thing in common; you look at that *Quadrophenia* film poster, we're all still alive.'

Sadly, though, some of *Quadrophenia*'s associate cast would not survive to witness the film's continued success. Michael Elphick maintained his association with Franc Roddam in the classic ITV comedy *Auf Wiedersehen, Pet*. Enhancing his cult credentials, he appeared in *Withnail and I* (1987), a film with a similarly rabid following to *Quadrophenia*. The long-running TV series *Boon* earned Elphick household-name status, many warming to the tale of the despatch rider cum private investigator. After a long struggle with alcoholism, Elphick died of a heart attack in 2002. Gary Holt, one of the Rockers in *Quadrophenia*, found a more sustained role in *Auf Wiedersehen, Pet* as well as further adventures in the musical field – some with fellow *Quadrophenia* alumnus Gary Shail. Aged only 33, Holt died of a drug overdose in 1985.

With his directorial tour de force behind him, Franc Roddam moved on to other cinematic productions such as *Lords of Discipline* (1983), *The Bride* (1985), *Aria* (1987), *War Party* (1988) and *K2* (1991). On the small screen, Roddam created the ground-breaking comedy drama *Auf Wiedersehen, Pet* in 1983, a production that would bring *Quadrophenia* veterans Timothy Spall, Gary Holt and Michael Elphick to a wider audience. More recently, Roddam concentrated his efforts on TV adaptations of *Moby Dick*, *Cleopatra* and *Canterbury Tales*. A creation of a totally different kind, Roddam was the brains behind *MasterChef*, arguably the first television programme to address the art of cooking seriously. Nonetheless, despite Roddam's diverse creative talents, it's undeniable that *Quadrophenia* will remain his signature film, and he's immensely proud of what he helped to create.

'I think that good films are timeless,' he says. 'Quadrophenia has an enduring quality because it looks at all those problems and passions and then says. "It's okay to be no good, it's okay to be useless, it's okay not to be good at sex, not to be good at fighting, not to like your parents, to be fired at work." It's all those things. I was always interested in how passionate you feel about everything when you are young. Those passions don't last very long, but they're very powerful. And in that sense, I think it's an instructive film in that it says, "I embrace what you're thinking and what you're feeling, and I understand what you feel 'cos I felt the same. It's great to fight, it's great to fuck, it's great to take drugs," but it also has a bit of objectivity, too, you know – "Don't do yourself in".'

Brian Tufano, the man who photographed Quadrophenia in 1978, went on to film numerous projects over the years. In 1995 he was chosen for Trainspotting, arguably Quadrophenia's stylistic successor. With director Danny Boyle a fan of the film, the energy, gang culture and sense of belonging that was integral to Quadrophenia was successfully imported into the screen version of Irvine Welsh's cult novel.

In 1980 Martin Stellman, the man who brought such verisimilitude to Quadrophenia's script, worked on the screen realisation of Babylon. Much like Quadrophenia, Babylon was highly praised for its authenticity. In 2018 Stellman wrote the acclaimed Yardie. Directed by Idris Elba, the film examined the dynamics of criminality and loyalty in seventies Kingston and eighties Hackney.

Having created a multitude of conceptual projects throughout his career, Quadrophenia appears to be something of a constant for its creator Pete Townshend. Given a new lease of life following The Who's break-up in 1982, Townshend concentrated on another 'Jimmy' for his 1985 featurette White City, based around the less romantic minefields of midlife challenges and breakdowns. While the protagonist hails from the same environs as Quadrophenia's Jimmy, there is little else to connect the two roles. The lead character seemingly trapped in a multitude of conflicts, White City attracted notable interest and spawned a coveted South Bank Show documentary on its making. Despite its authenticity, the film's modest one-hour length didn't allow the concept to reach any definitive answers. More conclusive was Townshend's score for the film, the excellent soundtrack renewing interest in his often overshadowed solo career.

While occasional songs from Quadrophenia remained in The Who's setlist over the years, it wasn't until the mid-nineties that the concept underwent a serious revival, with retrospectives of the work being played to audiences in 1996 and 2012. While The Who's album is clearly a thing apart from the film, there is an obvious symbiosis that will ensure Quadrophenia's longevity, in all its varied forms.

> **'I WAS ALWAYS INTERESTED IN HOW PASSIONATE YOU FEEL ABOUT EVERYTHING WHEN YOU ARE YOUNG.'**
>
> **FRANC RODDAM**

In 2012 Pete Townshend and Roger Daltrey revived Quadrophenia for a series of concerts. Playing to sell-out venues in America and Europe, it reignited the concept for a new generation. What proved to be the most extraordinary aspect to the revival was the age group of the audiences, ranging from the very young to those in Daltrey and Townshend's peer group – a fact not lost on Quadrophenia's creator in 2012. 'What does delight me is the fact that people still connect with Quadrophenia. For new audiences coming to it, it's a story about the travails of being young. But also there is a poignancy that we get from the older fans of Quadrophenia, people of our age or even a little older who reconnected with the story without there being any nostalgia.' ●

CHAPTER TWELVE

'THE AMERICANS HAD *GREASE* BUT WE HAD AND STILL HAVE *QUADROPHENIA*, AND AT THE END OF THE DAY, WOULD YOU RATHER BE PONCING ROUND TO "GREASE LIGHTNING" GOING "WELL-A-WELL-A-WELL-OOO" OR WOULD YOU RATHER BE DRIVING THROUGH SUSSEX ON A SCOOTER WITH NO HELMET ON KNOWING YOU'RE GOING TO HAVE IT OFF WITH LESLIE ASH IN BRIGHTON.'

—*LOADED*, NOVEMBER 1995

With *Tommy* having successfully transferred to the stage in both New York and London, it seemed predictable that *Quadrophenia* would also be suitable for a dramatic stage representation. The idea had been under discussion for many years, and in Los Angeles during November 2005, an adaptation of *Quadrophenia* was unveiled. In 2009, following an early plan to stage the musical in London's West End, an expanded version of the play was rolled out across the UK to generally upbeat reviews.

Cinema always receptive to any opportunity to revisit past successes, it was predictable that a sequel to the film would be ripe for exploration. For many, the film's enigmatic ending clearly invited questions as to what the future had in store for Jimmy. The film's continuous popularity only fuelled the demand for answers.

'It was talked about quite a lot,' recalled Franc Roddam in 1999. 'Roy Baird wanted him to become an advertising executive. What they were thinking was, "What is the next movement? Can he get into it?" He would probably have ended up supporting Margaret Thatcher…'

While potential concepts suggesting that Jimmy had embarked on the hippie trail (one idea was entitled 'Jimmy Goes to India') or moved into a career in advertising were shelved, it was apparent that those close to The Who were receptive to an imaginative extension to the film.

In 1988 *Won't Get Fooled Again*, a script co-written by *Quadrophenia*'s producer Roy Baird, was completed at the request of The Who's management. Set ten years after the original film, there was talk of the cast reuniting to reassume their roles. For whatever reasons, the film didn't advance beyond script stage, although this did little to prevent speculation about a possible sequel.

In 2011 a more realistic approach to a sequel was mooted. Written by the film's original screenwriter Martin Stellman, a new slant to the *Quadrophenia* saga was being lined up. With ex-Skids frontman turned director Richard Jobson set to direct,

OPPOSITE: Mark Wingett and Josh Farley pose for shots on Brighton beach for Devlin Crow's *Quadrophenia* inspired film, *Being*.

the few nuggets of information that escaped suggested that the story would follow on from Jimmy's abandonment of Mod culture, ultimately seeing him enter into rock band management. While there was considerable excitement at the news, not all voices were in harmony with the proposal. 'Would I prefer there not to be a sequel? Probably,' said Franc Roddam. 'It breaks away from the authenticity. I'm not a great sequel kind of guy. It's a bit of commercialism, isn't it?'

Despite the fanfare of publicity, no shooting date for what is called *Quadrophenia 2* has been announced. With a deafening silence on the film's progress since 2011, it appears that the creative energies at Who Films have now been refocused on a TV series, entitled *Mods and Rockers*. With a brief to occupy the 'same kind of world as *Quadrophenia*', noted director Simon West (*Con Air, Lara Croft: Tomb Raider*) has been signed up to oversee filming. 'It covers the Rockers' side of the story,' says West today. '[It] spills out into the wider world of Swinging Sixties London, taking in gangsters, music and fashion.'

Ⓠ 'WOULD I PREFER THERE NOT TO BE A SEQUEL? PROBABLY. IT BREAKS AWAY FROM THE AUTHENTICITY.'
FRANC RODDAM

While there are no scheduled dates as yet for The Who's TV series, three other projects, while not being *Quadrophenia* remakes or sequels, wove the ambience of the film into their respective plotlines. In 2016 news broke that a film based on Peter Meadows' book *To Be Someone* was about to start shooting. Meadows' novel was subtitled 'Jimmy's Story Continues – Inspired by *Quadrophenia*', and with reported approval from Pete Townshend, a script was developed from the book. The project evidently found favour with original cast members Phil Daniels, Trevor Laird,

OPPOSITE: Cinema poster for *Being*.

Mark Wingett and Toyah Wilcox, all of whom expressed interest in the project. Although not being touted as a sequel or remake, the putative script reportedly saw its protagonist on an odyssey of crime and disorder following his Mod life crisis back in the sixties – replete with many elements that were in the ether around *Quadrophenia*.

A veteran of numerous British cult classics, the film's director and one-time actor Ray Burdis was effusive in his excitement for the project. 'It wasn't difficult to get the cast members signed up as they all loved the script,' he reported to the *Daily Mirror*. 'Now we've got the core main cast in place, we're constructing the other characters carefully and slowly. I'm hoping it will spark a new generation of fans – kids have got nothing to grasp on to like the punk days, and we need something refreshing to come through.'

However, The Who's management were less than pleased with the association to what remained their creative property. In response to the blizzard of publicity surrounding the Meadows/Burdis proposal, a terse press release was issued to the media. 'As far as the group and original producer Bill Curbishley are concerned,' it ran, 'the new film is a blatant attempt to cash in on the original film's enduring popularity. *Quadrophenia* is a significant and influential film based on The Who's music, not some *Carry On* franchise. Any follow-up could only be made by the authors of the original and would need to be worthy of the name.'

While the problems surrounding *To Be Someone* are yet to be ironed out, two other Mod-related projects found themselves further along the road. *Being* is a charming and uplifting drama of a young boy's struggle to care for his mother who has multiple sclerosis. Utilising the rich backdrop of Brighton and featuring the talents of *Quadrophenia*'s frontline stars Mark Wingett and Trevor Laird, the film had echoes of *Quadrophenia* and Modernism running in tandem with its sensitive subject matter.

'I grew up in Brighton,' reported *Being*'s

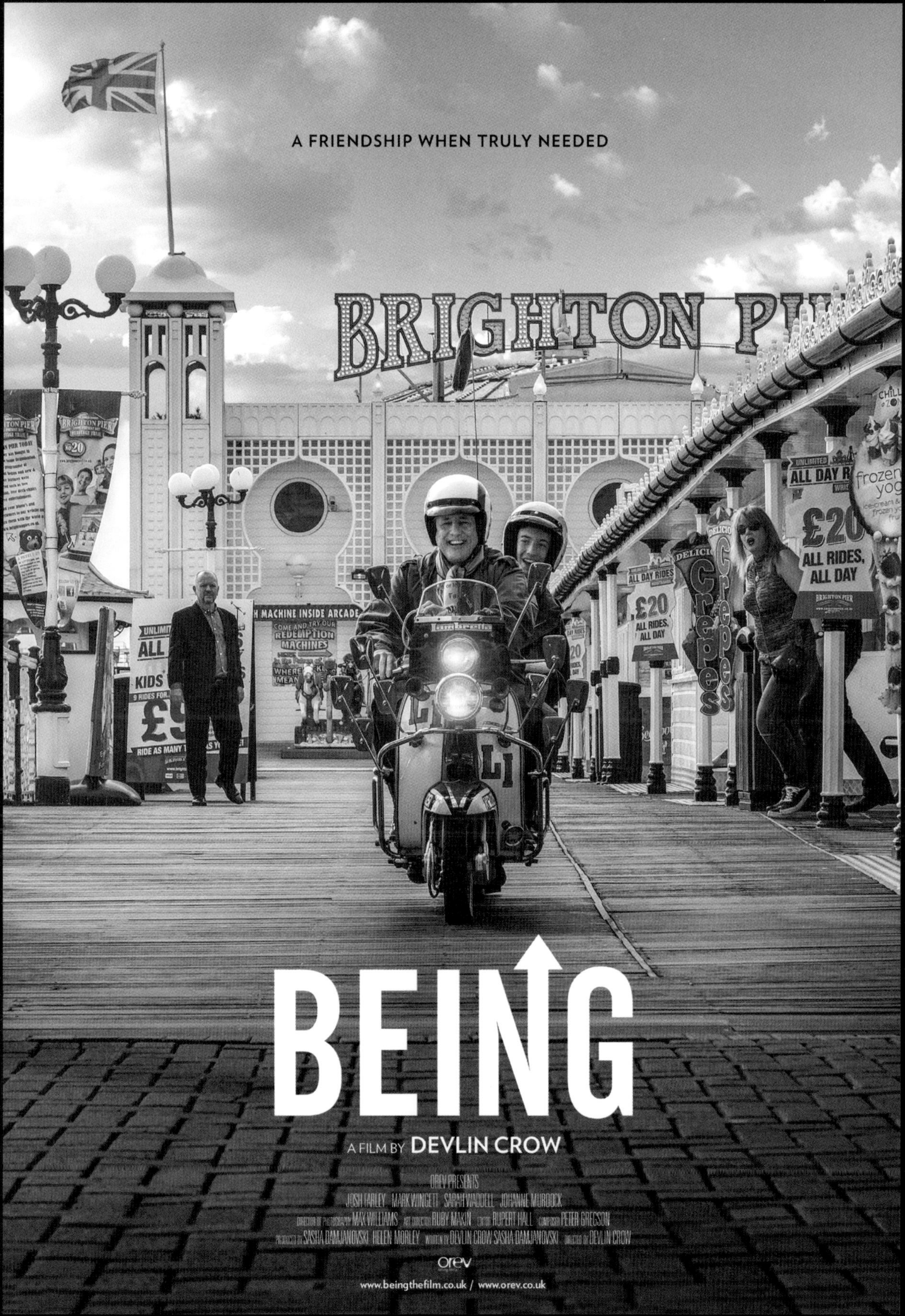

A FRIENDSHIP WHEN TRULY NEEDED

BRIGHTON PIER

BEING

A FILM BY DEVLIN CROW

OREV PRESENTS

JOSH FARLEY   MARK WINGETT   SARAH WADDELL   JOHANNE MURDOCK

DIRECTOR OF PHOTOGRAPHY MAX WILLIAMS   ART DIRECTOR RUBY MASON   EDITOR RUPERT HALL   COMPOSER PETER GREGSON

PRODUCED BY SASHA DAMJANOVSKI   HELEN MORLEY   WRITTEN BY DEVLIN CROW SASHA DAMJANOVSKI   DIRECTED BY DEVLIN CROW

OREV

www.beingthefilm.co.uk / www.orev.co.uk

director Devlin Crow to the author. 'I remember the Mods coming down as a young boy. *Quadrophenia* was central to my growing up. I could relate to Jimmy and his adolescent frustration. My youth and view of Brighton is fused with the film and the Mod scene… *Being* is not a sequel or remake, although it does have a nod to *Quadrophenia* and The Who. It's a heart-warming story about dealing with adversity and the dynamics of a mother and son who are fans of sixties music and The Who.'

With the full blessing of The Who's management, *Being*'s finance was raised through crowd-funding and it has garnered a wide community of supporters during its gestation. The film having done the rounds of the festivals and destined for a DVD release, once again the enduring interest in *Quadrophenia* was celebrated.

Another project that benefited from the crowd-funding platform was *The Pebble and the Boy*. While not linked directly to *Quadrophenia* as such, the Modernist theme and the pull of Brighton are omnipresent factors throughout. Much like *Being*, *The Pebble and the Boy* is a heart-warming exploration of a young boy dealing with adversity – in this case, a youngster coming to terms with the death of his father. The film takes its name from a Paul Weller song from his 2007 album *As Is Now*. The film's director/screenwriter is Chris Green, who told the author: 'It's a road movie of discovery. The lead character John, he's not a Mod, but his dad just died and he was entrenched in Mod sensibility. The plan is for his son to scatter his ashes in the sea at Brighton. As the film moves on, his son begins to realise he's following in his father's footsteps.'

Much like *Being*, the groundswell of interest in *The Pebble and the Boy* encouraged many to get involved directly with the production; supporters were filling walk-on parts, bands were queuing up to contribute songs, and Mods lent scooters for the picture.

On the commercial front line of film, *Quadrophenia*'s bright colours still find their way into mainstream pictures. The underwhelming remake of *Brighton Rock* in 2011 reintroduced sixties-era Mods and Rockers, and with The Who and Modernism still in vogue, there is obviously a guaranteed audience for any future *Quadrophenia* product.

⊕ 'IT PULLED ME RIGHT IN, THE FILM PLAYED WITH MY HEAD IN A SENSE.'
TONY PHILLIPS

Quadrophenia remains a defining moment in many people's lives. The film's multitude of emotions and themes succeeded in propelling many people towards a lifestyle that would live with them for ever. Those who are now in their fifties with children of their own, appear happy to recall their halcyon youth to which *Quadrophenia* was such a vibrant reflection. For many, the film acted as a blueprint for Modernism's brighter colours, something that was clearly more attractive than the harsh reality of late seventies Britain. Similarly, with the austerity-ravaged landscape of this decade offering little hope, looking back appears to be a far more attractive proposition. While the term 'Golden Age' seems an overused description these days, for many who make up the *Quadrophenia* generation, a large part of their youth is defined by the film.

Tony Phillips was a 17-year-old living in Tunbridge Wells at the time of the film's release. He recalled to the author his first viewing of *Quadrophenia* in 1979 and the strong impact it had on him.

'I had just left school and while I had seen The Jam on television, I didn't think

much of them and thought they were more of a punk band. I didn't know what Mods really were about to be honest. Anyway, the word went around that this film was worth watching and because the local cinema wasn't that hot on security, a few of us bunked in – seeing as it was an X-certificate we had to enter via a fire door. For me at least, it pulled me right in. The film played with my head in a sense, and much of what went on in the film, the partying and language, was exactly what we were all doing to an extent. Anyway, as a result of the film, I bought a parka and

ABOVE: *Being* star Josh Farley and director Devlin Crow on Brighton's Palace Pier.

Robert Joseph was another suburbanite pulled in by the film's powerful Mod manifesto. Living in Farnham, Surrey during the late seventies, viewing *Quadrophenia* was nothing more than a call to arms.

'I was 17 when I saw the film for the first time. I remember coming away thinking that it was amazing, as it appeared to mirror everything me and my mates were going through at the time. Definitely the party scene, which was something I'd experienced loads of time around Farnham, where there were loads of posh houses we used to gatecrash. At first, I didn't really get the Mod thing but then when everyone started dressing up and buying scooters, I got into it. I remember going to Brighton and seeing The Jam in 1980, around the time of the film's release. There were thousands of Mods everywhere; it was amazing and just like a scene in the film. Many of us went down to the beach after the gig and relived Jimmy's moment by the sea. It was funny, as I recall there were loads of us doing the same – all involved in our own little homage to the film. Later the violence came in and, to be honest, that was my signal to get out. I'll never forget those days though.'

Graham Lentz hailed from the commuter belt of East Grinstead in Sussex. He recalls the overwhelming imprint the film made on him at the time, even in such wealthy environs of West Sussex.

'By the time *Quadrophenia* hit the cinemas, I had already been a committed Mod for two years. The Jam and their first single "In The City" was my starting point. Richard Barnes' Mods book and stuff my dad told me about fifties Modernists were my reference points. When *Quadrophenia*

ABOVE: Chris Green's film, *The Pebble and the Boy*, also revisits the landscape of *Quadrophenia.*

then got a scooter the following year. I started hanging out with other Mods in the area, riding to Brighton on Bank Holidays and things like that. As I recall, the fighting was pretty embarrassing, although it was mainly the skinheads who were out to get us. Mind you, one of the best moments for me was walking down the promenade with a group of fellow Mods chanting, "We are the Mods. We are the Mods", just like in the film. I don't ride a scooter now, but I still like to watch the film occasionally to remind me of my youth. I'm 50 now and have got two kids, but they don't really get what it was all about.'

came out, I was in with a handful of Mods who all congregated at the Glandfield pub in East Grinstead, Sussex. When it finally got to our cinema I saw that film four times in the first week. Through the press, I knew that the film was due out for months before its release, so I was desperate to see it. I loved it then and still do today. It's a great British film. I still go on a rollercoaster of emotions when I watch it because it made such an impact and I identified with all those characters (I was South London born and bred after all). It also put me off purple hearts for life!

'It also brings back memories... Some of the lads with scooters had gone to Reigate to meet other Mods. While they were there, a biker gang known as the Road Rats from Boxhill also paid them a visit and it kicked off. But, as I recall, the Road Rats got more than they bargained for and one or two got a good kicking.

'About a week later I was in the Glandfield with three of my Mod mates at Sunday lunchtime. Suddenly we could hear this intense roar of bikes coming down the road. We thought the Road Rats had found us and were looking for revenge. This engine roar stopped right outside the pub. Dudley (the landlord and a top man) went out with a baseball bat to see what was going on. We tooled up with bottles and anything we could find and decided to fight it out in the pub itself. Then Dudley walked back in with a smile on his face, followed by about thirty Mods! They had come from the Carshalton area just to find this bunch who went by the name of the Defiance Scooter Club because they'd heard we'd turned the Rats over. We all had a drink and a chat, then we walked on mass to the cinema and... yep... we watched *Quadrophenia*.

'After the film, we all walked back to the pub but, for some reason, I wanted to drift to the back of the bunch. As they got slightly ahead of me, my brain took a snapshot of that moment. Thirty or forty Mods marching toward a pub car park literally filled with scooters. And every time I watch the film, my mind recalls that moment. Priceless (as they say).'

Mark Baxter was a 16-year-old living in Camberwell, South London. He recalled the seismic effect the film had on him and his peer group on its release.

'The news about the film spread like wildfire on our estate in Camberwell. "You have got to see this film, it's brilliant, mate." I asked its name. "*Quadrophenia*." "Quadro what? What's all that about then?"

'See, I had missed the album of the same name by The Who. I was too young at the time of its release in 1973 for it to have any impact on my life. But the film with the same name had come along just at the right time. I was now 16, coming up to 17. I was devouring the *NME* on a weekly basis and a band called The Jam had caught my eye. I had begun to buy their classic run of singles and also begun to adopt some of the clothing I had seen their singer wearing. The cut of his jib reminded me of photos my mum had of a couple of my uncles who were Mods in the mid-sixties. This fella Paul Weller was sporting the same "look" that they had adopted, which was one I also began to strongly identify with.

'It was the look of the Modernist.

'I finally got to see the film a week or so after being tipped off about it. I absolutely loved it and I went back at least three times to soak it all up further. I desperately wanted to live the same lifestyle depicted in it. I wanted to dance to the same music, I wanted to have the same suits made and most of all, I wanted a girlfriend who looked like Leslie Ash!

'Well, over the past thirty-five years or so, the decade of the sixties has been my fascination, some would say an obsession. The music and clothing styles from that era have been central to my everyday life. And that will be there until my dying day. Thank you, *Quadrophenia*.'

Jonny Bance was a 14-year-old living in Leicester when he first saw *Quadrophenia* on television. He came to the film in 1988, a little later than the first generation of devotees. Despite the time lag, he still had a charismatic conversion on seeing the film.

'On a cold rainy night in November 1988, I sat down to watch, for the very first time, a film that would change my life. I was 14 years old and looking for an identity, to belong and to have a meaning. That was found for me, and millions of others, in *Quadrophenia*. It was a heavily edited version shown on ITV and I was recommended to watch it by my cousin, who had been a Mod in the '79 revival. The film blew me away and made my head spin faster than the wheels of a Lambretta on Brighton promenade. I rushed out to buy the full X-certificate version on VHS and watched it over and over, memorising every line and scene. It was just what I was looking for, an instant connection, a powerful driving and influential film that led me to buy my first parka, my first Jam album, a seat for The Who's '89 tour and a ticket to see Phil Daniels on stage in *A Clockwork Orange*. Since those heady teenage days, the film has continued to

play a big part in my life; it got me an 'A' when I chose it as my dissertation in media college, helped towards getting me my first radio job as the programme controller was equally obsessive. It led me to meet the cast at a convention and interview Gary Shail (Spider). It also introduced me to the wonderful worlds of northern soul, rarer Mod tunes, literature, other British cinema, some fabulous friendships; it forever remains a huge part of my life. We are the Mods!!!!!!!!!'

All genres have their experts – someone who has done more, seen more and knows more about their subject than anyone else on the planet. While society rewards eminent scholars in conventional disciplines with Pulitzer Prizes, honorary degrees or even Empire medals in recognition of their devotion, cult film experts are rarely, if ever, rewarded for their remarkable work. *Quadrophenia*'s own Emeritus Professor is Kieran McAleer, a status qualified by over thirty-five years of devotion to the film, and his relationship with *Quadrophenia* proving more of a lifestyle than an interest. Not a trace of an anorak in sight, the affable and likeable McAleer, a musician and BBC soundman by profession, is clearly in awe of his subject matter, and has lived and breathed the residual energy left by the film since its initial release.

'I first saw *Quadrophenia* in 1979 at my local cinema in St Albans with a group of Mods,' he says today. 'When we came out, got on scooters and went home, it was one of the most euphoric feelings I had ever had. All I could hear in my head on the way home was the music, the opening titles, "The Real Me". I felt as though these scooters were like chariots and we were like gladiators.'

McAleer would maintain a strong interest in the film over the following years, building a replica scooter like Jimmy's and attending parties in his Hertfordshire locale – many of them mirroring closely the action in *Quadrophenia*. '*Quadrophenia* was just like the life we were living. It's become a bit of a clichéd old phrase that we use as a joke that "It's just like *Quadrophenia*, isn't it?" But at the time, it was a mirror of what was happening in my day-to-day life.'

Like many cult film aficionados, McAleer has watched *Quadrophenia* countless times. It may seem ridiculous to view a film more than a couple of times to the average filmgoer, but he reveals that he detects new elements to the film on each viewing. It has also proved fortuitous in many ways. 'I've no idea how many times I've watched it. It's immeasurable to the point that I've got different versions. I've got a great black-and-white version dubbed into French, which is amazing. It looks and feels completely different, it's incredible. It really helped – I had a French girlfriend for nine years and it helped me learn French because I knew the script.'

Location sleuthing pre-internet was an arduous task but McAleer approached his subject matter with a zeal that Sherlock Holmes would envy. 'On several occasions, I went to the cinema with a notepad and a torch in my mouth. Some of the street signs were visible and it helped me find the locations.'

McAleer's remarkable sleuthing has determined all but a few of the locations. Experiencing a sense of wonder on discovering the alley, the party house and the street on which we see Jimmy and Steph's emotional argument, like many, McAleer felt a deep sense of connection, as if allowed an exclusive entrée into the film itself. These moments would be enhanced when he'd recognise certain innocuous elements such as a paving stone or a fence post that were in the film. These discoveries, in their own way, took him closer to his subject matter, deepening his relationship with the film.

But beyond this, McAleer belongs to the select few whose sense of attachment to the film demands an even greater ownership. When Alfredo's Café (a London location that featured twice in the film) closed in the early part of the millennium, he sensed an opportunity to acquire an exclusive part of *Quadrophenia* – the unique art deco signage that hung above the premises – even though it only occupies a split second of screen time in the film.

'It was all boarded up,' recalls McAleer today. 'I thought, "That's going to get taken over soon and the signs on the front are all going to get skipped." I went to a hardware shop on the Essex Road and I bought a high-vis jacket, a set of ladders, hard hat and various tools.'

'AT THE TIME, IT WAS A MIRROR OF WHAT WAS HAPPENING IN MY DAY-TO-DAY LIFE.'

KIERAN MCALEER

After parking his car alongside the café, McAleer climbed up the ladder in broad daylight – pedestrians, shoppers and office workers unaware of his bold act of preservation. 'It was very precarious. The ladder was wobbling. I was up there with a Stanley knife trying to cut these boards off – I didn't realise how big they were.'

Manhandling the cumbersome signage down the ladder onto the busy North London street, McAleer placed the precious artefacts in his car and drove a few streets away. Viewing his booty with a joy normally reserved for religious worship, McAleer had achieved a rare feat – ownership of an integral part of the film. Having stored away the items and aware of their unique value, McAleer ultimately informed the current owners of its appropriation, but they were happy to let him keep the signage. Evidently, *Quadrophenia*'s heritage is far safer with its fans than with the contrary machinations of modern life. Ultimately, McAleer has got to the heart and soul of *Quadrophenia*, searching way beyond the film stock and the predictable one-dimensional interpretations of the average filmgoer.

'With *Quadrophenia*,' he says today, 'I don't want to be someone who just watches the film. That's not enough, because there are loads of people who do that. I want to know more.' To McAleer, *Quadrophenia* is truly 'a way of life'.

My first book on *Quadrophenia* was published some years ago and, despite its obvious limitations, it helped to document the extensive interest that still surrounds the film. As I expected, I received quite a few emails concerning the book following its publication, but one message that affected me particularly deeply was from 'Alan'. In my innocence, I had ignored the fact that *Quadrophenia* has acted as a beacon to sufferers of mental illness.

'I didn't dive into the book like most people probably,' wrote 'Alan'. 'For me suffering from BPD I wasn't sure how it was going to make me feel as there was no way I was going to be able to read this book without all the Mod memories coming back & the reasons for becoming a Mod as well. I've had to put it down a few times as it's bloody difficult trying to read with a film of your life playing over you as your memories come flashing back lol, I've found myself drifting off into the cobwebbed filled recesses of my mind that I thought were long forgotten only to be amazed that their being relayed back to me in only what I can describe as Blu-ray quality. As I said the memories it's brought back are overwhelming some good some not so good and some damn right shitty but it was being that Mod helped. As mental as I was and am, I was part of something I would not only give my right arm but my right no! hang on, both me nuts to get back there as they were the absolute best days of my life.'

This film, so preciously guarded by its devotees, was barely acknowledged by the loftier elements of film illuminati. The British Film Institute's largely respected chart of the Top 100 British films failed to include the film, despite having similarly cult-interest entries such as *Withnail and I*, *The Wicker Man* and *Get Carter*. Predictably, it was down to more street publications such as *Hotdog*, *MOJO* and *NME* to rightfully recognise its seminal importance. In 2005 *MOJO* included *Quadrophenia* in their listing of the 'Greatest Rock 'n' Roll Movies of All Time'.

Despite its perennial status in the hearts and minds of its aficionados, *Quadrophenia* has only had one official cinematic re-release. This occurred in the winter of 1997, at the zenith of the Britpop phenomenon. The film had been doing brisk business at outdoor screenings, drawing huge crowds of admirers, many of whom echoed the dialogue on screen as it unfolded. Helping matters no end was The Who's mammoth *Quadrophenia*-themed concert in Hyde Park the year before and the re-release of the original album on a remastered CD. With healthy sales of the film on VHS about to dovetail with the DVD, it was evident that *Quadrophenia* was ready to engage a new generation.

Launching the re-release, a special screening was arranged in Brighton for cast, crew and other associated flotsam and jetsam of the current scene. 'We have confirmation from people like Blur, Pulp, Irvine Welsh, Richard E. Grant and Ewan McGregor,' announced Will Clarke of the Feature Film Company. 'The Who and the original cast are coming as well. Oasis want to be there, and – fingers crossed – Sting will make it too.'

While none of those celebrities actually showed up, many of *Quadrophenia*'s cast made their way down to Brighton. Maximising every atom of publicity, Polygram chartered a train to Brighton for the night of Wednesday, January 29th, 1997. Labelled the *Quadrophenia Express*, the train couldn't find an appropriately iconic 5.15 p.m. slot for the jaunt, and so they left London's Victoria station terminus at 6.43 p.m., arriving in Brighton a little under an hour later.

While the majority of the cast took advantage of the train ride, Phil Daniels flew down from Manchester to be met by ecstatic crowds – and a wall of security. Ironically, it was an establishment figure in the shape of the Mayor of Brighton who introduced the film at Brighton's Odeon Cinema, with an atmosphere akin to an army reunion. Old hostilities forgotten, this army of Mods was royally welcomed back into the fold.

Following the excitable screening event, a party was convened at a nightclub in the basement of Brighton's Grand Hotel – its connection to *Quadrophenia* now enshrined for eternity. The entrance to the club, the Midnight Blue, was situated just a few feet away from the position where Sting's scooter was situated before Jimmy steals it for his spectacular finale. With a predictable ensemble of media freeloaders, journalists and celebrities drawn from all spheres, those present tucked into buckshee fish and chips and drinks.

The party went on into the early hours, and it was left to Brighton's very own Fatboy Slim (aka Norman Cook) to engage the partygoers with his take on the hits of the period as well as a sprinkling of more contemporary material. As the wee hours approached, a fleet of buses and taxis waited to take *Quadrophenia*'s merry cast back to the station for the return trip to London. As the last few stragglers left the club, the film's alignment with nineties culture had been successfully completed.

Franc Roddam was one of the last to leave the Grand Hotel, the sound of sixties dance music morphing into that of the soft waves crashing onto the nearby beach. As he walked down the hotel's marble steps, a large anonymous-looking man in his thirties tapped him on the shoulder. He'd been noticed by many, waiting outside the club since the festivities began, and had cut an unusual presence. Walking up to the director, he said, 'Your film saved my life,' and without waiting for a reply, the man walked off into the darkness. ●

QUADROPHENIA

Released 1979

Directed by:
Franc Roddam

Writing credits:
Franc Roddam

Martin Stellman

Dave Humphries

Pete Townshend

Chris Stamp

Alan Fletcher

Cast:

Phil Daniels	Jimmy	George Innes	Café Owner
Leslie Ash	Steph	John Bindon	Harry
Philip Davis	Chalky	P.H. Moriarty	Barman at Villain's Pub
Mark Wingett	Dave	Hugh Lloyd	Mr. Cale
Sting	Ace Face	Cross Section	The Band
Ray Winstone	Kevin (credited as Raymond Winstone)	John Altman	John
Garry Cooper	Peter	Jesse Birdsall	Aggressive Rocker
Gary Shail	Spider	Loren Day	Girl with Steph
Toyah Willcox	Monkey	Harry Fielder	Policeman
Trevor Laird	Ferdy	Julian Firth	Mod in Bathroom
Kate Williams	Mother	John Blundell	Lead Rocker
Michael Elphick	Father	Linda Regan	Lead Rocker Girl
Kim Neve	Yvonne	Simon Gipps-Kent	Boy at Party
Benjamin Whitrow	Mr. Fulford	Gary Holton	Aggressive Rocker
Daniel Peacock	Danny	Tom Ingram	Rocker in Police van
Jeremy Child	Agency Man	Derek Lyons	Jimmy's Gang Member
John Phillips	Magistrate	Peter McNamara	Mod
Timothy Spall	Projectionist	Glen Murphy	Fighting Rocker
Olivier Pierre	Tailor		

Produced by:

Roy Baird	Producer	Keith Moon	Executive Producer
Bill Curbishley	Producer	John Peverall	Associate Producer
Roger Daltrey	Executive Producer	David Gideon Thomson	Executive Producer
John Entwistle	Executive Producer	Pete Townshend	Executive Producer

Cinematography by:

Brian Tufano .... Director of Photography

Film Editing by:

Sean Barton

Mike Taylor

Casting by:

Patsy Pollock

Production Design by:

Simon Holland

Makeup Department:

Simon Thompson ....Hair Styles Creator

Gilly Wakeford .... Makeup Artist (as Gilli Wakeford)

Second Unit Director/Assistant Director:

Ray Corbett ....Assistant Director

Kieron Phipps.............................Second Assistant Director

Art Department:

Jack Carter .... Construction Manager

Andrew Sanders...................................Assistant Art Director

Terry Wells .... Property Master

Ken Wheatley.. Set Dresser

Adrian Start ....Painter

Sound Department:

Albert Bailey..Boom Operator

John Ireland .... Sound Editor

Bill Rowe.. Dubbing Mixer

Christian Wangler .... Sound Recordist (as Christian Wrangler)

Jon Astley.. Sound Engineer

Malcolm Hirst ....Second Boom Operator/

Sound Maintenance

Special Effects by:

Steve Hamilton .... Special Effects Technician

Camera and Electrical Department:

Martin Evans............ Electrical Supervisor: Lee Electrics Ltd

Jeff Paynter...Focus Puller

Frank Connor ....Still Photographer

Geoff Mulligan ....Camera Operator: Second Unit

Ronnie Rampton ....Best Boy

Derek Suter .... Clapper Loader

Costume/Wardrobe Department:

Joyce Stoneman ....Wardrobe Supervisor

Music Department:

Roger Daltrey...Musical Director

John Entwistle........................Music Producer and Director

Cy Langston ....Music Re-mix Engineer

Mike Shaw ....Music Coordinator

Pete Townshend ....Musical Director

Other Departments:

David Anderson ....Location Manager

Peter Brayham... Action Arranger

Alan Fletcher.. Story Consultant

Caroline Hagen....................................Production Assistant

Redmond Morris.....................................Location Manager

Kevin O'Driscoll .... Production Accountant

Melinda Rees .... Continuity

Christopher Stamp .... Story Consultant (as Chris Stamp)

Pete Townshend .... Story Consultant

Ken Tuohy...Producer's Assistant

Geoff Freeman.. Unit Publicist

Gillian Gregory/

Jeff Dexter..Choreographers

Richard Morrison..Title Designer

Freddie Haayen .... Special thanks

James Swann... Special thanks

Select Bibliography

Ash, Leslie, *My Life Behaving Badly: The Autobiography* (Orion, 2007)

Barrie, Amanda, *It's Not a Rehearsal: The Autobiography* (Headline, 2002)

Catterall, Ali & Wells, Simon, *Your Face Here: British Cult Movies Since the Sixties* (Fourth Estate, 2001)

Daniels, Phil, *Class Actor: My Autobiography* (Simon & Schuster, 2010)

Elphick, Kate, *Elphick: The Great Pretender* (The History Press, 2013)

Hamblett, Charles & Deverson, Jane, *Generation X* (Tandem Books, 1964)

Kent, Matt & Neil, Andy, *Anyway Anyhow Anywhere: The Complete Chronicle of The Who 1958–1978* (Sterling, 2009)

Marsh, Dave, *Before I Get Old: The Story of The Who* (Plexus, 1983)

Patterson, Layne, *Quadrophenia: The Complete Guide* (CreateSpace, 2017)

Wharton, Gary, *Chasing The Wind: A Quadrophenia Anthology* (Lushington Publishing, 2002)

Articles

Empire, February 1997

Films and Filming, September 1979

Film Review, February 1997

Loaded, November 1995

New Musical Express, May 12th, 1979

Premiere, February 1997

Scootering, August 2017 & March–May 2018

Total Film, February 1997

Audio/Visual Sources

**Commentaries for DVD releases
(Rhino, Universal, Criterion)**

Leslie Ash (2006)

Phil Daniels (2012)

Franc Roddam (2001, 2006, 2012)

Brian Tufano (2012)

Video Documentaries

The Who, the Mods and the Quadrophenia Connection (Sexy Intellectual, 2009)

Quadrophenia: A Way of Life (Universal, 2006)

Television

Cast and Crew (BBC, 2005)

The London Weekend Show: Mods (London Weekend Television, 1978)

Radio

The Modcast: August 2011

Interviews with Sean Barton, Phil Davis, Franc Roddam, Martin Stellman, Toyah Wilcox and Mark Wingett recorded at Institut Français du Royaume-Uni, London on Spetember 23rd, 2013.

Acknowledgements

In bringing this all together, I am especially grateful to the following:

John Altman, Brett 'Buddy' Ascott, Jonny Bance, Mark Baxter, John Blundell, Donna Boardman, Devlin Crow, Bill Curbishley, Rob Dady, Jeff Dexter, Gary Crowley, Phil Davis, Alan Fletcher (1999), Martin Gainsford, Chris Green, Paolo Hewitt, Robert Joseph, Andy Johns, Trevor Laird (1999), Graham Lentz, Mark Lewisohn, Paul McEvoy, Kieran McAleer, Bertie Nicholas, Ian O'Sullivan, Layne Patterson, Tony Phillips, David Price, Terry Rawlings, Franc Roddam, Michael W. Salter, Alan Shine, Gary Shail, Drew Stansall, Martin Stellman, Pete Townshend (1999 & 2018), Paul Weller (1999), Rob Williams, Dave Worrell.

Apologies to anyone I've missed – my thanks remain as large and bold.

On a personal note, I'd like to thank my family, my friends and everyone in the people's republic of Forest Row, Sussex.